W9-BUJ-651

Saul Bellow
In Defense of Man

JOHN JACOB CLAYTON

Saul Bellow
In Defense of Man

SECOND EDITION

INDIANA UNIVERSITY PRESS

Bloomington • *London*

Manufactured in the United States of America

Library of Congress Cataloging in Publication Data
Clayton, John Jacob.
Saul Bellow: in defense of man.
Bibliography: p.
Includes index.
1. Bellow, Saul — Criticism and interpretation.
PS3503.E4488Z6   1979   813'.5'2   78-19554
ISBN 0-253-14995-9   2 3 4 5 83 82 81 80

For my Uncle Lloyd and Aunt Grace

with love

Contents

Preface to the
Second Edition

My critical consciousness has changed a good deal during the ten years since I finished the first edition of this book. I have become more politically aware, for one thing. This awareness is reflected particularly in the new section on "The Politics of Oedipus: *Mr. Sammler's Planet* and *To Jerusalem and Back*." That title also indicates my developing interest in seeing Bellow with a psychoanalytic lens, a lens also at work in the new chapter on *Humboldt's Gift*. In other ways, too, I have changed as a critic. I find myself more suspicious now, less able to identify with Bellow's own moral and spiritual perspective, readier to step back and examine that perspective.

And yet I agree fundamentally with the work of my younger self. The book as a whole still represents the most useful approach I am able to make to a writer whose work I admire greatly. And I find it even more true today than it was ten years ago: Saul Bellow is our most important contemporary novelist.

J.J.C.

ACKNOWLEDGMENTS

I am indebted to James Justus for his assistance and advice, to James Hoffman for his insights and encouragement, to Marcus Klein for his suggestions, and to my students in an experimental seminar at Boston University for their stimulating ideas.

Saul Bellow
In Defense of Man

-1-

Introduction

ABBREVIATIONS
USED IN TEXT AND NOTES

AM   *The Adventures of Augie March*
DM   *Dangling Man*
EH   *The Eternal Husband* (Dostoyevsky)
H   *Herzog*
HG   *Humboldt's Gift*
HRK   *Henderson the Rain King*
MSP   *Mr. Sammler's Planet*
N   *Nausea* (Sartre)
NU   *Notes from Underground* (Dostoyevsky)
SD   *Seize the Day*
V   *The Victim*

CHAPTER ONE

In Desperate Affirmation

Saul Bellow is America's most important living novelist. His humanity and compassion radiate from every novel; his interests are the interests of this culture—he knows *where we're at;* his skill is incredible–in particular, his ability to describe experience in a human voice so that the texture of the experience comes through, and his ability to convey the philosophical-moral complexities of human life without losing that life itself. If Bellow doesn't enter the nightmare world of John Hawkes or attempt avant garde innovation, it is because he stands as a spokesman for our culture, as a defender of the Western cultural tradition. He can define the Darkness but never enter it; he can examine cultural nihilism but never share it.

But is this true? For if Bellow is a spokesman for our culture, he voices its uncertainties, its complexities, its paradoxes. Who can speak for us otherwise?

And so Saul Bellow's fiction contains three interrelated contradictions. First—Bellow takes a stand against the cultural nihilism of the twentieth century: against Dada, against the Wasteland, against the denigration of human life in modern society. Yet Bellow is himself essentially a depressive; and his imagination is as horrified by the emptiness of modern life as is Ionesco's.

Second—Bellow rejects the tradition of alienation in modern literature, and his fiction emphasizes the value of brotherhood and community; yet his main characters are all masochists and alienatees.

Third—Bellow is particularly hostile to the devaluation of the "separate self" in modern literature, and he values individuality nearly as highly as did Emerson. Yet in novel after novel he is forced to *discard* individuality, not simply because the individual is insignificant in the face of terrible forces, but also because individuality is undesirable, a burden which keeps the human being from love. The state of grace which his heroes approach is an anonymous state which is the polar opposite of the individuality Bellow loves and wishes to defend; but it is a state which enables Bellow to keep faith in the human being and in the possibility of his union with others.

We can better understand these contradictions by understanding their origins in Bellow's characters. They feel guilty, unworthy to live; they defend the human being in order to defend themselves. And so the Darkness and the struggle to escape the Darkness describe the psychic condition of Bellow's heroes before they describe the human condition; Bellow is a psychological novelist before he is a social novelist or moral spokesman. And the solution to the contradiction over individuality is also psychological before intellectual; that is, the heroes find that only by becoming unburdened of their guilty selves and entering the "shared condition of all" can they hope to become worthy.

1

Augie March, thinking about the fierceness of nature in Mexico, about an "element too strong for life," remembers the glory of the eagle being trained by Thea, remembers the eagle flying high over volcanic craters. Augie associates the eagle with Aldebaran, the bright star which the Aztec priests watched to determine "whether or not life would go on for another cycle."[1] The name *Augie* comes from *augury,* from the Latin *augur,* the name for the Roman priests who divined the future by regarding the flights of birds. Thus Augie is like both the Aztec priests auguring from stars and the Roman priests auguring from birds: Augie, like all Bellow's heroes, is Bellow's representative in determining whether life can go on. This is Bellow's main question, and his answer is an anguished *yes*. In "The Writer as Moralist" Bellow argues, "Either we want life to continue or we do not. . . . If we do want it to continue . . . in what form shall life be justified?" To answer this question is the writer's moral function.[2]

Certainly it is the function Bellow has taken on in his fiction. In this role Bellow affirms the possibilities of meaningful individual life, but he knows its difficulties and costs; he knows that the Aztec priests, "when they received their astronomical sign, built their new fire inside the split and empty chest of a human sacrifice" (*AM*, p.338). The cost of a continuance of civilization seems to be murder. Bellow doesn't hide: he believes with Blake that you must "Drive your cart and your plow over the bones of the dead"; he does not pretend that we ride a concrete freeway. With Doctor Pep ("A Sermon by Doctor Pep") he would reject disguising the dead animals we eat by making hamburgers and croquettes. He knows that if we live, we live off death. Bellow may write sympathetically of Joyce Cary's work, "It asserts that there are powerful and original natures to be found still, that genius exists, that striving is not necessarily monomaniac, happiness not extinct, hopes not unjustified."[3] But his own hope is tempered by a look at the worst. His friend Alfred Kazin says that Bellow was from the start "a wrestler in the old Greek style,"[4] and that reality is, for Bellow, "one man's contest with terrible powers." It is this wrestling to achieve affirmation that shows Fiedler wrong when he calls Bellow a sellout to middle-class optimism.[5] Middle-class optimism doesn't wrestle: it comes from seeing only what's comfortable.

But if Bellow is going to affirm the possibility of meaningful individual life in contemporary America, he has to affirm a changed life. If life as it is offers cause for despair and if the individual is both product and producer of this life, then the individual must be redeemed. Through his redemption society will be redeemed. So Bellow, unlike Herman Wouk, affirms not the present individual and the present society but their possibilities. And it is because Bellow refuses to lie, to simplify the difficulties of redemption, that his novels end so tentatively. Each (with the partial exception of *Augie March*) has this form: a hero tries to face the worst and cast it off, tries to throw off the burdens of his own past which prevent him from becoming human.[6]

An unusually comic version of this form can be seen in Bellow's wild one-act play, "The Wrecker."[7] The hero, refusing the city's $1000 compensation for moving from a tenement which is to be razed, smashes the apartment himself. Not only does he refuse to submit to the bulldozers of an administration concerned more with efficiency than with people; much more, he needs to smash the burdens of his life and to break free of his deceptions and miseries, which seem to have permeated the walls. So he smashes the walls. In a spirit of play and Reichian acting-out, he destroys the places of his and his wife's sorrows and quarrels. The husband argues that they must break free of their past. "You can't drag your heavy, heavy history around with you" (p.203). His mother-in-law thinks him mad, and his wife swears to leave if he smashes the bedroom—that would show her failure; but when she begins to swing the axe, she, too, finds it liberating, and she becomes more anxious than he is to smash the bedroom, whose ceiling she had always had a grudge against. Now he's the one to be a little hurt, but together they go off to smash the old life into shards and to start fresh. What is especially important is that Bellow sees this act of personal liberation as an act of cultural liberation. The husband compares himself to Samson in the temple; he thinks of himself as a racial hero: "Today I'm a man of deeds, like a hero out of Homer, like a man who does something for civilization" (p.197).

This act of seeming alienation is in fact performed for the community. As in so much of Bellow's fiction—*Dangling Man, Seize the Day, Henderson the Rain King*—there is an alienated hero struggling to redeem his own life—and, by extension, the common life—by ridding himself of a past seen in the metaphor of a burden (generally a burden more internal, and so less theatrical than in "The Wrecker"). Often the burden weighing down the hero is actually his own ego, which is the accumulation of his past. Bellow's heroes are strangely like the despairing, negativistic LeRoi Jones (with whom Bellow has little sympathy), who asks: What man

> . . . on the littered sidewalks of his personal
> history, can continue to believe in his own dignity or intelligence.

and who complains:

> . . . Each
> act of my life, with me now, till death. Themselves,
> the reasons for it. They are stones, in my mouth
> and ears. Whole forests on my shoulders.

This is the meaning of the gross flesh of Bellow's characters; this is why Asa heaves under the weight of New York heat, why Tommy sees himself as a hippopotamus, "the carrier of a load which was his own self . . ." (*SD*, p.39). The burdens must be cast off so that the hero as representative man can be redeemed, so that the life of the individual may be meaningful and beautiful. It is the struggle itself which proves that the individual's life is not a "dusty irrelevancy,"[8] but that dignity can be salvaged from the wreckage. In "The Wrecker," as in Bellow's later fiction (*Henderson, Herzog*), dignity is likened to that of traditional racial heroes but is in the end quite different: it is more the dignity of the holy fool of Yiddish literary tradition.

In a comic vein, in *The Last Analysis,* the ex-ratcatcher Bertram reads from the script Bummidge has prepared: "To disown the individual altogether is nihilism, which isn't funny at all. But suppose all we fumblers and bumblers, we cranks and cripples, we proud, sniffing, ragged-assed paupers of heart and soul, sick with every personal vice, rattled, proud, spoiled and distracted—suppose we look again for the manhood we are born to inherit."[9] And indeed, though the play is largely a satire on efforts at self-transcendence, we find that each of Bummidge's cynical, selfish hangers-on is by the end infected with the longing to become human. If Bellow, like most modern writers, writes of burdened, alienated, impotent people, he believes that a man "should have at least sufficient power to overcome ignominy and to complete his own life. His suffering, feebleness, servitude then have a meaning." Bellow does not avoid conditions of alienation and despair; but he insists that through them the power of the imagination "should reveal the greatness of man."[10] He insists that we are "not gods, not beasts, but savages of a somewhat damaged but not extinguished nobility,"[11] and he asks that the writer pay, like Dreiser, an "admission of allegiance to life."[12]

To pay this allegiance is not to demand adherence to some special idea of life—he attacks F. R. Leavis for asking just this; rather the writer indicates his faith by the concern he shows for his characters. "To believe in the existence of human beings as such is love," Bellow quotes Simone Weil: the writer's job is to manifest this love.[13] Just as the novelist must see his characters as real and important, so, too, must living human beings see one another. This love in itself affirms the value of human beings. "Dora" tells of a seamstress who, returning to her single room after baby-sitting, hears a thud. The "ordinary person" next door, a man she's never spoken to, has had a stroke. Shocked at how unattached he is, she sees the emptiness of her lonely life multiplied many times in his. He represents for her the terrible cries from an unknown window in the night, the cries that make her afraid. And she thinks: "It is shocking to me when someone who dies is not a person [but only a social security number]. . . . If you don't care about the differences . . . it might as well be the trunk falling as the man falling."[14] And in a quixotic gesture of refusal to see the individual's life as without importance, she dresses up every day and visits him at the hospital, although he remains in a coma. Totally alone and lacking the social texture which allows one to accept ready-made values, she is forced to create values existentially by her concern for her neighbor.

At the core of all Bellow's novels there is concern for other human beings, a concern which is evident especially in the transformation of the hero. The only significant moment of truth in *Dangling Man* is one in which Joseph feels a flow of affection for his wife; Asa's story in *The Victim* is one of learning to care about other people: his brother and his enemy Allbee. The proof of his transformation is that he can call his wife home. Augie sings of love throughout *The Adventures of Augie March.* At the turning point of the novel he discovers that he has never fully loved. Henderson cries out at his moment of truth, "I heard a voice that said I want! *I* want? I? It should have told me *she* wants, he wants, *they* want. And moreover, it's love that makes reality. The opposite makes the opposite" (*HRK,* p.286). Herzog's story turns partly on new awareness of other people as real and on his love for his daughter. The obstacles to learning to go beyond the self and be concerned for others make up much of the substance of Bellow's novels. Bellow's characters and Bellow himself pay "allegiance to life."

2

In saying human life can go on, Bellow feels that he is not struggling so much against the current of modern life as against the current of modern literature; and indeed, Lionel Trilling has placed Bellow as a spokesman against the culture of what he calls the "second environment." Trilling explains that young people, by means of the kind of literary education introduced in Sedgwick's and Arnold's time, have been taught to transcend their environment on the basis of certain values. But now, "there stands ready to receive him another 'environment' in which he is pretty sure to be tolerably comfortable. . . ."[15] This is the environment of art and freedom, its morality based on style. Trilling must be thinking of Susan Sontag's article on "camp" (originally printed in *Partisan Review*) in which she speaks of style and taste as criteria for the value of ideas, people, and morality.[16] And he must be considering, too, Genet's criterion of "elegance" in morality. Trilling agrees with his colleague William Phillips, who in "The New Immoralists" says he is "not ready to abandon morality to any aesthetic stance."[17] As Trilling puts it, quoting Keats: "an eagle is not so fine a thing as a truth" ("Environments," p.13). Both Trilling and Phillips fear the lack of a moral center in the "second environment"; Trilling accuses it of a trivialization like that of the philistine environment in opposition to which it was created.

Bellow, who as Trilling says is certainly no philistine, has also rejected this trivialization. He has "dissociated himself from the company of those writers who accept the belief that modern society is frightful, brutal, hostile to whatever is pure in the human spirit, a wasteland and a horror" ("Environments," p.12). This represents a trivialization because, Bellow would argue, it is an essentially *literary* attitude: "Literature has for several generations been its own source": a literary attitude developing out of late Romanticism. As Bellow put it in his Library of Congress address in 1963:

Writers have inherited a tone of bitterness from the great poems and novels of this century, many of which lament the passing of a more stable and beautiful age demolished by the barbarous intrusion of an industrial and metropolitan society of masses or proles who will, after many upheavals, be tamed by bureaucracies and oligarchies in brave new worlds, human anthills. . . . There are modern novelists who take all of this for granted as fully proven and implicit in the human condition and who complain as steadily as they write, viewing modern life with a bitterness to which they themselves have not established clear title, and it is this unearned bitterness that I speak of.[18]

Edenic past, present wasteland, future anthill. Raymond Williams shows that this formulation began with the industrial revolution and is to be found in Burke and Blake, developed in Carlyle and Mill, Newman and Arnold, Pugin, Ruskin, and Morris, to find its twentieth century exponents in Lawrence, Eliot, and Orwell.[19] The City of Dreadful Night becomes Eliot's Unreal City, which in projection becomes 1984, which in imitation becomes Jack Kerouac's "CityCityCity," a science fiction nightmare of people living in a thought-controlled world of steel and glass. Conrad's horror hidden in the heart of Africa and in the heart of man becomes the nightmare world of Burroughs' biological fantasies and cities of monsters (*Naked Lunch*) or Selby's realistic jungle of cruelty and drugged confusion (*Last Exit to Brooklyn*) or Rechy's grotesque, loveless world of homosexual prostitution and empty kicks (*City of Night*) or Gelber's vision of life as meaningless and spent in the isolation and despair of drug addiction, a whole society passing the time until it "scores"—with heroin, or by extension, alcohol or Cadillacs (*The Connection*). Ginsburg sees instead of the "lost America of love" ("Supermarket in California") a giant suburb of two-car garages, and juxtaposes images of homosexual love with images of political insanity and social sterility. Miller and Mailer set off a kind of sexual *Ubermensch* against a decadent civilization (*Rosy Crucifixion, Air-Conditioned Nightmare, Deer Park,* "Time of Her Time"). For Ed Dorn, "an alien world lives up in the hills" around Seattle. The old race of men is gone. From the new, alien world comes

the woman purchasing lotions to take off, then, in a great convertible over hills, in fresh breezes. What is the dark? America, it is all that is hidden under your hat. Your hot tropical afternoon when all the desperate groans creep out. It is our listless powerful voyage to oceania. Brings the disease of white morning. Brings waking, blinking, and the slow redawning that nothing is accomplished and already at your ears is the sound of the great raucous bells announcing a different race of men in the street, delivering truckloads of what you didn't even know existed and what you will patiently learn to want.[20]

Is twentieth century literary despair mostly literary? I don't think so. Leslie Fiedler is seeing one aspect of things when he speaks of "a weariness in the West which undercuts the struggle between socialism and capitalism, democracy and autocracy; a weariness with humanism itself which underlies all the movements of our world, a weariness with the striving to be men. It is the end of man which the school of Burroughs foretells, not in tones of doom, but of triumph." Bellow, however, rejects such visions of decadence; he refuses to believe that this is "the full crisis of dissolution."

Yet Bellow is *not* a spokesman for Trilling's first (philistine) environment. It isn't a vulgar or oversimplified explanation to say that the violence of his attack on art which despairs at or assumes cultural sterility and decay is a response to his own despair at our civilization. When Bellow declares that one of the "legacies from humanism is an idea of dignity which makes [one] . . . think a great deal of what he sees about him absurd,"[21] he is speaking of his own idea of dignity and his own sense of absurdity. Who knows the fragmented, isolated, materialistic life of a city better than the writer of *Seize the Day*, with its portrayal of loveless acquisitiveness? And it was Bellow, not Henry Miller, who wrote this passage:

In this modern power of luxury, with its battalions of service workers and engineers, it's the things themselves, the products that are distinguished, and the individual man isn't nearly equal to their great sum. Finally they are what becomes great—the multitude of baths with never-failing hot water, the enormous air-conditioning units and the elaborate machinery. No opposing greatness is allowed. . . . (*AM*, p.238)

In "Distractions of a Fiction Writer" Bellow tells of the difficulties facing the novelist:

. . . Sometimes he can feel in the very streets that the energies of the population have been withdrawn to mass activity, industry, and money. At mid-day in an American city you are aware of a certain emptiness about the houses. You hear the organ groaning in dissolution as the scenes of the soap opera change in the kitchen below. . . . And sometimes the suspicion arises that maybe the Studebaker, maybe the Bendix have absorbed man's highest powers. Can the intellectual, esthetic, moral genius of the human race have come to a stop? That's impossible. Aeronautical engineers have just shown that the globe can be circumnavigated in a forty-five hour non-stop flight. That is genius—to lift man and metal from the ground and send them around the face of the earth. Before such an achievement nobody ought to be bored and no one ought to feel isolated. The shuddering of the organ, the vacant dullness of a world that is (temporarily) not a temple have no great importance. The smell of beer on the dark stairs is nothing. The absence of human contact is merely temporary. The page in the typewriter describing a certain conversation that never actually took place is an offering placed on the altar of certain gods who—who aren't around just now. (pp.10–11)

This passage expresses not only despair at a culture from which intelligence, soul, and community are missing; but additionally Bellow's awareness of how much he needs to compensate for: the final phrase with its repeated "who" shows Bellow aware that his decision to affirm is a decision, that it requires determination.

Bellow's despair can be seen, in an extremely ironic vein, in "The Gonzoga Manuscripts" (*SD*, pp.161–92). Modelled after James' "The Aspern Papers," this story tells of a young scholar who goes to Spain in search of unpublished poems of the dead poet he loves, a poet whose work had given him new faith in life, in the common life, in communication between persons. But the search ends in failure. The scholar finds that (contrary to Gonzoga's faith) communication is mis-communication; that each man's concern for his own needs and each man's peculiarity of vision makes misunderstanding inevitable. In a final fiasco the scholar hopes to get the poems from the nephew of the woman for whom they were written. But his nephew is sure the scholar has come to purchase shares in a uranium mine, for to the Spanish, all Americans represent the bomb dropped on Hiroshima—over and over the scholar confronts this misconception. After a long session of mis-communication, the Spaniard explains —casually—that the poems were buried with the woman.

The burial of these poems represents the burial of those high hopes for man that the poet, and the scholar, and Bellow held. Here is the complement of the hopeful position in "Distractions of a Fiction Writer." Gonzoga's old friend wants to give the scholar the "dirt" on Gonzoga, and thus on mankind. Instead of communion there is suspicion (the police go through the scholar's luggage) and solitude, emotional and intellectual. The burial of the poems also symbolizes the death of European culture: the Spanish have no time for their past culture. They are all more interested in atomic warfare than in poems. Nobility has dwindled to a family of gigglers who mock both America and the dead military grandeur of their own country. The scholar, with his love for the unconsidered poems of a dead poet and with his belief in the noble, loving spirit of that poet, seems as quixotic a figure as Dora—or as Bellow himself, half afraid, in "Distractions of a Fiction Writer," that the novelist is an "anachronism" (p.20). But quixotic or not, what can he do? Bellow is aware (as in "Sealed Treasure") of the shopping-center life of the mass society. He recognizes that "the pressure of a vast public life" dwarfs the individual, and he writes, "One would have to be optimistic to the point of imbecility to raise the standard of pure affirmation and cry 'yea, yea' shrilly against the deep background of 'nays.' "22 But as he says in his Library of Congress address, "One would like to ask [Sartre, Ionesco, Beckett, Burroughs, Ginsberg] 'After nakedness, what?' 'After absurdity, what?' " (p.7).

3

So Bellow affirms; and he attacks the writer who, feeling the encroachment of the public realm on the private, responds by exhibiting his "power to despair."23 "Neither for himself nor for his fellows does he attack power and injustice directly and hotly. He simply defends his sensibility."

From the beginning of the novel as a genre there have been alienated heroes. The novel in fact derives from the conflict between the ideals of a hero and the reality he faces. In recent American fiction there have been the victimized edenic child, the lonely youth, the Negro without identity, the Jew involved in guilt and self-betrayal, the grotesque, the underdog, the disinherited American—all marginal, disaffiliated characters. Bellow writes: "The individual in American fiction often comes through to us . . . as a colonist who has been sent to a remote place, some Alaska of the soul. . . . The writer of sensibility assumes that only private exploration and inner development are possible and accepts the opposition of public and private as fixed and indissoluble."[24] But Bellow does not accept a purely private life; indeed, he feels its shame (*Herzog* was written partly out of this feeling).[25] He may believe that the men in power are "in some sense barbarians,"[26] but he believes that an individual must try to relate himself to power and to institutions (although not, he wants to make clear, by acquiescence to the mob).

Bellow, it is clear then, refuses to indulge himself in the romantic tradition of alienation. He is, moreover, attacking the poseur of alienation; so that while he lauds Thoreau for retaining his solitary connection with nature, cut off from his neighbors,[27] he attacks Thoreau's twentieth century descendant Jack Kerouac, who goes off to the coastal mountains of California to nurse his infantile ego (*Big Sur*). He attacks Kerouac's gesture just as he attacks the retreat of Updike into style and sensibility ("Pigeon Feather"). He insists there is "grandeur in cursing the heavens, not our socks,"[28] and laughs that American writers often "have the feeling of being Promethean when they're only having a tantrum." "Vehement declarations of alienation" and "polymorphous sexuality are not going to produce great works of art."[29]

4

We have seen Bellow's attack on literary prophets of doom; we have also seen his attack on poseurs of romantic despair and alienation, on those writers who groan too loudly about the misfortunes of the "sovereign self." The complement to over-concern with the individual is a belief in his insignificance, a third focus of Bellow's attack.

There are both over-concern and underestimation in the novels of Samuel Beckett, each one the portrait of the same insulated, interior world. If, as Bellow says, "dialogue is impoverished in Joyce,"[30] it is nonexistent in Beckett. Molloy and Malone are waiting, immobile, for death. The Unnameable is already dead. The end of total insulation is annihilation, and not the annihilation of an existential hero like Ahab, who smashes himself against the blank wall that refuses to explain. It is the entropy—Wylie Sypher has made the analogy—of the post-heroic self.[31] In the Zen analogy to human experience, if there is no moon, the water cannot shine. And so, the end of the nineteenth century over-concern with the sovereignty of the individual leads to the disappearance of that individual. The existential, Promethean hero, roaring "No" in thunder, gives way to the absurd hero, who, in Charles Glicksberg's words, "bears the knowledge of his own insignificance in the cosmic scheme of things."[32] Perhaps even better than Beckett's insulated hero, Mauriac's "I" in *All Women Are Fatal* exemplifies the devalued self:

We've renounced the feeling that we're different. At sixteen, I thought I was irreplaceable, like everyone else. Early one morning of my nineteenth year, it was August, I had a revelation of the nothingness of my life. Standing on a straw chair, I stared out the window at the squat steeple of Saint-Germain-des-Prés surrounded by brown roofs. Still impregnated with darkness the sky was turning translucent. Silent dawn. A woman was lying behind me. Yvette has an importance in my life only on account of that moment of which she was the sleeping witness. I had been taught to believe myself unique. Yet nothing distinguished me from the host of the living. A banal, simple truth, but so bitter that I had the impression of having known nothing until that moment. Happiness didn't matter. But misery didn't either. I no longer risked anything. Since that day, death has no longer revolted me. There was no reason to live when others were dying.[33]

Bellow is disgusted with the new French literature which denigrates the individual, seeing all persons as essentially the same and therefore dismissing character from novels. He believes that

modern literature is not satisfied to dismiss a romantic, outmoded conception of the Self. It rends it, annihilates it. It would rather have the maddest chaos it can invoke than a conception of life it found false. But after this destruction, what?[34]

Nathalie Sarraute does not "curse" the Self; but she has eliminated characters from her novels because she simply does not believe in the self. If, as she writes of Dostoyevsky's characters, "each one knows that he is nothing but a fortuitous, more or less felicitious assemblage of elements derived from the same common source," if characters began to become "simple props," if they began to universalize, to become K or HCE (Here Comes Everybody), then finally the character ceases to exist. "Particularly . . . he has lost that most precious of all possessions, his personality—which belonged to him alone—and frequently even his name." The reader, Sarraute goes on, "has watched the watertight partitions that used to separate the characters from one another give way, and the hero become an arbitrary limitation, a conventional figure cut from the common woof. . . ."[35] Thus in Sarraute's novels there are no Moses Herzogs but only *he, she, they, I*—and these blend so that their edges blur.

As Bellow writes, "Valéry, Joyce, Lawrence have questioned the stability of the experiencing self, have dissolved it . . . and altogether made us aware that the sovereign individual . . . was simply a fabrication. . . ."[36] Hesse's *Steppenwolf* shows us the fluidity of the self. Fragmenting the self at the Magic Theater, Steppenwolf finds he has not two parts—man plus wolf—but thousands, and that these thousands, like chess pieces, can be played in infinite combination. The human self Harry Haller had thought was his turns out to be a mere bourgeois compromise. And underneath is a freedom universal rather than individual.

The disintegration of the self is more extreme in Burroughs' *Naked Lunch*. Fiedler writes, perhaps over-dramatically: " 'Let the focussed consciousness blur into the cosmic night. . .' is Burroughs' lesson."[37] If *Naked Lunch* is a derivative of 1920's surrealism, it is an extreme derivative. Freud's dictum, "Where id was let ego be," is in Burroughs, "Where ego was let id be."

The self is exploded or, as in Ionesco, Mauriac, Robbe-Grillet, the self is anonymous, and by implication people are anonymous: there *is* no individual any more. It is this implication which

Bellow attacks. In his address before the Library of Congress, Bellow speaks of German phenomenology as one source for the attack on the self. Certainly it is true that Husserl's method of phenomenological reduction distinguishes between the ego and pure consciousness. The ego is a construct; it is no longer the *self*. Heidegger, whose thinking derives partly from Husserl, distinguishes between *Selfhood*—a substratum of personality, a *thing* —and the Person, whose essential nature is relation rather than substance—a standing-out-from rather than a thing. Sartre, similarly, identifies the ego as something created by free consciousness as a way of escaping freedom. He attacks the notion of an essential self, demonstrating that the ground of our behavior is not an essential self but pure freedom—or (another way of saying the same thing)—*nothing:* consciousness creates being but has no being of its own. What, then, is the individual? He appears to be a mask, created for protection from the void underneath him. The Self is an illusion.

Nathalie Sarraute has been heavily influenced by this phenomenological analysis. In *Portrait of a Man Unknown* the anonymous "I" says that he finds the characters in Tolstoy novels more "real," more sharp and clear, than persons he knows. "And, like the people we know best—even those nearest to us . . . each one of them appears to us as a finished, perfect, whole, entirely enclosed on every side, a solid, hard block, without a single fissure. . . ." But the people whom the narrator is seeking to comprehend in this book are not like that but "trembling shadows . . . ghosts. . . ." Indeed, *no* persons finally have firm outlines for the narrator:

When, occasionally, these "live" persons or these characters, condescend to come near me too, all I am able to do is to hover about them and try with fanatical eagerness to find the crack, the tiny crevice, the weak point, as delicate as a baby's fontanelle, at which I seem to see something that resembles a barely perceptible pulsation suddenly swell and begin to throb gently. I cling to it and press upon it. And then I feel a strange substance trickling from them in an endless stream, a substance as anonymous as lymph, or blood, an

insipid liquid that flows through my hands and spills. . . . And all
that remains of the firm, rosy, velvety flesh of these "live" persons is a
shapeless gray covering, from which all blood has been drained
away.[38]

This anonymous substance which people try to hide behind a
firm mask is related to Sartre's pure existence, spontaneous
consciousness. But more to the point, it is the anonymous, fluid
being we all share.

John Barth's heroes—derived from Sartrean ideas—have a non-
essence which they cannot hide from themselves. Jacob Horner, the
"hero" of *End of the Road*, begins the novel, "In a sense, I am
Jacob Horner." He is a cipher of whom Rennie, the wife of his
friend, says, "You know what I've come to think, Jake? I think
you don't even exist at all. . . . It's more than just masks. . . .
You cancel yourself out." And Horner knows that on certain days,
"Jacob Horner, except in a meaningless metabolic sense, ceased
to exist altogether, for I was without a character, without a
personality: there was no *ego;* no I."[39]

Most clearly derived from Sartrean existentialism are the characters of Genet. Each acts out a role to gain security and self-
justification. Although the Balcony is a brothel, it is mainly a
brothel of illusions: the clients pay to become generals, judges, or
archbishops. They pay for the privilege of being fixed essences, of
entering dramatic scenes in which they wear the clothes of the
chosen figures and stand on cothurni, which help establish them
as more than human. They are anonymous selves pretending to
be individual essences.

This loss of the individual is found not only in literature; there
are the movies of Buñuel, the interest in Zen for its loss of
personality, the cubist portraits by Picasso. Even more clear is the
recent attempt of techniques in the arts to remove individuated
vision—remove the artist in a more drastic way than Flaubert-
Joyce-James ever contemplated. In machine-made paintings, tire
track paintings, or paintings of optical effects, the spirit of a
creator is intentionally absent. Just as anonymous are the "land-

scapes" of Dubuffet, who feels himself a *medium* for the mud or
ink, a way for the natural world to express itself. Similarly, pop
art accepts the social surface—the artist is absorbed by popular
culture and finally refuses, like Andy Warhol, to sign his own
work: the end of a cycle that began in the thirteenth century.
Instead of the creation of a unique work by a unique individual,
the pop artist may, like Robert Indiana, reproduce a sign, or, like
Roy Lichtenstein, a cartoon, or, like Warhol, duplicate a silk-
screen copy of an existing photo.

We find this anonymity in certain modern literary techniques.
Gertrude Stein's automatic writing becomes Ginsberg's poems
written under peyote and mescalin; or Burroughs' cut-up technique, in which, as he explains, "I place a page of one text folded
down the middle of a page of another text (my own or someone
else's)—The composite text is read across half from one text and
half from the other. . . ."[40] Note that the texts do not even have
to be the writer's own. This technique (with its variations) is not
new: Dada used it first. But it has gained new life and authority;
moreover, it is used with greater seriousness than during the
1920's. Whether or not theoretical statements such as Burroughs'
are "boring" and "nonsensical" as Bellow claims,[41] he is correct
that they indicate a cultural trend, a trend which he wishes to
combat, searching for ways to recover a civilized self.

The loss of individuality and the sense of the "nothingness" of
individual life are precisely what Bellow wishes to combat. He
attacks the cheapening of individual life, noting how far the
human being has sunk from Von Aschenbach (*Death in Venice*)
to Humbert Humbert (*Lolita*)—his similar passion a joke—and
to Wright Morris' professors in Venice (*What a Way to Go*),
knowing the insignificance of their own lives and joking about
the Mann novella.[42] Bellow perceives the difficulty of ennobling
the individual in an age in which so many millions became hair,
gold teeth, and ashes; in which whole populations were sacrificed
to "make the world safe for democracy" or to build socialism.[43]
He realizes that the nineteenth century concept of Self is out-

moded—that it is only a "painted millstone," a "rude, impoverished mass-produced figure that a civilization in need of a . . .
docile public . . . has brought into being"; and Bellow seems to
agree with Lawrence's view that the surface "personality" is "a
wastepaper basket filled with ready-made notions."[44] As he says
of the films of Buñuel, "the old self pursuing the old goals [is
seen as] . . . unreal. The great question seems to me to be:
When will we see men . . . [in] higher forms of individuality,
purged of old sicknesses and corrected by a deeper awareness of
what all men have in common?" ("Saul Bellow on the Modern
Novel," a radio broadcast.) In other words, while he seeks a new
conception of individuality, one which distinguishes between the
presentation self and the true self, he will not "give up on" the
individual. Indeed, this is more than belief; it is the substance of
Bellow's fiction.

In the superb short story "Looking for Mr. Green" (*SD*,
pp.135–60), for example, the hero's attempt to locate an unemployed, crippled Negro so that he can give him a relief check
becomes the attempt to prove that the ordinary individual's life is
meaningful. Grebe rejects the cynicism of the Italian storekeeper,
who is disgusted with the slum dwellers he considers "worse than
animals" (p.150). The storekeeper conjures up for the case-
worker "a huge, hugging, despairing knot, a human wheel of
heads, legs, bellies, arms, rolling through his shop." Grebe insists,
" 'All the same . . . there must be a way to find a person' "
(p.151). "It was important that there was a real Mr. Green"
(p.160), because only if Green exists can Grebe feel that his own
existence, almost as marginal as Green's, is meaningful. A down-
and-out humanist, Grebe seems to fear not only what his boss
tells him—that the depression has cancelled the value of philosophical studies and that only the most brutal facts have any
reality—but is afraid also that concern for the individual in such
a world is anachronistic. Yet is it? We see Staika in the relief
office shouting for her rights and making the officials give them to
her—Staika, the " 'blood mother of Federal Street' " who might

"'submerge everybody in time, and that includes nations and governments'" (p.149). And we see Winston Field, who insists on identifying himself with a "Social Security card, relief certification, letters from the state hospital in Manterro, and a naval discharge . . ." (p.152). Field is declaring that in spite of circumstances, *I matter*. "'You got to know who I am,' the old man said." And so Grebe listens with respect to his scheme for making the Negro race well-off, and he goes away determined to find Green. The clearest formulation of the significance of the story comes near the conclusion: "'It almost doesn't do any good to have a name if you can't be found by it. It doesn't stand for anything. He might as well not have any'" (p.157). With this appeal Grebe touches one of Green's neighbors, who tells him where Green lives. And even the fact that finally he has to give the check to a naked, drunken woman doesn't take away Grebe's victory: "Whoever she was, the woman stood for Mr. Green" (p.160). Green, and therefore Grebe (the similarity of names indicates the similarity of condition), exists as a separate self. The individual's life means something.

5

Bellow wants Herzog to be a "marvelous Herzog" (*H*, p.93); he wants to consider men as "a little lower than the angels," not as insignificant or anonymous. Therefore he rejects the attitude that ordinary life is trivial and banal, conventional or mechanical; that men live secondhand, unauthentic lives, rejecting spontaneity; that their lives are not of quiet desperation but of backslapping complacency; that ordinary life has fallen into the quotidian. Bellow asks in *Herzog:* "Dear Doktor Professor Heidegger, I should like to know what you mean by the expression 'the fall into the quotidian.' When did this fall occur? Where were we standing when it happened?" (*H*, p.49).

Ionesco is one who sees common life as banal, indeed as unreal: thus the chatter in *Bald Soprano*, the empty chairs in *The*

Chairs, the disembodied voices we hear from the street for the first fifteen minutes of Act II of *The Killer,* the easy acceptance of conformity in *Rhinoceros.* Before the playwrights of the Absurd, this attitude was to be found in Rice's *Adding Machine,* Huxley's *Brave New World,* and Eliot's early poems. In fact, the attitude derives from nineteenth century existentialist tradition (Kierkegaard's being *in the crowd* or *in the truth*), nineteenth century Romantic tradition, and the Victorian disgust with "the mob." The plays of Harold Pinter with their brilliant handling of the cliché, a novel like *Lolita,* which sees America as gaudy banality, a parody-novel like *Candy,* which sees the "sincere," Fromm-reading, self-fulfilling college girl as a bundle of secondhand ideas surrounding a core of dull selfishness—these are different in form and extent but not in kind from the nineteenth century *Bouvard et Pécouchet.* As in that work, human relationships, especially those expressed in language, are without value and meaningless. Here is an illustration from *Jack, or The Submission:*

ROBERTA II: In the cellar of my castle, everything is cat . . .
JACK: Everything is cat.
R II: All we need to designate things is one single word: cat. Cats are called cat, food: cat, insects: cat, chairs: cat, you: cat, me: cat, the roof: cat, the number one: cat, number two: cat, three: cat, twenty: cat, thirty: cat, all the adverbs: cat, all the prepositions: cat. It's easier to talk that way . . .
J. Oh yes! It's easy to talk now . . . in fact, it's scarcely worth the bother.[45]

Common life is seen as devoid of intelligence, and (unlike nineteenth century precursors) intelligence is useless in touching real existence. For this reason, the plays of the absurd are composed of ritual action, slapstick, clichés—but not many overt ideas. Life is seen as a game of pinball or ping pong; more than in 1920, it is in 1965 measured out with coffee spoons. Trying to exit from this quotidian existence, one finds himself unable to turn the door handle; a tryst is made impossible by bridge night and Parole Board meeting (Richardson, *Gallows Humor*).

Bellow does not deny that ordinary life is little conducive to human nobility. He agrees with De Tocqueville that "the language, the dress, and the daily actions of men in democracies are repugnant to ideal conceptions," that "a modern mass society has no place for such qualities, no vocabulary for them, and no ceremony . . . which makes them public. . . ." But, he insists, "human greatness can still be seen by us. . . . We are not members of a different species. Without a certain innate sympathy we could not read Shakespeare and Cervantes."[46] Bellow affirms the possibilities still to be found in the common life, and he says of the ordinary people of Kansas and Oklahoma of whom no novelist writes, "They're human beings—they belong to the same species as Moses and Socrates." And he insists there must be more to their lives than banalities tossed back and forth over the breakfast table. He believes "these bakers' daughters may have revelations."[47]

6

Thus, Bellow rejects the denigration of the ordinary life of the individual and tries to show in his fiction the possibilities for finding meaning in such lives. In all his novels the defense of human dignity and human possibilities, even in a dehumanized age, stands central. Let me give three examples.

Joseph, the hero of *Dangling Man,* is an amateur philosopher, and before his alteration he had been preparing essays on Diderot and other philosophers of the Enlightenment. Already we see anticipated another of man's defenders, Moses Herzog. Already we see a moral intellectual focus. Joseph quotes Spinoza and he reflects on Goethe. Believing in reason, in man's potential beauty, Joseph is a humanist. In his breakdown can be seen the breakdown of humanism as a way of looking at the human condition. "My beliefs are inadequate; they do not guard me" (p.123). Humanism of any traditional kind, including Marxism (Joseph is an *ex*-Party member) is insufficient. He looks at

Chicago (Augie March's "somber city") and sees slums, "warehouses, billboards, culverts, electric signs blankly burning, parked cars and moving cars, and the occasional bare plan of a tree" (p.24). He looks at "the lack of the human in the all-too-human" (p.153), and the bleak despair he feels makes him ask, "Where was there a particle of what, elsewhere, or in the past, had spoken in man's favor?" (p.24).

His humanism is not viable in Chicago, but he tries throughout the novel to sustain it. He looks for signs of men's common humanity. He does so because "I was involved with them" (p.25), and if the race is condemned, so is he. Thus he defends traditional humanistic values—perhaps Western values would be more accurate—individuality, moral integrity, brotherhood: the individual *and* humanity, joined by love.

"He is a person," Joseph writes about himself, "greatly concerned with keeping intact and free from encumbrance a sense of his own being, its importance" (p.27). In a society of uniforms, military or civilian, he too wears "the uniform of his times" but only "so that he can give all his attention to defending his inner differences, the ones that really matter" (p.27). He wants to preserve the self, its dignity and freedom. In doing so, he cites Spinoza; but of course the tradition goes back without a break to the Renaissance humanists and from Spinoza on to all important nineteenth century writers, including the existentialists Bellow attacks, and to the Americans Emerson and Thoreau, both of whom saw that "the mass of men lead lives of quiet desperation," both of whom sang, with Whitman, "the simple separate person":

> I celebrate myself and sing myself
> And what I assume you shall assume
> For every atom belonging to me as well belongs to you.

Whitman can sing both terms—he can celebrate himself and humanity because he makes a poetic merger, and they become one. In *Dangling Man* Bellow is unable to perform this magic;

Joseph is unable to end his alienation, although he wants to. Once again: "Goodness is achieved not in a vacuum, but in the company of other men, attended by love." If Joseph cannot be part of society as a whole, can he at least be part of a "colony of the spirit, or a group whose covenants forbade spite, bloodiness, and cruelty" (p.38)? He does not find such a colony because it is not in him to find it, but he longs for it, as surely Bellow does.

The defense of human life in America stands at the center of *Augie March*. Indeed, Bellow wrote the book as a conscious act of affirmation. I shall show later that Bellow's affirmation hides negation and despair, and that the novelist of *The Victim* and *Seize the Day* can be heard beneath Augie's lyric exuberance. But what matters at this point is that through Augie—his style, which expresses joy and possibilities, his open-ended life not confined by naturalistic conventions, his life-crammed picaresque—Bellow wishes to affirm. Although agreeing with Kayo Obermark that "Everyone has bitterness in his chosen thing," Augie keeps hope: "There may gods turn up anywhere" (p.260). He defends the possibility of human happiness, telling cynical Mimi "how pleasant" his life has been (p.254). He rejects, as does Bellow, the low view of human life, held by Moulton, who liked "to show that ill, miserable things and rubbish supplied the unity of the world" (p.366). Padilla tells Augie, "The big investigation today is into how *bad* a guy can be, not how good he can be. You don't keep up with the times" (p.431). Augie refuses to believe that only low motives inspired men like Rousseau and Marx (p.329). Perhaps he cannot go along with the Reverend Beecher "telling his congregation, 'ye are Gods, you are crystalline, your faces are radiant!'" But he was "and has always been ready to venture as far as possible" (p.76). As Clem says, "You want there should be Man with a capital *M*, with great stature. . . . O King David! O Plutarch and Seneca! O chivalry, O Abbot Suger! O Strozzi Palace, O Weimar! O Don Giovanni, O lineaments of gratified desire! O godlike man! Tell me, pal, am I getting warm or not?" (pp.434–35).

Augie admits it. He believes in human greatness—or at least longs for it. In fact, much of the novel is built on implied or stated comparisons between the present and the noble past, comparisons meant to dignify and magnify the modern individual.

To understand the importance of such comparisons you have to feel their accumulated bulk. His "grandma" was one of many "Machiavellis" (p.4). Writing of his mother, who had three bastard children by a traveling man, Augie compares her to "those women whom Zeus got the better of in animal form. . . ." (p.10). Mrs. Klein was "pope-like and liberal with pardons and indulgences" (p.35). Simon, Augie says, "intended to carry me along with him, when it was time, the way Napoleon did his brother" (p.53). When Grandma Lausch locks her door it is "a change in the main established order." Her falling on election day is called an "election day fall" and clearly "she sensed that new days were pushing out the last of an old regime, the time when counselors and ministers see the finish of their glory, and Switzers and Praetorian Guards get restless" (p.55). Later, "it was Simon who took care of the surplus, and no longer Grandma, as in the old administration" (p.93). When she goes off to the old age home, "she made retirement out of banishment, and the newly created republicans, the wax not yet cool on their constitution, had the last pang of loyalty to the deposed, when mobs, silent, see off the limousine, and the prince and princely family have the last word in the history of wrongs" (p.96). Einhorn, similarly, is compared to Caesar, Ulysses, Machiavelli, Pope Alexander. He teaches "lessons and theories of power" (p.98). "The Crash was Einhorn's Cyrus and the bank failures his pyre, the poolroom his exile from Lydia and the hoodlums Cambyses. . . ." (p.106). His success in cheating Nosey Mutchnik is "a specimen triumph of the kind—only bigger and bigger—he

wanted his whole history to consist of" (p.118). Later in the
novel Lucy is compared to Phaedra, the eagle gets the name of a
Roman emperor, Caligula, the relationship between Augie and
Thea is compared to that of Leicester and Elizabeth, and the
novel ends with Augie comparing himself to Columbus. Nor do
these cited comparisons begin to exhaust those in the novel.
Bellow loves and idolizes the great man, and throughout *Augie
March* he shows greatness to be a present human potential.

Seize the Day is again an affirmation of human life; an affirmation of the possibility that the "salesman" need not go to his
"death," need not live a life given to him by others and follow a
masochistic strategy to preserve his childish self.

This affirmation is found most clearly in the poem which the
charlatan-psychologist Dr. Tamkin presents to Tommy Wilhelm:

> *Mechanism vs Functionalism: Ism vs Hism*
>
> If thee thyself couldst only see
> Thy greatness that is and yet to be,
> Thou would feel joy-beauty-what ecstasy.
> They are at thy feet, earth-moon-sea, the trinity.
>
> Why-forth then dost thou tarry
> And partake thee only of the crust
> And skim the earth's surface narry
> When all creations art thy just?
>
> Seek ye then that which art not there
> In thine own glory let thyself rest.
> Witness. Thy power is not bare.
> Thou art King. Thou art at thy best.
>
> Look then right before thee.
> Open thine eyes and see.
> At the foot of Mt. Serenity
> Is thy cradle to eternity. (p.75)

When Tommy asks Tamkin "who this Thou is," Tamkin tells him,
"Thou is you" (p.76). He explains, "You were in my mind when I
composed it. Of course the hero of the poem is sick humanity. If

it would open its eyes it would be great" (p.77). Tommy is, then, a representative man, an Everyman. To heal Tommy is to indicate the possibilities for healing the human race, to affirm the greatness of man. In none of Bellow's novels is it so clear that this greatness is dependent on a transformation of the individual. It is a transformation seen in terms of religious conversion: death and baptism and resurrection.

Tommy asks, "Yes, but how do I get into this?" He means, how does the poem refer to him; but, more broadly, the question means, how can he become the king that he is potentially, how can he reach the "greatness that is and yet to be"? The answer is given in the poem under the pompous, amateurish surface: reject the superficial of life and take its real prize, which is readily available if you can open your eyes. Opening them, you will become a child again and without striving you will reach "eternity." Seizing the present moment is equivalent to seizing the eternal.

The poem is a clumsy vehicle for ideas out of Blake (human divinity, eternity in the present), Reich (blindness of men due to character armor, as in *Listen Little Man*), and Gestalt therapists such as Goodman (living in the here-and-now). Bellow discounts the ideas by vulgarizing them. One of his continuing interests is in the reductions and debasements of great ideas. Through vulgarization, however, he is able to introduce healing ideas without sounding like a ventriloquist. For these *are* healing ideas. Bellow proposes that man can be great, that even Tommy, the common man who sees himself as more hippopotamus than man, can be great: he need only open his eyes.

Modern writers sin, says Bellow, if they pretend to know that the individual is defunct. "The subject of the novelist is not knowable in any such way. The mystery increases, it does not grow less as types of literature wear out. It is . . . Symbolism or Realism or Sensibility wearing out, and not the mystery of mankind."[48]

CHAPTER TWO

Bellow's Cultural Context

1

Saul Bellow's defense of man has been made in the cultural confluence of two main streams: the Jewish experience and the American experience.

Bellow grew up a Jew in a Montreal slum. He is not merely a Jew by birth—he comes from a strongly Jewish household. His mother "lived strictly in the nineteenth century and her sole ambition," Bellow has said, "was for me to become a Talmudic scholar like everyone else in her family."[1] He attended *cheder*, where he learned Hebrew thoroughly, and at home he spoke Yiddish (as well as English, and French). His Yiddish is fluent; he has translated a number of stories, including Singer's "Gimpel the Fool," and he has written an introduction to a collection of Jewish short stories.

There is evidence in his work of this Jewish background. *The Victim* deals largely with the Jewish sense of persecution and the Jewish yearning for brotherhood; the early scenes of *Augie March* portray the lives of the urban Jewish poor and lower middle class; the characters in *Seize the Day* are recognizable New York Jewish types; and in *Herzog* there is the portrayal of a Jewish childhood and an emphasis on Jewish family feeling. Then, too, as his work progresses, one finds a quasi-Yiddish style—shown in sentence construction and in a mixture of mundane and ideal—which becomes more and more pronounced.

How exactly has this cultural background contributed to Bel-

low's belief in man and allegiance to life? Such belief is basic to
Jewish culture—and indeed, it would have to be; it has served as
armor against the despair resulting from the blows inflicted on
the Jewish community throughout history. Maurice Samuel uses
the Yiddish word *bitochon,* meaning *certainty, assurance, trust;*
he writes that *bitochon,* an "instinctive faith in every form of life
[was] part of the equipment of survival."[2] Whether in fact there
was more *bitochon* found in the *shtetl* than in any other peasant
community is beside the point. What is important is the Jewish
self-consciousness of a yea-saying found throughout Jewish literature. It is a yea-saying very much the same as the *amor fati*
Bellow longs to express in his work.

How has the Jew said *Yes* in the face of the grimmest facts?
Essentially, he has been conscious of the presence of an ideal
world lying not outside but within the everyday world. The ideal
world is not a heavenly Jerusalem but the earthly Jerusalem
returned. The Jew returns not as a disembodied soul but as a
living Jew. Heaven is this world, redeemed. So while there is
great tension between the world as it is and the world as it will
be, both poles are immediately present. As Mendele, the "father"
of modern Yiddish literature, wrote, "Israel is the Diogenes of
the nations; while his head towers in the heavens and is occupied
with a deep meditation concerning God and his wonders, he
himself lives in a barrel. . . ."[3] This accounts for what Rosenberg calls the "Jewish vertigo." The Jew totters between the
everyday world and the miraculous one at hand.[4] Buber,
Heschel, and others have shown that analogous to the miraculous
world is the Sabbath—a kind of image of what the redeemed life
will be like: essentially, a time of joy and of a holiness come to
reside in this world. The Jew longs for the final Sabbath when the
redeemer will come; longing, he greets the Sabbath that is. And
he has the power, at least according to the Hasidic tradition, of
making the everyday actions of his life sacred by the manner in
which he performs them; the *zaddik* teaches Torah by the way he
ties his shoes, washes dishes, dances. Hasidism teaches that

common life itself can be sanctified, *what is* can be made *what ought to be*. Through the piety of the Jews the redeemer will come. In Jewish fiction this duality accounts for the combination of a realistic portrayal of everyday life with a fervent idealism. Isaac Rosenfeld describes Tevye as a Sancho Panza whose Don Quixote is God—or who has within him both Sancho and the Don.[5]

Bellow has said of the "Jewish feeling" within him that it resists the claims of twentieth century apocalyptic romanticism;[6] it rejects the belief that man is finished and that the world must be destroyed. The world is, on the contrary, sanctified. Thus we find the struggling householder Tevye (of Sholem Aleichem) celebrating, not cursing, poverty. We find Gimpel ("Gimpel the Fool") humiliated by an extraordinarily unfaithful wife but converting his suffering into an acceptance of life and celebration of God. Gimpel comes from a long line of Jewish fools who praise life; there is Bontsha the Silent (Peretz), who never complains in life and in heaven asks only for a roll and butter each morning; there is also, as we shall see, Moishe Herzog. In Pinski's "And Then He Wept" there is a celebration of endurance in which a poor man accidentally smashes the family's one possession, the bed, and still jokes at misfortune (although his laughter turns to tears when his wife's fury breaks and she cries). In Reisen's stories of poor Jews holding their heads up in poverty, there is again a celebration of common life.

The common life was all the Jews of Eastern Europe had; but it was not denigrated. Indeed, the world is supposed by the Jews to be sustained by the holiness of thirty-six secret saints, unknown even to themselves, men who live as ordinary beggars, cobblers, merchants. Then, too, any beggar may be the prophet Elijah come to earth, and each beggar must be entertained as if he were. The sense of the holiness of Everyman, not limited to the Jewish tradition, was sustained longer in the insulated, semi-medieval Jewish communities than in Christian Europe. Rabbi Pinhas once said to his wife (Buber relates), "I tremble before

Hershele [the water carrier]—because he is so precious."[7] It is partly out of this tradition that Bellow can say, "these bakers' daughters may have revelations."[8] Thus, the *shlemiel* Tevye, dragged off by a horse in the midst of his prayers, remains a man of dignity. "Against the rising tide of despair, Tevye tries to spin the thread of rational discourse."[9] He talks to God not as a miserable sinner but as a man with some virtue on his side.

There is no literature of the "hollow man" in Jewish culture. A Jew is the descendant of Old Testament heroes: not figuratively, but literally. When the Messiah comes, each Jew will enter his Old Testament condition, so that the men around him may be Saul, may be Moses. As Rosenberg writes, "Each Jew is three thousand years old."[10] Each Jew is to consider himself at *seder* as having personally escaped from Egypt. Now, as then, we may be slaves—but we will not be slaves, for we are chosen. Therefore one Jewish writer after another rejects the devaluation of man, knowing in his heart, even if he rejects God, that a man is a profound and holy mystery. The "legacy of wonder" from the Jewish religious tradition[11] is a counterweight to despair over the insignificance of man. It seems no coincidence that the Jewish-American novelist Bernard Malamud, when he received his National Book Award, said almost precisely what Bellow himself said in his own National Book Award address. Malamud declared:

I am quite tired of this colossally deceitful devaluation of man in this day; for whatever explanation: that life is cheap amid a prevalence of wars; or because we are drugged by totalitarian successes into a sneaking belief in their dehumanizing processes; creators of our own thing-ridden society. . . . Whatever the reason, his fall from grace in his eyes is betrayed in the words he has invented to describe himself as he is now: fragmented, abbreviated, other-directed, organizational, anonymous man, a victim, in the words that are used to describe him, of a kind of synecdochic irony, the part for the whole. The devaluation exists because he accepts it without protest.[12]

Jewish culture is essentially affirmative. Howe writes, "These writers—let us call them the writers of sweetness—do not assume

evil to be the last word about man. . . . They do not condescend
to the ordinary, or scorn the domestic affections, or suppose
heroism to be incompatible with humbleness. . . . We are repeatedly struck by the tone of love, that final register of moral
poise, with which such masters as Sholem Aleichem and Peretz
faced the grimmest facts of life."[13]

Howe could be writing of Saul Bellow. Still, Maxwell Geismar
is not completely wrong in seeing Bellow's *amor fati* as something
intended more than something achieved.[14] Bellow is not only a
part of the affirmative Jewish tradition; he is self-consciously a
part of it. He knows that Jewish writers have said *Yes* in the face
of suffering, and he longs also to say *Yes;* thus he stands in a
more complex relation to the tradition than earlier Yiddish
writers or even the contemporary I. B. Singer, who wears the
tradition like his own skin.

Jewish culture *hopes.* Isaac Rosenfeld's "The Hand That Fed
Me" tells of an isolated writer—a Jew in "exile"—who has been
pared to the core. He writes without humiliation to a girl he loves
after one meeting three years before. What is important here is
that even in a story very much in the tradition of alienation, the
hero is hopeful—he believes in happiness. We sense in the tone,
in spite of the incredible over-ratiocination, a spirit of love and of
hope. In Lamed Shapiro's "The Rebbe and the Rebbetsin" the
couple longs for a son, and although they grow old, they never
stop hoping. Even after death, the air of the house seems to sing
with their hopes. Jewish culture hopes; yet it is also true that the
Jew looks backward. As Rosenberg puts it, he "struggles forward
to the halls of yesterday."[15]

While this phenomenon derives from the fact and myth of the
diaspora, it has broader significance: the Jew is, if not a slave to
traditions, a devotee of them; the *shtetls* and the ghettoes, forced
in upon themselves, nourished themselves upon their own culture. It must be remembered that the Hasidic emphasis upon
spontaneity (1) was not a norm but an antidote to a rigid,
tradition-bound rabbinate more concerned with the letter than

the spirit of the Law; and (2) never meant to deny tradition but only to inject the spiritual blood of holy joy into existing traditions. Indeed it is probable that the fact that Jews are closer (even now) to their traditions than gentiles largely accounts for the interest in Jewish-American fiction and Yiddish fiction.[16] At a time when the values and traditions of Westerners have lost power and community has become fluid and without a spiritual center, The Jewish writer provides at least ersatz tradition. Writers like I. B. Singer and Bernard Malamud present a world in which sorrow is meaningful; they present a person with a core. Bellow writes: "I think the Jewish feeling resists romanticism and insists on an older set of facts."[17] It is this older set of facts which has served as a basis for Bellow's affirmation of the value of man.

At the center of Jewish culture and Jewish fiction is this kind of moral concern for man—a moral seriousness which pervades even the comic writing. Art was never, Howe explains, "its own excuse for being." Beauty was not separated from good; "one spoke not of a beautiful thing but of a beautiful deed or event. . . ."[18] Nor was intellect, in theory at least, separated from morality: a scholar was a Talmudic scholar; further, his scholarship had to go beyond mere cleverness—in numerous legends the clever scholar, like the "clever" Zen monk who "stinks of Zen," loses all his knowledge and must become a simple servant in the house of study. In reality, the clever scholar more likely married the rabbi's daughter; nevertheless, the ideal of goodness is there. "I should rather be devout than clever," Rabbi Pinhas said, "but rather than both devout and clever, I should like to be good."[19] This open concern with goodness pervades Bellow's work. Joseph believes his only talent is for goodness; Asa learns what goodness means; Tommy longs to be good. What is required is not certain actions but a goodness of heart, an openness to others. It is a quality to be found continually in Jewish writers: there is Malamud's responsivé and responsible hero of *A New Life;* we think of the lesson his Fidelman has to learn from the

shnorrer Suskind in "The Last Mohican"; we remember the love
that blooms in the heart of the *shlemiel* Stern at the end of
Friedman's novel; and we call to mind Singer's old scholar who
learns human love and says to his rationalistic idol Spinoza,
"Divine Spinoza, forgive me. I have become a fool"[20]—a sainted
fool, like the self-forgiven Moishe Herzog.

Related to the Jew's moral concern for others and the writer's
moral concern for those he writes about (see Bellow, "Distractions") is the Jew's belief in community. If the Jew is a proto-
typical alienatee, he is also the product of an ingrown community. Howe notes that the Jewish child was loved and beaten and
turned into a little *Mensch* terribly young—but was never ignored.[21] The strong family ties and the sense of community are
responsible for the fact that the Jews of Bellow's generation may
despair, may be filled with childhood guilt, but they are not
hollow men isolated from one another like Beckett's Unnamable.

The tension between what is and what might be, between the
everyday and the sabbath, underlies the joke of the "chosen
people"—chosen, yet suffering; highest, yet lowest. Herzog is
baffled that his noble father, whose "I" had such dignity, could
be beaten by hijackers. Throughout *Herzog* and *Augie March* we
find the ironic contrast, not always comic by any means, between
the ideal of greatness people set for themselves and the reality of
foolishness or age or poverty. The joke, "My son was beaten by
the police and sent to Siberia. But does he write a fine Hebrew,"
is one that runs through *Augie March*. We remember particularly
that in the final scene Jacqueline, the Marches' maid, a woman of
sagging breasts, varicose veins, and many beatings, tells Augie,
" 'Ah, the dream of my life is to go to Mexico!' " (*AM*, p.535). As
Malin says, Bellow's heroes "walk the line between dream and
fact, laughing at their precarious position. They are Jewish
ironists."[22]

The ironic disparity between dream and fact and the tradition
of moral seriousness is responsible for the mixture in Jewish
fiction of realistic detail with parable and fantasy. In Kafka and

in his American-Jewish pupil Isaac Rosenfeld the interest in parables aiming at elucidating moral-metaphysical problems is clear. Rosenfeld's "King Solomon," whose irony is very much concerned with the disparity between actual and ideal, tells of a paunchy, middle-aged Solomon: is this the wise man? His wisdom (as all wisdom) is that of a fumbling human being. The story mixes slang and concrete details with a focus on the mystery of human greatness and human fallibility. Realistic parables, from the Talmud to Kafka's "A Country Doctor" to Buber's retelling of *Tales of the Hasidim* are a part of the Jewish tradition. So too is fantasy. One Yiddish genre is the demon tale, found in modern form in the bizarre and humane demon stories of Isaac Singer. Fantasy is also found in Peretz' reworking of folk material (as in "The Golem"), Malamud's tale of sorrow after death, "Take Pity," or his "Jew Bird" or "Angel Levine"; Kafka's "A Country Doctor" or his "The Bucket Rider"; Sholem Aleichem's Kafka-like tale of the town whose dead came alive to run things ("The Dead Town"). But even when not so obviously fantastic, Jewish tradition has its mixture of the surreal: Marc Chagall's vision arises much more out of his Jewish childhood than out of the influence of his contemporaries. I think of West's *Day of the Locust* or the surrealist scene at the close of Henry Roth's *Call It Sleep,* both books written at a time when subjectivity and fantasy were passé in American fiction; I think of Heller's fantastic satire *Catch-22,* of Friedman's *Stern,* with its West-ian scene in the sanatorium, its reliance on imagination: " 'Yes,' said Mrs. Spenser, a skeletal woman Stern imagined had been worn down by her husband's dignified but fetishistic love-making requests."[23]

Bellow, like Philip Roth, has much less of the fantastic in his fiction than Friedman. But he does derive from both the American and the Jewish tradition a delight in half-real, half-symbolic flights of imagination: iguana hunting in Mexico with a poor millionairess who stores money in her refrigerator; becoming Sungo of an African tribe, meeting Reichian African princes, discussing theories of boredom in a lifeboat, writing unmailed, wild letters to dead philosophers, and performing a psychodrama of personal problems on closed circuit television to a mixed audience of scientists and entrepreneurs, aided in performance by a sponging son, an ex-wife, a current mistress, and an ex-rat-catcher. But more important than the fantastic is Bellow's use of parable for the discovery of moral and metaphysical truth. In Bellow, such parables are in the form of dreams, and these dreams are nearly always moral as well as psychological.

In fact, this is true of Bellow's fiction in general: it is moral fiction; it is not concerned with style for its own sake nor even with psychological revelation for its own sake; it considers such moral-metaphysical problems as the demarcation of human responsibility (*The Victim*) and the relationship of the individual to the world of power (*Herzog*). Always it seeks to know *why*. Always it is concerned with the question of goodness—the failure or success of the sympathetic heart. It believes in man and in the potentiality of holiness and joy within the common life, the possibility of meaningful existence. To this extent it is *Jewish* fiction.

2

Bellow came to Chicago when he was nine. He lived in its libraries, yet found time to become an "Indian"—Chicago's only Jewish Indian, he says.[24] Thus, although he remained a religious Jew, he began to imbibe American culture. He studied at the University of Chicago (its "Great Books" program under Hutchins was then in operation), and later switched to Northwestern, to graduate with a degree in anthropology and sociology. Caught up in the depression, Bellow worked for the WPA Writers Project, preparing short biographies of American writers, and taught for four years at a teachers' college in Chicago before turning seriously to his own fiction. Thus he became a special kind of American—a cosmopolitan intellectual with a deep strain of liberal humanism.

The influence on Bellow's fiction of the American cultural tradition is strong, although sometimes hard to distinguish since that tradition is so much a product of eighteenth century enlightenment humanism and nineteenth century romanticism, and since it is parallel in many ways to the Jewish cultural tradition.

The spirit of America as seen in Bellow is largely the spirit of the individual whom he wishes to defend—the individual's significance, his freedom. To say this seems strange perhaps; for ever since the publication of Leslie Fiedler's *Love and Death in the American Novel* (influenced by Lawrence's *Studies in Classic American Literature*) it has become fashionable to see American literature as one of secret terror, of loneliness, of horror and death hidden in children's books.[25] As Fiedler says in *Waiting for the End*, "It is the dream of exile as freedom which has made America; but it is the experience of exile as terror that has forged the self-consciousness of Americans."[26] Beneath the dream of a promised land is the nightmare of confrontation with death, the absurd, and the subterranean forces in the psyche.

Fiedler is right. Yet it is also true that Bellow's defense of human dignity is peculiarly American. In its negation American literature still affirms human dignity. The gothic tradition reveals a horror which, as Fiedler notes in his introduction to *Love and Death,* was liberated with the liberation of the Western psyche from God and reason. Hawthorne's gothic curse on the Pyncheon family; Poe's use of gothic atmosphere and his journeys to disintegration; Bierce's satanic irony; Faulkner's vision of childhood terror and adult castration, of unburied corpses and rotting societies; West's surrealist nightmare (which has nearly turned into reality) of Los Angeles destroyed by the dissatisfied, of cripples and of a costume world hiding emptiness and death; Capote's decadence and mystery; Ellison's scene of psychic fragmentation in the factory infirmary; John Hawkes' vision of nightmares becoming real, his habit of preparing the reader for horror until the repeated imagery of destruction causes incredible anxiety—the list could be extended indefinitely. Such a tradition is not, however, opposed to belief in the individual; indeed, only a literature with an overburdened emphasis on the significance of the individual could have such a tradition.

The same is true of the naysayers in American literature. Hester Prynne and Ahab say No, and *for that reason* have majesty. Like Camus' Rebel, the American hero denies metaphysical and social injustice, saying, "All right, then, I'll *go* to hell." But this is not a shadowy figure out of a junk nightmare nor a package of clichés nor a disembodied voice. We have our gentle witches: Hester Prynne in a book, Emily Dickinson writing books; we have our Bartlebys who "would prefer not to"; we have the grandfather of the Invisible Man who tells his grandson, "Live with your head in the lion's mouth. I want you to overcome 'em with yesses, undermine 'em with grins, agree 'em to death and destruction, let 'em swoller you till they vomit or bust wide open."[27] These social and metaphysical rebels are in some sense victims of the streets or of the seven mad gods who rule the seas. Innocent, they rebel.[28] Our literature is full of rebellious innocents combating a hostile, brutal, or indifferent world. From Natty Bumppo to Billy Budd to Daisy Miller to Nick Adams to Holden Caulfield our heroes are purer than the world around them.

And so, while horror and alienation are integral to American fiction from Irving and Cooper to the present, yet it is a fiction which believes in the significance of the individual. But integral also to American fiction are a return to society and an affirmation of human possibilities; Fiedler and Hassan underplay this side of American literature. Hester Prynne's A for Adulteress becomes an A for Angel. Ahab goes out, Ishmael returns, healed. Thoreau in *Walden* moves between the pond and the town, isolation and community, as does Huck Finn. Marcus Klein shows in his brilliant *After Alienation* that contemporary American literature also swings between the poles of alienation and accommodation; the hero is fearful of losing his identity yet longs for a union of self and society.[29] The outsider doesn't want to stay outside. At the end of *Invisible Man* the hero chooses to return to the community to play a "socially responsible role" rather than to remain in isolation or to equip himself with protective disguise and move from role to role like Rhinehart. Baldwin returns from expatriation and enters the fight for civil rights; his *Go Tell It on the Mountain* works toward an integration of the hero into his community; *Another Country* ends with the reunion of the two lovers, Eric and Yves (Eve), at the airport—a return to Eden that takes place in America, not in exile.

Perhaps the most intense "accommodationist" in American literature is also the most intense champion of the individual: Whitman is able to sing both of the dynamic, nonconforming individual and of the union of such individualists into a community of love. This is truly America as Eden.

Bellow is clearly a part of this tradition, out of which come the magnificent individualists of his novels: out of the transcendentalist glorification of the individual, out of the Hucks and Ahabs of our fiction come Augie (Huck) and Henderson (Ahab). "The function of American fiction," Hassan writes, "is to mediate between the hero's outrageous dream and the sadness of human mortality."[30] Augie, that "sort of Columbus" (*AM*, p.536) after an impossible Eden, setting the force of his Self against the stubbornness of *moha;* Henderson, revolting against death, his great heart booming, "I want, I want"—these are specifically (indeed, self-consciously) American heroes.

Bellow's attempt, in *Augie March* and in his later novels, to catch the spirit of America is part of a tradition going back to Emerson's "American Scholar" address and, more concretely, to the local colorists, to the identification with America by Walt Whitman, to the tradition of attempts to write the "Great American Novel," and to certain great American novels such as *Sister Carrie, USA,* and *Grapes of Wrath.* For many of these writers the spirit of America is the spirit of dynamic life and openness; and as the form of the greatest works has been extremely loose or nonexistent, as in *Song of Myself, Moby Dick, Adventures of*

Huckleberry Finn, USA, so the style has been—at least in the "redskin" tradition—crude. Bellow says, "Dreiser could handle his reality without a recourse to style."[31] Of course, Bellow is an extremely self-conscious stylist. But his style has become wild and rough, attempting to be "in the American grain": "I am an American, Chicago born," Augie begins, "and go at things as I have taught myself, free style. . . ." Similarly he opens up the journal form of the first novel and the Dostoyevskian form of the second to a picaresque looseness in *Augie March* and *Henderson the Rain King,* a looseness which says "life," says "America."

Malcolm Bradbury has shown how Bellow derives partly from Dreiser and the American naturalist tradition, but also how he transcends this tradition in favor of lyric intensity and metaphysical concern.[32] This is true. *Seize the Day* (as well as *The Victim*) is in the broadest sense a naturalistic novel, but one raised to searing, poignant power in the celebration of Tommy Wilhelm's attempt to transcend the terms of the naturalistic novel. Hassan has spoken of Bellow's "sense of cosmic wonder." And Bellow himself has shown his supranaturalistic concern in the questions he raises as essential to the novelist and to all the artists: "Why were we born? What are we doing here? Where are we going? In its eternal naïveté the imagination keeps coming back to these things."[33] These are questions which show that Bellow, while he is a participant in the "cult of experience," looks for gods who transcend this mystery. In doing so, Bellow is both Jewish and American, out of the metaphysical tradition of Hawthorne, Melville, Poe, Whitman, and the transcendentalists.

Emerson ennobled man as a fountain of divine truth, a piece of the godhead: to rely on the self is finally to rely on the godhead of which each one is a part. Bellow is like the American romantics, particularly in their mixture of realistic detail and fable or parable using symbolical or allegorical machinery. It is a mixture which derives partly from the attempt to "reconcile high principles with low fact"—a problem Bellow finds in American writing generally, particularly in Emerson, Thoreau, and Whitman.[34] It is very much Bellow's own problem as well.

3

The two streams of Jewish and American humanism join in the work of contemporary American cosmopolitan intellectuals, mostly Jewish, who write for such magazines as *Partisan Review*. Indeed, this magazine published Bellow's first two stories, "Two Morning Monologues" and "The Mexican General," and has since published much of his fiction and nonfiction.

During the 1940's and 1950's the *Partisan Review* group included such men as Bellow himself, Lionel Trilling and William Phillips (editors of *Partisan Review*), Philip Rahv, Delmore Schwartz, Bellow's friend Isaac Rosenfeld, Wallace Markfield, and Paul Goodman. The group is indeed amorphous: Fiedler remarks that it would resent being thought of as a group at all.[35] Goodman, a libertarian socialist, shares few ideas with the moderate liberal Lionel Trilling; the acceptance for a time of Wilhelm Reich by Schwartz, Bellow, Rosenfeld, and Goodman (whose Gestalt therapy derives partly from Reich) was never shared by Trilling. But they all do partake of an interest in important contemporary international ideas, a serious political concern which has outlived *Partisan Review's* Marxist beginnings, a moral intellectualism that derives more from Jewish tradition than from Matthew Arnold, a rejection of aestheticism in favor of a morally engaged art, an interest in depth psychology, and a belief in man and civilization.

Susan Sontag, in an article on "camp," said, "The two pioneering forces of modern sensibility are Jewish moral seriousness and homosexual estheticism and irony." When she speaks of Jewish moral seriousness she is certainly thinking primarily of *Partisan Review*, in which her article was published.[36] At any rate, *Partisan Review* is strongly opposed—and has been throughout the reign of the New Criticism—to a purely esthetic view of art or life. Trilling is opposed to the esthetic attitude of the "second environment" and its concern with style; he is opposed, too, to a criticism which does not test art by life, which does not ask whether a writer has anything important to say. Using the responses to Bellow's speech as illustration, he writes, "Almost certainly no one will consider in a consequential way whether what was said was right or wrong. . . . It will be carried into the realm of gossip, that great new transcendent gossip of the second environment, where it will be used to understand the quality of being, the grace or lack of grace, of those who think it right and of those who think it wrong." Against such trivialization Trilling sets the example of Sedgwick, who, when he saw a conflict between self-interest and altruism in Mill's system, "set himself to 'examine methodically the relation of Interest and Duty' " so that he might act accordingly.[37] William Phillips has attacked the formalism of the New Critics as well as the estheticism of the New Immoralists, demanding a morally committed criticism and art. Paul Goodman's work, whether it is sociological, literary, architectural, or educational, is concerned with the liberation and development of man's powers so that in a better world he may live a fulfilled life of both freedom and community. Making little distinction between essay, address, fiction, and personal support for political causes, he is a committed writer. Again, Lionel Trilling has not divided his art from the life of the country. His *Middle of the Journey* is, like *Dangling Man*, a novel about a man at the end of his ideological rope. At the beginning of the novel Laskell is recovering from scarlet fever, both physical and political. Recuperating, he finds himself a liberal having only a moral humanism to guide him. Trilling's novel is, like *Herzog*, a novel of ideas similar to what is proposed by Philip Rahv in "The Cult of Experience in American Writing." Indeed, what Rahv says of *Herzog* in his review in *The Herald Tribune* could be said of either novel: "This novel radiates intelligence. . . ."[38] *Middle of the Journey* tries to work toward a political and moral way of life viable for the postwar period. Trilling's brilliant short story, "The Other Margaret," deals with the sadness of maturity, the lesson of moral complexities—a theme similar to but in a different key from *Middle of the Journey*. Isaac Rosenfeld specialized in a kind of parable which combined the intense, complicated thought of the Talmudic analysis or rabbinical *reponsa* with the charm and sophistication of the urban intellectual, and this put to the service of a study of moral responsibility. In his stories, too, such as "George," we are directed to the moral life. "George" concerns a modern, secular *Hasid* who, in protest against the self-destructive ugliness of his intellectual friends at a party, walks out of a window and on down the street (with a broken leg). Like Bellow he believes in goodness. We are reminded of King Dahfu saying, "Good impresses you, eh, Mr. Henderson" (*HRK*, p.149).

Bellow is certainly one of these men. In *Herzog* he attacks the merely "aesthetic critique of modern history" which he finds in modern writers (pp.74–75). No one represents better than he the moral seriousness Miss Sontag contrasts to contemporary estheticism. Often, as in "A Sermon of Doctor Pep" and "Address by Gooley MacDowell," he makes fun of his own propensities to sermonize, making his eccentrics deliver their sermons to a street crowd in Bughouse Square and to the Hasbeens Club of Chicago. Indeed, Doctor Pep attacks sentimental idealism and Gooley is sick of ideas meant to improve mankind, yet both are sermonizing for mankind's health. Then, too, when Bellow began a periodical, it was entitled not *Chicago Literary Review* but *The Noble Savage*. Bellow, like the others, rejects estheticism.

Trilling writes that Bellow is "reassuringly *modern*"; yet he looks to literature for the same moral impulse that Sedgwick and Arnold found. Trilling continues, "The classic defense of literary study holds that, from the mobilizing and liberalizing of the sentiments which the study of literature brings about, there results, or can be made to result, an improvement in the intelligence, and especially the intelligence as it touches the moral life."[39] At a time when intelligence and the moral life are both passé, Bellow has Herzog write to a dean:

> Look, Smithers, I do have a good idea for a new course. . . . The people who come to evening classes are only ostensibly after culture. Their great need, their hunger, is for good sense, clarity, truth—even an atom of it. People are dying—it is no metaphor—for lack of something real to carry home when day is done. See how willing they are to accept the wildest nonsense. O Smithers, my whiskered brother! What a responsibility we bear in this fat country of ours! Think what America could mean to the world (H. p.28).

In modern form, here is the moral seriousness of Matthew Arnold in "Rugby Chapel." Bellow, like Arnold, wishes to serve the cause of truth and virtue (the fact that the words are embarrassing may signify how anachronistic they seem). He has called the nineteenth century writer a "curer of souls" and has regretted the writer's loss of this function. He himself has not lost it.

As the *Partisan Review* grew less and less partisan, breaking first with the Communists, then with the popular front of the early 1940's, it seems likely that Saul Bellow went through a similar transformation. As a young man he was a "moon-faced ideologue," and I surmise that Joseph's break with the Communists in *Dangling Man* may be a reflection of Bellow's own youth. In discussing Bellow's development as a novelist I shall show that Bellow's movement away from the unhappy first two novels to the joyous—self-consciously joyous—*Augie March* again parallels the movement of Trilling and *Partisan Review;* for the 1952, the year before the affirmative *Augie* was published, *Partisan Review* held an extremely affirmative symposium celebrating the possibilities for the individual, particularly the artist, in American culture.

It is obvious, then, that the Jewish and the American experiences, commingling in the American-Jewish urban intelligentsia, are the traditions behind Bellow's writing which affirm human dignity and possibility.

- 2 -

The Psychic Pattern of
Bellow's Fiction

CHAPTER THREE

Alienation and Masochism

1

Bellow affirms. But if Bellow affirms so *hard*, it is because he has to compensate for so much that he sees in the culture. But let me go further: it is not only what Bellow *sees* in the culture but what he *brings* to the culture. He has within him the seeds of the despair which he attacks. He is reviling that side of himself which concurs with the prophets of doom and hucksters of the void.

Partly this despair derives from a frustrated idealism. Bellow is like the humanist he criticizes in the *Times Literary Supplement* for judging by a system of ideals deriving from eighteenth century humanism (and nineteenth century romanticism) and therefore seeing the life around him as bitterly disappointing, as absurd. Believing in nobility, Bellow looks around him—and within him—and fears it isn't there.

Of course, Bellow is aware of the fallacy of setting impossible standards—for example, as in his "Sermon of Doctor Pep" or the satire on idealism in *Augie March* and *Henderson the Rain King*. But beneath the satire he is like Augie: "You want there should be Man with a capital *M*, with great stature" (*AM*, p.434). He lyricizes over Father Herzog: "His *I* had such dignity" (*H*, p.149). He sorrows over a world from which nobility and greatness and dignity seem to be missing. The complement of such idealism and love of greatness is an anguish at what society and the individual really are.

Perhaps this anguish is particularly Jewish. The other side of Jewish hope for the individual and faith in the common life is Jewish despair, Jewish guilt and self-hatred, Jewish masochism. As Maurice Samuels has written of the Jewish people with their lofty idealism: "It was because they had undertaken to be so much better that they felt themselves to be so much worse."[1] Here again, in Rosenberg's phrase, is the "Jewish vertigo"—but this time with its tragic side: the Jew's "refusal to accept from life less than the full satisfaction in the face of all obstacles,"[2]—a refusal leading to despair.

Bellow's despair is typically Jewish. For while it is true that the Jew has transformed suffering by means of irony and a celebration of endurance, it is also true that Jews are expert sufferers. Howe says, "The virtue of powerlessness, the power of helplessness, the company of the dispossessed, the sanctity of the insulted and injured—these, finally, are the great themes of Yiddish literature."[3] In each phrase of this statement we see the underside of *bitochon* (faith in life): helplessness, alienation, injury. We think of the tradition of suffering on the Yiddish stage, of stories of helplessness such as Schneour's "Revenge"—the "revenge" for the murder of a young man's family in a pogrom being only the killing of a gentile's dog—followed by anxiety: "the gentile must have overheard!" We think of the stories of sorrow like that of "Munie the Bird Dealer": openly cuckolded by his wife, "Munie sat down with his hands on the floor, and remained there, motionless, not like a human being, but like a piece of broken gray stone."[4] We think of Kafka's projections of guilt and masochism, of Henry Roth's *Call It Sleep*, a novel of guilt, of a child's punishment and misery, of a victory achieved at the cost of a retreat into the self. Indeed, when critics say that the Jewish writer now speaks for all men and that this is the root of his current popularity, they refer primarily to the "voices of powerlessness speaking in situations of humiliation, nakedness, and weakness. . . ." This is the Jewish voice "that speaks most directly about the nature of present experience."[5] Fiedler agrees: "It is the Jew who has been best able to recast this old American wisdom (that home is exile, that it is the nature of man to feel himself everywhere alienated) in terms valid for twentieth century Americans, which is to say, for dwellers in cities."[6] Similarly Isaac Rosenfeld sees the Jew as the perfect "insider" in a complex age precisely because he is so much an "outsider."[7]

Hence, in attacking the tradition of alienation and despair in modern literature, Bellow is attacking also a Jewish tradition very much his own. The *diaspora*—the scattering of the Jews into exile—is threefold: from the promised land to the shtetl, from the shtetl to the Jewish slum (Napoleon Street in *Herzog*), from the ghetto to the modern world (Chicago in *Herzog*). (We remember the hero of Philip Roth's "Eli the Fanatic" discovering his alienation in the midst of the suburbs by being forced to recognize his identification with the refugee in the black suit and hat.) Swados, like Bellow in asking writers to rejoin the human race, attacks the Jewish writer's "tradition of alienation" and argues, "The reader who does not approach these Jewish writers with romantic preconceptions finds himself continuously stumbling on their ill-concealed self-hatred, despair, and masochism."[8] This is reminiscent of Wallace Markfield's *To an Early Grave*, which, while it treats with gentle irony the suffering of the sensitive, ego-ridden, world-beaten hero, also celebrates that suffering. In a beautiful prayer to the dead "Leslie" (a character modelled after Isaac Rosenfeld), Morroe thinks:

Leslie . . . intercede for me.
I am no big intellect. I am no bargain. I watch too much television. I read, but I do not retain. I am not lost, exactly, but still I am nowhere. I am the servant of no great end. I follow the recommendations of the *Consumer's Research Bulletin*.
But do me this favor, anyway. Keep them off. For they hem me in from all sides now. They wait deep in the dark. They put in my mouth the taste of darkness. They set grief and despair upon me like savage dogs. They give me queer feelings, they get me all balled up. When

I turn my head or open an eye they will rip me with tooth and claw. They will throw me from awful heights. They will drown me in a drop of water. They will put me in a grave.[9]

The following line—"And then he got a whiff of far-off ocean"—is a portent of hope, showing that Markfield is not wallowing in despair. But the novel is in the tradition that Swados attacks. So too is Friedman's *Stern* about a man "whose Jewishness," as Fiedler says, "survives only as a psychological disease. . . ."[10] Weighted down with guilt for paying too little for his house, for not fighting his anti-Semitic neighbor, for being a Jew, he may buy his son a trampoline to watch him rise free into the sky, he may cultivate sophisticated Negro friends, he may join the Air Force—but he is *nach-shlepper*, a *shlemiel*, guilty still. And still alienated, he gets sick aboard a general's B-17: "Cowardly Jewish vomit staining a golden aircraft."[11] For Malamud in *The Assistant*, to be a Jew means to accept suffering. Frank Alpine, converting to Judaism at the end, must undergo circumcision, the pain of which foreshadows his life as a Jew (which is to say, for Malamud, as a *man:* the Jew is simply the prototypal human being).

Noting the positive and negative sides of the Jewish tradition, Maxwell Geismar feels that "Judaism in Bellow's work is a source . . . of guilt and anxiety rather than of pride and pleasure." He feels that Bellow is *oppressed* by his moral tradition of Judaism. Indeed, he says (mistakenly) of *The Victim* that

the whole 'Jewish' concept in this hero (and in the author?) is so close to paranoia and madness, so fraught with guilt, anxiety, and fear and so lacking in warmth, humor and joy, that it is no longer in the historic sense, Jewish. There is all the Jewish guilt without the Jewish pride, there is all the agony of life but no enjoyment, there is the heavy vestigial morality with none of the deep or wild human impulses which necessitated this morality.[12]

This attack is unfair (what of Schlossberg? what of the humanizing, the learning to love, that Asa goes through?), and so one-sided that the criticism seems personally motivated and looks forward to Geismar's vicious personal attack on Bellow in *Ram-parts*. But Geismar is not totally wrong; the guilt and the agony are strong in Bellow's fiction. Indeed, Norman Podhoretz calls the tone of *The Victim* "oppressively pessimistic." "I call it oppressive," Podhoretz goes on, "because it is a pessimism over the human condition even darker than Freud's in *Civilization and Its Discontents*. In *The Victim*, the making of a settlement (that is, the stifling of the instincts) is seen as bringing no positive rewards or compensations of any significance—no increase of energy through sublimation, no powerful Faustian drive; it merely has the negative virtue of preventing the outbreak of 'cannibalism.' "[13] Certainly Bellow's view of the world includes what he calls "the darkness"—the presence in nature and in the human heart of that which has no concern for man; the presence of death under the "social sugars"; the presence of cannibalism under the breaded chickenburger; the chaos under the civilized ego. And so, he isn't speaking out of facile optimism when he asks: "After absurdity, what? After nakedness, what?"

Bellow himself has said, "Well, I am a melancholic—a depressive temperament. But I long ago stopped enjoying melancholy—I got heartily sick of my own character about fifteen years ago. Sometimes I think these comic outbursts [in *Augie March*] are directed against my own depressive tendencies."[14] I would argue that his affirmation of man is also directed against his own bitter nature.

2

In spite of his desire to be affirmative, Bellow's depressive tendencies are seen in nearly all his fiction. One would expect in a writer who wishes to affirm human life and to defend the individual to find characters with strength, grace, even nobility. But Bellow's characters are lonely, despairing, cut off not only from society but from friends and wives. Moreover, they are pathological social masochists, filled with guilt and self-hatred, needing to suffer and to fail.

"A Father-to-Be" is a good example (*SD*, pp.121–33). Filled with despair and masochism relieved only by the humanity of the sufferer and the humor of his imagination, it contains in short form many of the essential elements of Bellow's characters.

The sufferer, Rogin, is like Tommy Wilhelm in his awkward bulk and like Herzog in his masochistic submission to a "bitch." In Joan, indeed, we have the first glimpse of Herzog's Madeline —beautiful, with a Roman nose, sociable, aristocratic, money-devouring, man-devouring. Just as she now locks up her dog in the bedroom "where he jumped persistently against the door with a rhythmic sound of claws on the wood" (p.132), so she will, when they marry, lock up Rogin.

The story tells of Rogin's subway ride to his fiancee's—what he sees and thinks. Rogin feels annoyed by the bills Joan is already piling up before marriage. Paying for her psychiatrist (a whim), her gifts to her rich roommate, her food, he feels weighed down, "under pressure." He generalizes, "Who is free? No one is free. Who has no burdens? Everyone is under pressure. The very rocks, the waters of the earth, beasts, men, children—everyone has some weight to carry" (p.123). Similarly, he sees two tall men, "shapeless in their winter clothes, as if their coats concealed suits of chain mail" (p.125).

As in *Seize the Day*, the world is a loveless one. Rogin, a person with a warm heart, sees one man indifferent to his friend's confession of heavy drinking, sees a father fussing with his daughter "as if he were trying to change her into something else." Another child comes in with the same muff. The parents are annoyed; and "it seemed to Rogin that each child was in love with its own muff and didn't even see the other" (p.127). His own mother, who had always spoiled him, was becoming difficult. "She had sat at the table motionless, with her long-suffering face, severe, and she let him cut his own meat, a thing she almost never did" (p.126).

Indeed, Rogin is not sure, as he recalls his dream of carrying a woman on his head, whether the woman was fiancee or mother.

He feels that they both are extracting their price—"Oh Lord, how he had to pay, and it had never even occurred to him formerly that these things might have a price" (p.126)—leaving it uncertain as to what the price is or why he must pay it.

His most awful vision is of a fellow-passenger, handsome but empty looking, well-dressed—a dandy of respectability—cold: "he seemed to draw about himself a circle of privilege, notifying all others to mind their own business and let him read his paper" (p.128). As Rogin, who is an inventor and possessor of strange notions, watches, he imagines that this respectable fellow-passenger might be his own son by Joan, a son in whom his own traits are recessive. He feels not like an individual but like an instrument working toward ends "we thought were our own. But no! The whole thing was so unjust. To suffer, to labor, to toil and force your way through the spikes of life . . . only to become the father of a fourth-rate man of the world like this. . . ." (p.129). It is a vision of his own extinction—and not only his, but of the human future, in which his kind of man would be gone. We are reminded of Rogin's other dream—of refusing to allow an undertaker to cut his hair—that is, of refusing to die. Now this subway vision of his own death makes him irate; the reader wonders, will he be able to throw off his burdens or will he submit to "death"?

As the tragicomic fantasy continues, Rogin grumbles at Joan's door: " 'I won't be used. . . . I have my own right to exist.' " But quickly we know that he *will* be used. She plies him with baby talk—" 'Oh my baby. You're covered with snow. Why didn't you wear your hat? It's all over its little head'—her favorite third-person endearment" (p.131). And although he thinks of telling her, " 'Do you think . . . that I alone was made to carry the burden of the whole world on me? Do you think I was born just to be taken advantage of and sacrificed?' " (p.132), he says nothing.

And so, he defends his individuality, his dignity, his manhood —but only in his thoughts. When Joan comes back, he bows his head and lets her shampoo his hair; his "secret loving spirit" overflows into the sink, and he forgets the words he had rehearsed (p.133).

Certainly the "water-filled hollow of the sink" is meant to be a symbol of the womb and his "pink" scalp a symbol of infancy. This is Rogin's birth, but an ironic birth: he, not the man in the subway, is his son, Joan's son, in whom his own traits will be recessive and hers dominant. In effect this "spoiled child" is changing his mother. His uncertainty over which woman shall be "on his head" is over; it will be Joan, who is shampooing him. However, in a more important sense, Rogin is here acceding to death. In his dream he had refused to let the undertaker cut his hair; now he accepts Joan's shampoo.

Thus Rogin will never drop his burdens. He has submitted to a masochistic relationship, submitted to being "bled" like Tommy Wilhelm and Moses Herzog. Unlike *Seize the Day* and *Herzog*, this short story does not delve into the origins of Rogin's masochism. What is clear quite simply is the masochism; and it is clear too that the story, despairing of saving Rogin from his burdens, illustrates Bellow's own depressive temperament. Further, in his defeat as an individual, Rogin is symptomatic of a larger defeat of humanity. "Would this [cold, indifferent dandy] perhaps be general forty years from now?" (p.130). Bellow, then, finds himself unable to defend the ordinary individual whom he so desires to vindicate. The masochism of Rogin makes it impossible for him to affirm the potentialities of his humanity, as it makes it impossible for Bellow to defend the human being.

It would be helpful now to consider these attitudes in three of the novels: *Dangling Man, Augie March,* and *Seize the Day*.

Isolates and depressives appear in all Bellow's novels and often his heroes are cut off from those who love them. There is, for instance, Joseph in *Dangling Man,* who can talk only to himself, and that fact accounts for the form of the novel as a journal, the proper form for an isolate. Bellow says of Gide in a review article, "he is an autobiographer, in fact, who hopes to be transformed into an historian, an excellent monologist who wants to advance to dialogue. . . . Sadly enough, the number of intelligent people whose most vital conversation is with themselves is growing."[15] This criticism of Gide applies to the Dangling Man (and to most of Bellow's characters): Joseph is an intelligent monologist.[16] He is living with Iva, his wife, but she might as well be visiting her mother, as does Asa's wife in *The Victim:* there is only one conversation between them and that is an argument. He is as alone as Asa, as Tommy Wilhelm (*SD*), as Herzog. He has to invent a Spirit of Alternatives to talk to so that his ideas can have a sounding board—his friends, he affronts; his family, he rejects. There is no organized plot, no dramatic interaction among characters working toward a resolution: the problems and their resolution remain internal. The journal entries are flat, unemotional, yet quietly ironic; for example the January 16 entry: "Fairly quiet day." In the midst of so many fairly quiet days, this entry is self-lacerating. As Hassan says, the book leaves the impression "of a man who screams out in laughter to see his guts dangling from his belly."[17] In quiet laughter: the screaming is internal.

It seems especially strange that Bellow, a defender of Man against writers of alienation and the void, should create in *Dangling Man* a novel so close in form and spirit to that classic novel of alienation and the absurdity of existence, Sartre's *Nausea*.[18] There are so many similarities that it seems certain Bellow in 1944 was consciously drawing on Sartre's 1938 novel. Both novels are in the form of journals. Roquentin and Joseph start their journals for the same reason: an important change has come over them. "Something has happened to me" (*N*, p.11), both heroes say in effect; they are trying to understand what it is. Both men are isolates: Roquentin has occasional sexual intercourse with Françoise the café owner, Joseph is married to Iva, but we hear little of these relationships; the emotional lives of the two men are equally barren. Each one is "pushed upon [himself] entirely," and for both this puts "the very facts of simple existence in doubt" (*DM*, p.190). Both feel boredom and weariness, a disgust for life.

Both are amateur writers studying eighteenth century figures. Both are unable to continue their writing, feeling, in Joseph's case (besides paralysis) that the ideas of the eighteenth century cannot answer his questions, and in Roquentin's case that his M. Rollebon had been only false security—a way for Roquentin to avoid feeling his own existence, a "Purpose" in life. Neither acts purposefully while he writes his journal; Joseph reads the newspapers, goes for walks, Roquentin walks, eats, thinks. Around them they see a fragmented and trivial environment: Roquentin sees disjointed hands, cards, teeth, hears pieces of fatuous conversation; and Joseph:

> Since eleven I have been growing restless, imagining that I am hungry again. Into the silence of the house there fall accentuating sounds, the closing of a door in another room, the ticking of drops from a faucet, the rustling of the steam in the radiator, the thrum of a sewing machine upstairs. The unmade bed, the walls are brightly striped. The maid knocks and pushes open the door. She has a cigarette in her mouth. (*DM*, p.15)

Joseph, like Roquentin, wonders who he is. Roquentin feels he is "No one. Antoine Roquentin exists for no one. That amuses me. And just what is Antoine Roquentin? An abstraction. A pale reflection of myself wavers in my consciousness. Antoine Roquentin . . . and suddenly the 'I' pales, pales and fades out" (p.227). Is there a self? The more Roquentin writes about Rollebon, the more he finds that it is he himself who creates this character. Rollebon seems to have no fixed ego. Reports of his conduct do not seem to be about the same person. Joseph "suffers from a feeling of strangeness, of not quite belonging to the world, of lying under a cloud and looking up at it" (*DM*, p.300). No longer "the sort of person I had been," Joseph looks at himself, stands back and examines himself through the occasional use of third person description: "Joseph, aged twenty-seven, an employee of the Inter-American Travel Bureau, a tall, already slightly flabby but, nevertheless handsome young man, a graduate of the University of Wisconsin. . . ." (p.26). What is this strange object "Joseph"? "Only for legal purposes," he says, is he his old self. This is not the same, certainly, as to deny the existence of a self; but it is to question with Sartre its consistency and unity. How strange for a writer committed to the defense of the individual!

Joseph and Roquentin are separated from the world, and so too is Tommy Wilhelm in *Seize the Day*. Tommy is legally separated from his wife; his father has rejected him as a slob; he has no friends, and (with reason) he doesn't trust his one acquaintance, Tamkin; he feels that his children's affections have been poisoned against him; he believes that his wife wishes him dead. He is bitter, weighed down by grief, living on self-pity and pills; alienated from himself, accepting the world's values and rejecting himself, he sees himself as a swine, an elephant, a hippopotamus. Like Herzog, like Joseph, like Asa, he sees a cold, alien world which reflects his own isolation; what he sees, he is.

And was everybody crazy here? What sort of people did you see? Every other man spoke a language entirely his own, which he had figured out by private thinking; he had his own ideas and peculiar ways. If you wanted to talk about a glass of water, you had to start back with God creating the heavens and earth; the apple; Abraham; Moses and Jesus; Rome; the Middle Ages; gunpowder; the Revolution; back to Newton; up to Einstein; then war and Lenin and Hitler. After reviewing this and getting it all straight again you could proceed to talk about a glass of water. "I'm fainting, please get me a little water." You were lucky even then to make yourself understood. And this happened over and over and over with everyone you met. You had to translate and translate, explain and explain, back and forth, and it was the punishment of hell itself not to understand or be understood, not to know the crazy from the sane, the wise from the fools, the young from the old or the sick from the well. The fathers were no fathers and the sons no sons. You had to talk with yourself in the daytime and reason with yourself at night. Who else was there to talk to in a city like New York? (*SD*, pp.83–84)

Of course Tommy, like all of Bellow's heroes, does not want to cut himself off from other men. Just as Joseph longs for a "colony of the spirit" (*DM*, p.38) and believes that "Goodness is achieved not in a vacuum, but in the company of other men, attended by love (*DM*, p.92), so Tommy longs for merger into community, and, as we shall see, knows moments of loving communality. But in general his attachments have been to the cold nipple of the coke bottle and to the fantasy father who, even more terrible than the real father, persecutes him.

Happy-go-lucky Augie March may seem an exception, but he, too, is an alienatee. He has, it is true, many friends, many loves. Bellow turned to the affirmative *Augie March* after discarding a novel in progress, "The Crab and the Butterfly," of which one section, "The Trip to Galena," was published in *Partisan Review* in 1950. The hero is an alienatee like Joseph, only more aggressive and verbal, who rejects the practical advice of his sister, angry that she accepted a mediocre marriage. At the house of his future in-laws, he becomes sick, embarrasses everybody, and leaves early. Much more naturalistic then *Augie March*, the published excerpt offers few hints of the later novel's affirmations. The hero hates "romantic Hamlet melancholy," but unlike Augie, he exemplifies it.[19] As Bellow said later, "It was a grim book, in the spirit of the first two, when I suddenly decided, 'No.' Actually my feeling wasn't as mild as I'm describing it. I felt a great revulsion."[20] The result of this revulsion was the affirmative *Augie March*. But while Bellow seemingly discarded completely "The Crab and the Butterfly," we can see, comparing the published excerpt with *Augie March*, that the earlier novel is hidden away in the shell of the later one. In both there is a young man who had dealt with the black market in Europe, who had run with a rough crowd. In both, the hero's disreputable appearance and behavior bring shame to a sibling (brother in *Augie*, sister in *Crab*) who has accepted middle class life, which the hero rejects. In both, this sibling and spouse claim a kind of greatness, of nobility. In both, this sibling and also an old woman (an aunt in *Crab*, Grandma Lausch in *Augie*) want to plan the hero's life; the hero rejects these plans and strikes out on his own, criticizing the sibling for accepting too little, "While I, you see, was still campaigning" (p.791). We remember Kayo Obermark's question to Augie: How is your campaign for a worthwhile fate . . . ?" (p.432). But, far more important, in both the hero is, finally, a lonely outsider. As Tony Tanner says of Augie, "Underneath his exhilarating rhetoric one sometimes hears a faint echo of that saddest of lines from that loneliest of characters, Melville's Bartleby, who could only say, 'I would prefer not to.' "[21]

Augie cannot commit himself to anyone. After Thea leaves, Augie groans, "Me, love's servant? I wasn't at all!" (*AM*, p.400). Even at the end he is by himself, his wife in Paris, and driving alone he is a stranger in exile.

3

Bellow's heroes are not only alienated; they alienate *themselves*. Filled with guilt, they loathe themselves and, in most of the novels, need to heap suffering and indignity on their own heads. Joseph, Asa, Tommy, Henderson, Herzog—all are moral (social) masochists. Their literary ancestors are in the fiction of the underground, especially in Dostoyevsky. Bellow borrowed, for instance, the entire plot of *Eternal Husband* for *The Victim*, and in all his novels he uses Dostoyevskian imagery, imagery of almost psychotic strain—vivid, seemingly irrelevant impressions that touch at the antennae of the unconscious.

Dangling Man has even closer affinities of spirit to Dostoyevsky's fiction than to Sartre's. By pointing out these affinities, I will show that Bellow is close to the underground tradition he attacks. Like the Underground Man, Joseph is a self-alienated moral masochist:

> But what can a decent man speak of with most pleasure?
> Answer: of himself.
> Well, so I will talk about myself.[22]

So the Underground Man talks about himself, as does the Dangling Man. He does so from a wretched room—he seems pleased with its wretchedness and pleased with his own—at least he recites in detail all his disgusting traits, all his frustrations. He revels in his alienation, in his loathsomeness, in his spite. "People do pride themselves on their diseases" (*NU*, p.132). Joseph is like that too. As acidly self-analytic as Dostoyevsky's hero, he writes down every detail of his paralysis, of his disgust and boredom, of the frustrations that he faces. Like the Underground Man he is filled with self-hatred which reveals itself in his imagining or enlarging offenses against him. Both are "as suspicious and prone to take offence as a hunchback or a dwarf" (*NU*, p.133). Joseph is certain the maid disregards him; he is sure Iva is disgusted with him and wants him to earn his keep. The Almstadts treat him like a loafer and affront him by leaving a chicken feather in his orange juice. If Joseph reveals self-hatred by these projections, he demonstrates it also by explosive scenes very much like those the Underground Man indulges in with his friends from school. And as the Underground Man broods for years over the officer who, ignoring him, pushes past, so Joseph has to repay Burns, the Communist who ignores him presumably because Joseph is now a "renegade." Embarrassing the friend he is with, Joseph shouts that Burns is an "addict" and an "idiot"; then, going up to him, he makes Burns admit he knows him. Joseph, like the Underground Man, has a "great deal of *amour propre*" (*NU*, p.133). He does not *openly* delight, as the Underground Man does, in "the enjoyment of despair" (*NU*, p.133), but like him Joseph has "a mad fear of being slighted or scorned, an exacerbated 'honor'" (*DM*, p.147), a sign not of self-love but self-hatred.

Their self-hatred is the other side of their gigantic idealism. Both, trying to be more than human, are less. The Underground

Man wants nothing more than to be good. He has the noblest, loftiest sentiments; he is full of loving-kindness, and, although he is the first to recognize his baseness, he feels superior to those who ridicule him. Joseph, too, is a moral idealist: he sees himself as the thoughtful, good man. He asks, "How should a good man live?" (*DM*, p.39). In spite of his recognition that he has changed, that he is not so mild as he once was, he is terribly self-righteous. He thinks of his friends as having failed him because of their weaknesses; he feels morally superior to his successful brother, rejecting his friendship and help. He believes he has not understood the "likelihood of baseness in other people" (*DM*, p.78), and although recognizing that "the treasons I saw at the Servatius party were partly mine" (*DM*, p.147), he generally keeps the stance of the moral man in an immoral world. It is largely because they cannot sustain their ideals that the Underground Man and Dangling Man hate themselves so much and act as badly as they do.

Their guilt and self-hatred are especially responsible for their desire to suffer. Joseph's suffering really has two effects: it expiates guilt and it forms a stance of moral superiority. If it is true, as I have said, that Joseph does not *openly* delight in suffering as the Underground Man does (who goes into a tavern hoping to be thrown through the window), nevertheless Joseph secretly seeks to suffer, just as do Tommy Wilhelm, Henderson, and Herzog.

First, simply to write the journal is in itself to choose to lacerate oneself—though at the same time to give oneself comfort by admiring the size of the wound. On the first page Joseph rejects the Hemingway code of "hard-boiled-dom" current in America. He is not going to be afraid of expressing weakness: he is going to moan, he is going to open himself up. Actually he is bitterly terse, but his anguish is clear.

He comes to the world with a desire to *not achieve*. He prefers a menial job at a travel agency to a good position with his brother. He prefers poverty to luxury. He would rather die in war than benefit from it, would rather be "a victim than a beneficiary" (p.84). He does not want to raise himself by war, nor by anything else. Partly Joseph's sufferings are meant to assuage his guilt: it is significant that after his blood test—after blood has been taken from him—he is able for the first time to read all day. Partly, too, his suffering is a sign of his higher nature—he raises himself up by keeping himself down. He writes of Myron, whom he has just embarrassed in the scene with the Communist—"But then I may be expecting too much from Myron. He has the pride of what he has become: a successful young man, comfortable, respected, safe for the present from those craters of the spirit which I have lately looked into" (p.38). Thus, although he has just embarrassed Myron, he is superior because of what he has gone through.

We find, then, that the defender of the dignity and freedom of the individual, he who affirms humanity, is none other than an alienatee and a masochist similar in a number of ways to Dostoyevsky's anti-hero, the Underground Man. One scene in *Dangling Man* reveals with particular clarity a Dostoyevskian psychology from which emerge behavior patterns associated with figures like Raskolnikov and Velchaninov. This scene also shows the conflict between Joseph the spokesman and Joseph the dramatic character. Keith Opdahl has spoken of the difficulty of creating ironic distance in the journal form.[23] He points to various kinds of incongruities as enabling Bellow to separate author from character. Bellow is, in general, successful in making this separation; but in doing so, he makes it difficult for us to see Joseph as the reasonable defender of Western values.

Joseph takes Iva to his brother Amos' house for Christmas. Amos is disappointed in Joseph's choice of career—his choice of failure. After a quarrel at the dinner table during which Joseph refuses to consider becoming an officer, believing that to succeed would be to climb "upon the backs of the dead" (p.64), he rejects both Amos' present of a hundred dollars and Amos' way of life; then, climbing to the music room, he listens again and again to a Haydn divertimento for cello—a record he had given the family the year before. Interrupted by his teen-aged niece Eta, who wants to play a Cugat record, he becomes angry. "Beggars can't be choosers," she tells him (p.71), and, furious, he spanks her. When the family rushes upstairs to stop him, he is irate that they think him a rapist and thief (he had taken a pin from his sister-in-law's drawer and Eta had seen and reported him). After they go home, Iva weeps on the bed. "'Dearest!' I shouted. 'It's so nice to know that you at least have faith in me'" (p.74).

Somehow through all of this he feels essentially pure. He had gone upstairs to return the hundred dollar bill, had stayed to gain the knowledge of life that Haydn could give him, treated Eta like the spoiled brat she was, and left because his own family implied that he was a thief and a pervert.

But the reader isn't convinced. First, the humble voluntary poverty and refusal to advance himself over the backs of the dead are ways of gaining secret superiority over his brother and society at large: he will be—it is his comparison—like Socrates, a common soldier. This superiority is revealed by his quoting Isaiah with regard to his sister-in-law Dolly, and Eta: "Because the daughters of Zion are haughty, and walk with stretched forth necks and wanton eyes, walking and mincing as they go, and making a tinkling with their feet: therefore the Lord will smite with a scab the crown of the head of the daughters of Zion, and the Lord will discover their secret parts" (pp.60–61). It is revealed too by his "missionary eagerness" to save Eta from her family when she was twelve.

As Joseph introduces the scene he remembers the last time Amos offered him money. When he refused, Amos said, "I'd take it, by golly. I wouldn't be so proud and stiff-necked." A few lines further on Joseph quotes from Isaiah about "stretched-forth necks." Thus he is projecting his secret pride onto "the daughters of Zion," Eta and Dolly. On the following page Joseph reflects that Eta resembles him physically and later wonders about (though he rejects) affinities of another kind. Thus his judgment of Eta's pride is a displaced judgment of his own, and a displaced anxiety that he will be smitten for pride.

At the end of the scene Joseph's anger at his family's unspoken accusations is again projection. No one says or even hints that he was handling the girl for perverted sexual satisfaction; no one says—Dolly in fact denies—that he is a thief. Yet in some sense he must feel guilty of both crimes. Joseph mentions the passage from Isaiah in connection with the graceful necks of Dolly and Eta. He is astonished that Isaiah, like himself, associates the graceful delicate neck of a woman with her "secret parts" her "ancient machinery of procreation" (p.61). Thus he does see both Dolly and Eta as sexual objects. Upstairs, angry at Eta, he calls her an animal, and pulls her over his knees, "trapping both her legs in mine." As she struggles, it is her neck he remembers pressing down—and then he describes "her long hair reaching nearly to the floor and her round, nubile thighs bare" in his lap (p.71). Of course not all his description of the girl is sexual, but there is enough to make us feel that the hint of sexual offense is his own projection. The situation is not so clear concerning the charge of "thief." But in a general way, Joseph's attitude toward life is that of a guilty thief. As a moral masochist, anything Joseph takes feels like theft to him, just as in *The Victim*, Asa Leventhal feels that he has stolen his moderately good place in life.

Joseph's own place in life, he feels, is to suffer.

I have never found another street that resembled St. Dominique. It was in a slum between a market and a hospital. I was generally intensely preoccupied with what went on in it and watched from the stairs and the windows. Little since then has worked upon me with such force as, say, the sight of a driver trying to raise his fallen horse, of a funeral passing through the snow, or of a cripple who taunted his brother. And the pungency and staleness of its stores and cellars, the dogs, the boys, the French and immigrant women, the beggars with sores and deformities whose like I was not to meet again until I was old enough to read of Villon's Paris, the very breezes in the narrow course of that street, have remained so clear to me that I sometimes think it is the only place where I was ever allowed to encounter reality. (pp.85–86)

We are reminded strongly of Herzog, who recalls

Napoleon Street, rotten, toylike, crazy and filthy, riddled, flogged with harsh weather—the bootlegger's boys reciting ancient prayers. To this Moses' heart was attached with great power. Here was a wider range of human feelings than he had ever again been able to find. . . . What was wrong with Napoleon Street? thought Herzog. All he ever wanted was there. (*H*, p.140)

For both heroes reality is the world of their childhood, and this reality is one of suffering. Late in the book Joseph receives a letter from John Pearl, nostalgic for Chicago. Joseph interprets Pearl's feelings: "He thinks he would be safer in Chicago, where he grew up. Sentimentality! He doesn't mean Chicago. It's no less inhuman. He means his father's house and the few blocks adjacent" (p.153). It is the security of his own father's house that Joseph, like Herzog, longs for: two Jews yearning for the time their personal temples stood and the diaspora had not yet begun. Joseph remembers cleaning shoes at home as a child: the feeling of the room "closed off from the wet and fog of the street." He says, "nothing could have tempted me out of the house" (p.85). It is this shutaway, secure world he is trying to recapture in his isolation and suffering. It is only a partial truth, but a truth nonetheless, that isolation and suffering are Joseph's ticket home.

This truth sheds light on the passage in which Joseph listens to Haydn in the music room.

It was the first movement, the adagio, that I cared most about. Its sober opening notes, preliminary to a thoughtful confession, showed me that I was still an apprentice in suffering and humiliation. I had not even begun. I had, furthermore, no right to expect to avoid them. So much was immediately clear. Surely no one could plead for exception; that was not a human privilege. What I should do with them, how to meet them, was answered in the second declaration: with grace, without meanness. And though I could not as yet apply that answer to myself, I recognized its rightness and was vehemently moved by it. Not until I was a whole man could it be my answer, too. (p.67)

It is a beautiful passage, affirming the possibility of communication and of human nobility in the face of suffering. To say that Joseph finds what he needs in the music is certainly not to negate the truth of what he finds, any more than the wisdom of Dostoyevsky's Underground Man is negated by *his* masochism. But let us see Joseph as he is: isolated from others, gaining by his suffering self-justification, moral mastery, the reflection of childhood security, the reduction of guilt. If goodness is achieved not "in a vacuum but in the company of other men attended by love," Joseph is not achieving it; he removes himself from the others, isolates himself with *dead* company—Haydn—leaving Iva alone with Amos, Dolly, and Eta. He speaks of grace and the lack of meanness as the way to meet suffering and humiliation, yet ten minutes before, he met the "humiliation" of being handed money by attacking his brother, and five minutes later he will throw a tantrum and attack a teenaged girl for the humiliation he receives at her hands.[24] True, he admits that he has not yet become capable of applying Haydn's answer to his own life; but that is just the point: there is a schism between Joseph the spokesman and Joseph the character; the defense is qualified by the defender.

The defender is much like the Underground Man, who also yearns to love and to have faith in men (as is evident in the long, only partially ironic sermon to the prostitute), but whose pride leads him to scorn men and hate himself. Of course Dostoyevsky does not negate man. His characters are, like Joseph, alienatees, but also like Joseph, alienatees with souls. Bellow, like Dostoyevsky, does not want to plunge us into the void but to guide us away from it. But both authors have ambivalent attitudes toward life; much of Bellow's sympathy lies with Joseph the masochistic sufferer, despairer, alienatee, just as Dostoyevsky's sympathy is partly with Raskolnikov and Ivan. But when we say this, we must remember that Raskolnikov and Ivan, and Joseph, too, are themselves divided characters. Joseph, therefore, represents a good example of Bellow's desperate affirmation—his longing to affirm, but his inability to do so fully.

Seize the Day is still more obviously about a moral masochist, Tommy Wilhelm. Tommy is his own most difficult obstacle, his own worst enemy. What he believes to be his troubles are not his real troubles. He allows Margaret to place burden upon burden on him, when he knows that "no court would have awarded her the amounts he paid" (p.29). He chooses to live with a cold, carping father in a hotel for retired people. He chooses, out of pride, to leave the company where he had been employed, and does not look for other work.

Nor is it only present troubles that are self-imposed. Throughout his life Tommy has made bad decisions he knew in advance to be bad. "He had decided that it would be a bad mistake to go to Hollywood and then he went" (p.23). He did not accidentally give Tamkin his last $700. "From the moment when he tasted the peculiar flavor of fatality in Dr. Tamkin, he could no longer keep back the money" (p.58).

He constantly provokes his father into punishing him. Knowing his father's attitude toward his drug-taking, Tommy nevertheless (or rather, therefore) waits until they are together to swallow a phenaphen. He indulges in sloppy habits which disgust the old man. When he makes a scene in the restaurant, choking himself in demonstration of what Margaret does to him, he certainly knows that his father will snap, "Stop that—stop it!" (p.48). He begs for pity, "almost bringing his hands together in a clasp" (p.108), although he knows he can expect no pity. "Look out, Wilky, you're tiring my patience very much," his father says before he finally explodes (p.109). Tommy knows he is tiring his father's patience, and he wants to do so.

Yet Tommy only dimly suspects his self-destructive impulses. He, like Asa, sees himself as a victim: "It isn't my fault" (p.53)—

fate, the world, the hotel clerk are against him. He has bad luck at cards, takes a licking on the stock market. As Napoleon once told a young officer, *"Bonheur est aussi une qualité."* Tommy, however, believes that he is simply unfortunate. He is being murdered: "You must realize, you're killing me," he tells his wife. "Thou shalt not kill! Don't you remember that?" (p.112). When his father gives him advice, he reflects on how much the old man is *not* giving him. When his father says, "Well, Wilky, here we are under the same roof again, after all these years," Tommy is suspicious: "Wasn't his father saying, 'Why are you here in a hotel with me and not at home in Brooklyn with your wife and two boys?'" (p.27). The city itself is against him, slapping parking tickets on his car or frightening him with handbills that look like tickets.

But Tommy sees in the city what he is himself. Is the city grasping, money sucking, self-centered? So too is Tommy, who tries to drink or eat his way back to childhood security, who begs for love and pity. Tommy hates the city as he hates his own "pretender" soul.

Yet he has chosen the city. He remembers idyllically the suburbs around Boston. But no, "to be here in New York with his old father was more genuinely like his life." Indeed, he believes that to suffer is his fate, therefore his true occupation:

He received a suggestion from some remote element in his thoughts that the business of life—the real business—to carry his peculiar burden, to feel shame and impotence, to taste these quelled tears—the only important business, the highest business was being done. Maybe the making of mistakes expressed the very purpose of his life and the essence of his being here. (p.56)

What better summation could there be of the life of a moral masochist—or, in Reik's terminology, of a social masochist?[25]

Still, it is important to note that Tommy's masochism does not warp *Seize the Day,* and that this is not a novel expressing the author's masochism but a novel about a masochist. There is, to be sure, a persecuted little man here, but as in *Dangling Man* and

The Victim, it is a *self*-persecuted individual, created with the full awareness of the author. In other words, this is a far different thing from the authorial self-pity and masochism which Harvey Swados feels and attacks in Jewish writers.

Tommy needs to destroy himself and wants to see himself as a victim. There is social masochism, too, in the origin of his behavior and in its reinforcement.

According to Bernard Berliner, masochism does not result from the individual directing early sadism against the ego, but rather begins with another person and is from inception a pattern, literal or symbolic, directed toward a figure of both love and authority, a strong superego figure, generally a father.[26] The masochist, acting out his childhood relationship, fulfills the expectations of the father. As Weiss says, "Wilhelm has the masochistic necessity to fail, to be destroyed at the hands of the punishing father, in order, under the terms of the moral masochistic commitment, to retain his love, and, in less obvious ways, to memorialize certain events in the past."[27] It is for these motives that Tommy lives in New York, resides in his father's hotel, dresses and acts sloppily, behaves with cringing self-pity. I am reminded of Reik's discussion of the "provocative factor" found in both sexual and social (moral) masochism. Tommy acts the little boy; he provokes by childish behavior the punishment he needs to reproduce his childhood relationship with his father. Tommy uses Tamkin as a substitute father (*Tamkin* Tom-kin). Both are doctors, both give advice, and Tommy sees himself riding on the backs of both; thus to lose under the influence of Tamkin—to "take a licking" on the market—is to take a symbolic licking from his own father, a punishment which is a form of love. As Wilhelm Reich puts it, the masochist makes "demands for love in the form of provocation and spite."[28]

This explanation does not cancel Freud's idea that masochistic behavior is self-punishment to remove guilt, generally oedipal. "You have lots of guilt in you," Tamkin tells Tommy (p.73). He judges himself by his father's criteria, from his father's perspective. "When he was drunk he reproached himself horribly as Wilky," his father's nickname for him: "'You fool, you clunk, you Wilky!'" (p.25). And although in Hollywood he tried to break away from his father's judgment by changing his name (Wilhelm Adler to Tommy Wilhelm), he was unable to do so: "Wilky was his inescapable self" (p.25). He "knows" his father is right, "knows" he should not have trusted Tamkin, or gone to Hollywood, or married Margaret, or left Margaret, or resigned from his job.

But as Reik and Berliner both show, the masochist gets positive rewards as well as guilt-reduction. Berliner says, "suffering has come to mean being worthy of love."[29] "When I suffer—you aren't even sorry. That's because you have no affection for me, and you don't want any part of me" (p.54). This is the baldest statement of Tommy's secret goal. And although Dr. Adler does not provide pity, or phenaphen, he does provide a duplication of the more or less secure father-child relationship.[30] Tommy's worthiness of pity is in itself rewarding—whether or not he is actually pitied. It makes him feel, like Joseph, morally superior to his cold father. Thus, again like Joseph, Tommy refuses to dodge the draft during the war, becoming an ordinary GI rather than an officer. And, like Joseph and Augie, he feels superior to his father and Mr. Perls "because they adored money" (p.56). But Tommy's suffering must seem to come from outside sources, and therefore he must keep "his troubles before him." If he did not, "he risked losing them altogether, and he knew by experience that this was worse" (p.43). Worse not only because specific fear is milder than vague anxiety but also because his self-justifying construction might break down and, in confusion, his real motives would threaten to emerge.

Tommy luxuriates in his suffering. He sees himself as a sacrificial victim, remembers poem fragments like "Come then sorrow/Sweetest Sorrow! Like an own babe I nurse thee on my breast!" (p.89). He does not know why he remembers these lines, but it is clear to the reader: his vision of himself as dead,

his invitation of sorrow, his identification of sorrow with the state
of infancy. Both doctors, his own father and Tamkin, tell him:
"You make too much of your problems. . . . They ought not to
be turned into a career" (p.45, his father) ; "Don't marry suffering. Some people do" (p.98, Tamkin).

Tommy has married suffering. Even more than Joseph, he
moves toward death. He is in a hotel with old people waiting to
die. He constantly feels pains in the chest, or choked, or suffo-
cated, as he shows his father by strangling himself and telling
him, "Dad, I just can't breathe. My chest is all up—I feel choked"
(p.109). He is being bled to death: "When I had it, I flowed
money. They bled it away from me. I hemorrhaged money"
(p.40). Margaret is "trying to put an end to me" (p.47). Tommy
feels like the Brahma bull eaten by the piranha. "When I have
the money they eat me alive, like those piranha fish. . . . when
they ate up the Brahma bull in the river" (p.76).

The bull in the river—Tommy also refers to himself as "wallowing hippopotamus"—connects the images of death by being
devoured and death by water. Drowning is the most common
image of death in *Seize the Day*. Tommy remembers from a
college literature course the line, "Sunk though he be beneath the
wat'ry floor" from *Lycidas*, about the drowning of Edward King
(p.13). His father suggests a water cure, and in telling him to
forget his troubles, says, "Concentrate on real troubles—fatal
sickness, accidents" (p.45), a statement which seems an accidental invitation to die. Later, Tommy is afraid, "the waters of
the earth are going to roll over me" (p.77). When he discovered
the loss of his investment, "his washed tears rose and rose and he
looked like a man about to drown" (p.104). It is as if he were
going to drown in his own tears—a very precise symbolic statement. Choked, he visits his father by the pool in the steam room,
and there he is, in a sense, told to die: "I'll see you dead Wilky
. . ." (p.109); and at the stranger's funeral he symbolically does
die by drowning: his eyes are blind and wet, there is heavy sea-
like music which pours into him, he sinks "towards the consum-

mation of his heart's ultimate need" (p.118). Weiss exaggerates in believing that this scene represents Tommy's acceptance of the role of victim; but it is true that Tommy's self-pity and his drive toward self-destruction and even death are brought to climax here.

Augie March is not a novel about a social or moral masochist. As was pointed out earlier, Bellow developed in this book a conscious opposition to his own bitter nature. Yet in the conflict which Robert Alter considers between *Augie March* as a picaresque novel and *Augie March* as a *Bildungsroman*,[31] there are still hints of Bellow's depressive, masochistic characters.

The conflict of interests is present from the beginning: we are concerned both with the characters Augie meets, and with the adventures, as well as with his process of education. For much of the novel this education is secondary: Augie's "larkiness" carries him—and us—through. But from the beginning of the Mexican adventure with Thea, Augie grows more and more self-critical, less buoyant, less able to sustain himself by larkiness.[32]

Bellow has admitted that he cannot plan a whole book, that he gets "a book two-thirds done and I don't know how it is going to turn out."[33] Increasingly Bellow shows his dissatisfaction with Augie by his hero's self-criticism, criticisms by others, ironic contradictions, and apparent self-indulgence. *Self-criticism:* "I actually did intend to be as good as possible. That's how much I myself knew. But Jesus, Lord! Dissembling! Why, the master dissemblers there are around!" (p.369). *Criticism of others:* Thea tells him, "By a little flattery anyone can get what he wants from you, Augie. . . . I can't out-flatter everyone in the world" (p.387). *Ironic contradictions:* although Augie criticizes the ideal constructors with their monomanias, he says, "Clem had urged me to be engaged for six months. . . . but this advice was good for people who were merely shopping, not for someone who had lived all his life with one great object" (p.476); and although laughing at Utopians, he wants to form a community of orphans with his retarded brother as shoemaking instructor and charming, social Stella as housemother. *Self-indulgence*: when Thea leaves him, Augie carries on like an infant, ready to kill when he finds out that Thea has gone off with Talavera; and to a Russian who dares doubt that he, Augie, has suffered more than anyone, Augie says, "What do you mean, you runt! You cheese-cloth cossack you! After I've told you how I feel—" *I*. Augie has to recognize, "Why, he too had a life" (p.412).

Thus the quality of Augie's speech questions the image of adventuring picaro and at the same time questions the affirmation, as more and more strongly come refrains of the Darkness facing the individual. Late in the novel Augie looks over Chicago from the roof of a hospital:

Around was Chicago. In its repetition it exhausted your imagination of det..ils and units, more units than the cells of the brain and bricks of Babel. The Ezekiel cauldron of wrath, stoked with bones. In time the cauldron too would melt. A mysterious tremor, dust, vapor, emanation of stupendous effort traveled with the air, over me on top of the great establishment, so full as it was, and over the clinics, clinks, factories, flophouses, morgue, skid row. As before the work of Egypt and Assyria, as before a sea, you're nothing here. Nothing. (pp.458–59)

Here Augie, as much as any of the prophets of doom Bellow scourges, prophesies the end of the city, and *in* the city the negation of the individual. In contradiction to Bellow's style and in contradiction to his willed affirmation, the novel has sinister undercurrents.

In more subtle ways, as well, Augie is similar to Bellow's typical heroes. For instance, like Joseph and Asa, he cannot accept success. Augie may be like Huck, "lightin' out for the Territory" when Mrs. Renling or brother Simon want to tame him, but he is also suspiciously like Joseph, rejecting high position, insisting on a loser's role. And just as Tommy leaves Margaret, and Joseph is unable to accept the love of Iva *or* Kitty; just as Asa shuns Mary, and Henderson flees Lily, and Herzog runs from angelic Sono and domestic Daisy or sensual Ramona—

so, too, Augie is unable to accept the love of Thea or to stay with Sophie. I am reminded of Herzog running from the Sisslers, "not able to stand kindness at this time" (*H*, p.98). Even at the end, Augie driving through Europe on business has dropped a few hints that Stella, like Thea, is being unfaithful to him; Augie, like Herzog, sets himself up for being cuckolded.

Thus there is more similarity than appears between Bellow's overtly masochistic heroes and Augie. Augie is not a typical Bellow hero; Bellow produces enough noise and gaiety with the role of the picaro to mask alienation, self-hatred, and masochism. But in spite of him, hints of them appear.

What is true of Augie seems equally true of Bellow. Bellow, like his hero, is life-affirming, love-affirming, individual-affirming. But underneath the "yea" is a deep, persuasive "nay"— underneath belief in the individual and in the possibility of community is alienation, masochism, despair.

CHAPTER FOUR

Construction of Self and World

This is my whole idea. More than human, can you have any use for life? Less than human, you don't either.

(Schlossberg in *The Victim*, p. 133)

One of the important ways in which Bellow's heroes show alienation is in their attempt to go beyond human life: to live detached from mortality and weakness. In his analysis of the men who makes himself into an image, Bellow is extremely close to the analysis of Sartre in *Nausea* or Genet in *The Balcony*, writers from whom Bellow separates himself in his defense of human dignity.

To be "human" is, throughout Bellow's fiction, terrifying. And so his heroes turn themselves into ideal images in order to protect themselves. At the same time they turn the world into one in which they can live safely. This double creation of a self and of a world is a constant theme in Bellow.

Analysis of this double creation begins in Bellow's first novel, *Dangling Man*, which, as was earlier shown, is closely related to Sartre's *Nausea*. Both Bellow and Sartre see that people, uneasy without a consistent, unified self, create roles and limited versions of reality which enable them to be secure amid the chaos of reality and in the face of death. Sartre, believing that underlying the self is nothingness—i.e., that a person has no basis upon which to choose, that he is pure freedom—shows people who, fearing this freedom, create neat versions of themselves or let others create them. At one point Roquentin is disturbed by an anxious little man who sits near him in the café. The waitress, whom he calls "poor girl," cannot figure him out; Roquentin recognizes him as alone, like himself, perhaps waiting for the Nausea. All are uncomfortable until Dr. Rogé enters and puts the man in his place: "He's crazy as a loon, that's that." Rogé, a gross, pompous man—himself a mask of The Wise Old Doctor—has cleared the air: "He knows that the loony won't be angry, that he's going to smile. And there it is: the man smiles with humility. A crazy loon: he relaxes, he feels protected against himself: nothing will happen to him today. I am reassured too. A crazy old loon: so that was it, so that was all" (*N*, p.93).

Bellow's concept of the ideal construction, which is evident in all his novels, is fairly close to this formulation. "I could name hundreds of these ideal constructions," Joseph says, "each with its assertions and symbols, each finding—in conduct, in God, in art, in money—its particular answer and each proclaiming: 'This is the only possible way to meet chaos'" (p.140). An ideal construction is, then, a created self and a created reality. Thus, an ideal constructor can see things as a military man or behavioristic psychologist or clown or Communist Party member. Joseph's brother sees himself as a budding tycoon and the world as money. Jimmy Burns sees Joseph not as a person but as a "contemptible petty-bourgeois renegade" (p.36),—and so can cut him dead.

"The world of explanations and reasons is not the world of existence" (*N*, p.174). Or, as Bellow puts it through Joseph, who asks the Spirit of Alternatives: "But what of the gap between the ideal construction and the real world, the truth?" (*DM*, p.141). It is only at the expense of reality that a person can live by one of these ideal constructions. Roquentin finds similarly that as he tries to give an order to Rollebon's life, "the facts adapt themselves to the rigour of the order I wish to give them; but it remains outside of them. I have the feeling of doing a work of pure imagination" (*N*, p.23). In *Dangling Man* Alf Steidler, in order to keep up his image of the world as dramatic and of himself as a comic actor, "would willingly let go everything in his life that is not dramatic" (p.140). To Mr. Fanzel the world is buttons, needles, cloth, and money. Death is absent, suffering is absent. We are reminded of Kafka's narrator in "The Burrow," who is precisely an ideal constructor, trying to substitute a mentally created formulation for the real world.

The ideal construction is held not only at the expense of perceiving reality but at the expense of lived experience. We find this idea at the moment of truth in Dostoyevsky's *Notes from Underground*. The Underground Man says, "we are oppressed at being men—men with a real individual body and blood, we are ashamed of it, we think it a disgrace and try to be some sort of impossible generalized man" (*NU*, p.222). Here we are touching the core of existentialist thought with its concern with the subject, its rejection of anything external—codes, ideals, formulations—for the subject to act by, and its emphasis on the going-out-from-himself of a living person. It is strange to find Bellow, a critic of existentialists, employing so central an existentialist tenet. In *Nausea* Sartre contrasts actual existence with the creation of essences (like ideal constructions) which keep existence at bay. His central image for these essences is the work of art—the biography, the statue, the portrait. In the Bouville Museum there are realistic portraits of the dead leaders of the town. All have become frozen images of the roles they once played; none are more or less dead than they were as flesh and blood. The men portrayed are all great, sure of themselves and of their right to exist. Confronting them, Roquentin is unsure of his own existence: "My existence began to worry me seriously. Was I not a simple spectre?" (*N*, p.118). But then he begins to understand that not he but these figures have given up real existence. There is, for example, Jean Parrottin, once president of the S.A.B.: "This man was one-indeaed. Nothing more was left in him but bones, dead flesh and Pure Right" (*N*, p.121). As he looks closely, Roquentin sees that the man is a fraud—had created this image of himself. All the portraits were of masks. "Under the brush, their countenances had been stripped of the mysterious weakness of men's faces. Their faces, even the least powerful, were clear as porcelain." Now a humble man and woman, dressed in black of course, enter the hall. The man takes off his hat, " 'Ah!' the lady said, deeply touched." Whereas they have resigned their living reality to the dead essences on the walls, Roquentin refuses to do so. "Farewell, beautiful lilies, elegant in your painted little sanctuaries, goodby, lovely lilies, our pride and reason for existing, good-bye you bastards" (N, p.129). Bellow's condemnation of ideal constructions is similar. "They can consume us like parasites, eat us, drink us, and leave us lifelessly prostrate" (DM, p.88).

Perhaps the best example of this self-destructive nature of an ideal construction is that of the Christian Scientist. Joseph sees her often in the neighborhood with her shopping bag full of Christian Science literature. She is a fanatic and, ironically for a Christian Scientist, very sickly.

Her speech is memorized. I watch her chapped lips through which the words come, so dry and rapid. Often pronounced as though she did not understand them. The words, the words trip her fervor. She says she has talked to many young men who are about to go to war, who are going to face destruction. Her duty is to tell them that the means of saving themselves is at hand if they want it. . . .

Meanwhile her face and the hard brown shells of her eyes do not change. She writes on a pad while she is talking. . . . Her lips come together like the seams of a badly sewn baseball. Her face burns and wastes under your eyes. . . . When, after a long pause, you do not offer to buy one of the tracts, she walks away, her run-down shoes knocking on the pavement, her load swinging as heavily as a bag of sand.

Yesterday she was sicker than ever. Her skin was the color of brick dust; her breath was sour. In her old tam that half-covered the scar, and her rough blackened coat buttoned to the neck, she suggested the figure of a minor political leader in exile, unwelcome, burning with a double fever. (p.162)

Joseph describes the woman as a zombie—with memorized speech and unchanging eyes—as not only physically sick but dead to life, having substituted a dogma for a more uncertain flesh-and-blood life. In the final sentence of the passage Joseph generalizes by comparing her to another kind of ideal constructor, a minor Trotsky with a wall of ideas around him. As Joseph tells the Spirit of Alternatives: "The obsession exhausts the man. It can become his enemy. It often does" (p.141).

If anything, Bellow attacks the self even more strongly than Sartre. On the one hand Bellow defends individualism through Joseph, while on the other, he sees individualism—aggrandizing individualism—as an error.

> . . . We suffer from bottomless avidity. Our lives are so precious to us, we are so watchful of waste. Or perhaps a better name for it would be the Sense of Personal Destiny. Yes . . . shall my life by one-thousandth of an inch fall short of its ultimate possibility? . . . It is because we have been taught there is no limit to what a man can be. Six hundred years ago, a man was what he was born to be. Satan and the Church, representing God, did battle over him. He, by reason of his choice, partially decided the outcome. But whether, after life, he went to hell or heaven, his place among other men was given. It could not be contested. But since, the stage has been reset and human beings only walk on it, and, under this revision, we have, instead, history to answer to. We were important enough then for our souls to be fought over. Now, each of us is responsible for his own salvation, which is his greatness. (pp.88–89)

This search for greatness, for a Personal Destiny, the "I want, I want" is the same romantic error from which Henderson will have to recover and which Herzog will attack. It is the error of becoming more-than-human and so becoming less-than-human.

Joseph, of course, attacks greatness from the standpoint of a failure. But it is not just sour grapes. He has isolated a dangerous virus, a true disease—Blake's disease of Selfhood, Dante's of Pride. Morris Apt has all the symptoms. With a strong Sense of Personal Destiny he worked busily through college trying to be

"Lenin, Mozart, and Locke rolled into one." When he found that there was not time for all three, he settled on Locke. "Inevitably," Joseph says, "he fell short of his models. He would never admit that he wanted to become another Locke, but there he was, wearing himself thin with the effort of emulation, increasingly angry at himself and unable to admit that the scale of his ambition was defeating him" (p.88). When he goes to Washington as a political scientist, he writes Joseph a letter "rich in Washington gossip and explanations of current policy. Why we act as we do in North Africa and toward Spain, De Gaulle, Martinique. It amuses me to catch the subtle pride with which he mentions his familiarity with important figures" (p.151). The search for salvation through greatness is both self-destructive and isolating.

Alf Steidler, a comic, exuberant, theatrical type like those in *Augie March,* and a semi-bum, quite different from Apt, doesn't escape the disease. He tells the story of his conquest of a Norwegian beauty, and "The story wandered to its inevitable conclusion—the conquest, with the Norwegian learning at last to distinguish between his superior worth and his appearance. . . ." (p.150). The disease is found even in a little boy Joseph sees on the street "playing king in a paper crown. He wore a blanket over his shoulders and, for a scepter, he held a thin green stick in his thin fingers. Catching sight of me, he suddenly converted his scepter into a rifle. He drew a bead on me and fired, his lips moving as he said, 'Bang!'" (p.107). This episode hints at the destructive nature of the disease: me-up is you-down.

Joseph believes he has eschewed greatness. Yet we know his *amour propre,* we know that he cherishes his hidden differences as his mother once cherished his Buster Brown curls. We know the secret satisfaction he gets in refusing his brother's money, in refusing to be a "beneficiary." Very often in Bellow's fiction it is a fanatic who knows the truth—Dr. Tamkin or King Dahfu—here it is the Christian Scientist who tells Joseph, "You mustn't be proud" (p.163). But generally he wears greatness with a negative sign, holds the power of the suffering masochist. The point here is that selfhood, including Joseph's selfhood, is destructive: it is his selfhood which keeps him isolated, which makes him hurt those around him. Joseph, speaking of goodness, says:

> That greatness is the rock our hearts are abraded on. Great minds, great beauties, great lovers and criminals surround us. From the great sadness and desperation of Werthers and Don Juans we went to the great ruling images of Napoleons; from these to murderers who had that right over victims because they were greater than the victims . . . to dreams of greatly beautiful shadows embracing on a flawless screen. Because of these things we hate immoderately and punish ourselves and one another immoderately. The fear of lagging pursues and maddens us. The fear lies in us like a cloud. It makes an inner climate of darkness. And occasionally there is a storm and hate and wounding rain out of us. (p.89)

This is a passage which, like similar passages in *Herzog*, connects many sicknesses in our culture—political and personal, Hitler and Hollywood. Both Sartre and Bellow reject the shadow world of ego, the dream of greatness transcending life and so perhaps escaping death.

Bellow's analysis of the ideal construction and of selfhood in *Augie March* is similar to that in *Dangling Man*. But the canvas is bigger, the colors louder, the strokes broader—life turned into history and legend, the individual become a king. Much more than in *Dangling Man* Bellow here shows the individual wishing to magnify himself.

No one need compare Einhorn to a great man; he does it himself, comparing himself to Henry V and Socrates. Each character has a dream, a fixed idea of Self; each stands out from the mass. Near the end, dumpy Jacqueline, the Marches' maid, tells Augie, "Ah, the dream of my life is to go to Mexico!" Augie laughs at this battered woman "refusing to lead a disappointed life" (pp.535–36). It is a typical scene. Bateshaw, the paranoiac ship's carpenter who escapes with Augie from their torpedoed ship, remembers as a child swimming in the municipal swimming pool. "A thousand naked little bastards screaming, punching, pushing, kicking. . . . Skinny you. The shoving multitude bears down and you're nothing, a meaningless name, and not just obscure in eternity but right now. The soul cries out against this namelessness. And then it exaggerates. It tells you, 'You were meant to astonish the world. You, Hymie Bateshaw, *stupor mundi!*'" (p.503). This delightful final sentence—the name of a *nebish* plus the grandiose Latin phrase—sums up the desire of the individual to *matter*, hence, to be great. Many, not just Marx and Rousseau, want to "set themselves apart for great ends . . ." (p.329), want to be, like Simon, a prince of at least the Magnus family. Throughout, characters suffer, as in *Dangling Man*, from "bottomless avidity" (*DM*, p. 88). Grandma Lausch establishes this theme near the beginning of the novel: "Just so you want! Heaven and earth will be moved" (p.30). Many have this American—and Jewish—dream. In a parody of the Horatio Alger story, Simon, working as a newsboy among celebrities, "set off the hope that somehow greatness might gather him into its circle since it touched him already" (p.34). Here is Einhorn, sucking a pierced egg: "It was something humanly foxy, paw-handled, hungry above average need" (p.68). Mimi Villars, too, "had a large mouth, speaking for a soul of wild appetites, nothing barred . . ." (p.204). And Simon the Prince says, "I want money, and I mean *want*" (p.199).

These Machiavellians want to impose themselves on the world in a relationship of power. They remind one of Trotsky, who wrote in *Literature and Revolution*, "Man will occupy himself with re-registering mountains and rivers. . . . In the end he will have rebuilt the earth, if not in his own image, at least according to his own taste. . . . Man will command nature in its entirety. . . ."[1] Similarly, Thea forces the piano to do her bidding, captures snakes and puts them in cages, tames an eagle. Thea loves not the bird but her objective: "The motive of power over her, the same as afflicted practically everyone I had ever known in some fashion . . . carried and plunged us forward" (p.327). As Simon pistol-whips tough Poles and shoots rats and Thea kills crows and snakes, the millionaire Robey flits roaches. "He wildly raised hell as he worked the spray gun, full of lust" (p.444). In a more serious vein, the finest image of human desire and individuality is that implied by the soaring eagle:

> It was glorious how he would mount away high and seem to sit up there, really as if over fires of atmosphere, as if he was governing from up there. If his motive was rapaciousness and everything based on the act of murder, he also had a nature that felt the triumph of beating his way up to the highest air to which flesh and bone could rise. And doing it by will, not as other forms of life were at that altitude, the spores and parachute seeds who weren't there as individuals but messengers of species. (pp.338–39)

Gaining power and so stamping their individuality on the world, saying "You, Hymie Bateshaw, *stupor mundi!*", each person creates a version of the world and of the self with which to order reality (see Chapter Two). When a friend, running across Augie in Paris, is surprised to see him "in the City of Man," Augie wants to know, "Which Man was it the city of? Some version again. It's always some version or other" (p.521). "Every precious personality" gives his own order to reality: like the Utopians—Campanella, More, Machiavelli, St. Simon, Comte, Marx and Engels—whom Augie reads while in Mexico; or like the millionaire Robey, who brawls with cabdrivers and pays for stripteasers but wants to synthesize the history of culture into a single volume and so change the world. In this figure of Robey, Bellow is parodying those historians and philosophers who fit our civilization into a niche in their System, who presume the Jew, a Magian, to be an anachronism in a post-Magian era; Bellow is parodying all literary historians who tell us that the novel is dead; he is parodying all men who, like Laputans, try to fit reality into their schemes. Each person has his own version: "What this means is not a single Tower of Babel plotted in common, but hundreds of thousands of separate beginnings, the length and breadth of America" (p.152). Even Kreindl the marriage broker has *his* version: "To come together with a peepy little woman who sings in your ear. It's the life of the soul!" (p.184). For Simon the life of the soul is money and the seat of glory the "episcopal" barber chair.

Each person protects his version of reality. At the extreme there is Bateshaw tying up Augie in the lifeboat to prevent him from interfering with his "dominant idea" of creating life. More moderate is Stella, who lies a good deal—"or you can call it protection of your vision. . . . Stella looks happy and firm and wants me to look the same. . . . She's calm, intelligent, forceful, vital, tremendously handsome, and this is how she wants to put herself across. It's the vision" (p.522). It is partly to protect their own vision that nearly all the characters in *Augie March* are teachers. One after another wants to convince Augie that he has captured reality: if Augie doesn't see it, he's a fool.

Grandma Lausch shakes her teaching finger; so do William Einhorn, Anna Klein, and Mrs. Renling. Responding to the "something adoptional" about Augie, they want him to share their version of reality. Thinking Augie pliable to make "perfect," Mrs. Renling proposes to adopt him, but Augie "was not going to be built into Mrs. Renling's world, to consolidate what she affirmed she was" (p.151). He was not, that is, going to reassure her that yes, she had the final vision of the world. *Augie March* aims precisely at showing that no one has such a final vision; hence its expansive, open-ended quality. Mrs. Renling was one of "a class of people who trust they will be justified, that their thoughts will be as substantial as the seven hills to build on, and by spreading their power they will have an eternal city for vindication on the day when other founders have gone down, bricks and planks, whose thoughts were not real and who built on soft swamp" (p.152). Again the comparison with the world of history and political power: the point here is not Mrs. Renling's greatness but her need for greatness, akin to the needs of political leaders, akin to their illness.

Augie is no Machiavellian. "To tell the truth," he writes, "I'm good and tired of all these big personalities, destiny-moulders, and heavy-water brains, Machiavellis and wizard evildoers, big wheels and imposers-upon, absolutists" (p.524). In this criticism Augie agrees with Joseph, tired of "great minds, great beauties, great lovers and criminals" who claimed a special destiny (*DM*, p.89).

Yet Augie too is after a special destiny, a "worthwhile fate," a "higher, independent fate." As the novel progresses, and especially as Bellow begins to come down hard on his hero's clever innocence, the reader sees that Augie, too, has a "dominant idea" of un-encumbrance, of not being swallowed up, of a "place of my own"—the dominant idea of an orphan who wants a home but to whom nobody's home is his. It is an orphan's quest for a personal Eden.

Augie is, then, as Fiedler notes, Huck Finn, the innocent orphan.[2] But Bellow hints at his being like an even more illustrious orphan, Aeneas. Like Aeneas he leaves a collapsing home: "Tin showed, cracks, black spots where enamel was hit off, threadbarer, design scuffed out of the center of the rug, all the glamour, lacquer, massiveness, florescence, wiped out" (pp.58–59). Childhood has disintegrated for Augie; home is now just a deteriorating house. Coming at "the last of an old regime"—Grandma Lausch's—Augie's loss of the ancestral home announces his moment of departure, and like Aeneas he has not got the power to stop moving. Again and again we hear "It wasn't even in my power to be elsewhere, once we had started" (p.310). He carries a "father," Einhorn, on his back down the steps of a brothel, and compares himself to Aeneas "who carried his old dad Anchises in the burning of Troy, and *that* old man had been picked by Venus to be her lover. . . ." (p.122). Like Aeneas he regretfully leaves haven after haven—and many Didos—to seek his fate. Like Aeneas, he descends to the underworld (surely this is implied in the scene at the steambath) to gain wisdom about death and life from another "father," Mintouchian, a "monument" of a person, one who claims to have felt himself die and come back; and in an echo of the Sixth book of the *Aeneid*, Augie says of Mintouchian, "I returned him love for love." Like Aeneas he is the leader of men on a ship and is saved when the ship is wrecked. Like Aeneas again, Augie declares himself "love's servant" as Aeneas in Aphrodite's. And Augie deals with goddesses —Thea, meaning *goddess*; Sophie, from Sophia; and Stella, star, the star which Augie imagines as his goal. He is protected by at least two goddesses: Sophie saves him from a beating as Venus saves Aeneas from Turnus, and Thea saves him after a fall from a horse. Finally, like Aeneas he seeks a place of his own to replace his Troy, a place which he conceives of as a kind of orphan home where he would be, as Clem laughs, both father and king (Pater Aeneas). The analogy, since it is comic, is not sustained; Augie is a parodic Aeneas, just as Bloom is a parodic Ulysses; but the analogy exists and reveals Augie's sense of personal greatness.

As much as Moulton, the editor who could speak about his own life and nothing else, Augie has a sense of personal importance. "Nothing is ever good enough for you to stick to. Your old man must have been some aristocrat bastard" (p.452). At times Augie has the manner of an aristocrat, although his father drove a truck. As much as Hymie Bateshaw, Augie has "lived all his life with one great object" (p.476). As much as any of the Reality Teachers, he stars in his own play and gives others the supporting roles. He is sure, for example, that Stella wants what he wants; he is sure that her preoccupations are with him. It is only later that he discovers the truth: Stella has her own life with manifold secret compartments to keep herself important; her preoccupations are with herself. "What do you think it is," Augie laughs, "to drag people from their preoccupations, where they do their habitual toil?" (p.516). He himself is preoccupied with being a Columbus of the Spirit, as absorbed in his quest as Thea in her objective of taming Caligula.

Augie's self-concern is shown in his susceptibility to flattery. Thea is correct in accusing him of this flaw. Moulton's name for him—Bolingbroke—hints at it: Bolingbroke, the crowd-pleaser, the exiled hero become king. Augie is "flattered and smiling" when Clem tells him, "For you? Something exceptional. . . . When I think of you I have to think in terms of something exceptional. On the level of achievement. . . . Are you like one of the lousy crowd cheering the Coptics who row out to the boat? You are not. You are a distinguished personality. You are a man of feeling" (pp.433–34). This is almost a parody of that secret spot of self-importance in Augie's breast that says, as Henderson will later say, "I want, I want." Augie is *not* "groggy with glory" when he takes the eagle down on his arm (p.339); however, from his special kind of glory he is not immune. He, too, is less than human in his attempt to be more.

Generally (although for Augie this is only partly true) everyone "has bitterness in his chosen thing," as Kayo says. Each is disappointed in his dream, in his plan, in his dominant idea. Mimi and Mama are hurt by the love out of which they make their lives. Simon is deadened by his chosen thing, for with the drive for power comes an inner death, and with the money comes Charlotte. As Mintouchian tells Augie, "the thing that kills you is the thing you stand for" (p.484). More is implied here than that the individual is unsuccessful in his striving to be important; what is implied, as in *Dangling Man*, is that the very striving is self-destructive, "because you are the author of your death." A brief examination of this destructiveness will show that Bellow's critique of the reaching after personal uniqueness in *Augie March* is very similar to that in *Dangling Man*.

While the individual's need to assert himself and to refuse to be swallowed up is understandable, his attempt to climb out of the municipal swimming pool results in a rejection of the rest of humanity. To feel worthwhile, to feel safely removed from the Darkness, Thea's father in the rickshaw must not allow himself to feel made of the same clay and subject to the same terrors as the coolies around him. Again, me-up is you-down; so that when Simon is crossed, he has to assert his importance by pistol-whipping Guzynski. And in a very different way Augie, like Joseph and Tommy, is an alienatee. The search of this Columbus for an independent fate keeps him apart and aloof from humanity; he understands things and he laughs, but he laughs from the outside. He well represents a modern principle Bellow attacks in "Distractions of a Fiction Writer" (pp.4–5): "Don't give yourself wholly to any single thing." Bellow understands, with an insight very applicable to Augie, that: "By so doing we deny the power of death over us because as long as we're getting better there's no reason why we should die." Augie keeps aloof: his relationship with his wife seems incomplete and tentative; there is indication that she is cuckolding him. At the end of the novel he is wandering through Europe alone. As Augie's Russian friend says and Augie agrees, "I couldn't be hurt enough by the fate of other people" (p.453). Bellow's analysis of Augie is not so thoroughgoing as his analyses of Joseph and Tommy, but his is not a psychological novel and should not be read as one.

I have mentioned the creation of separate towers of Babel, each builder hoping to keep out chaos. The image of the Tower of Babel indicates the presumption and foolishness of the builders, who say, as in Genesis, "let us build us a city and a tower whose top may reach into heaven, and let us make us a name, lest we be scattered abroad upon the face of the whole earth" (Gen. XI). Perhaps Bellow was thinking of that "let us make us a name," and surely he was thinking of the result—the division of man from man, each speaking his own language. Now, says Augie, it is worse—each builds his own tower, so that common purpose and common understanding are impossible.

Tower building alienates you from other people; it alienates you also from reality. Bellow hints at this again and again. We find, for example, Charlotte's "real mouth . . . unconforming to the painted one." In broader ways this is a dominant motif in the novel. "Everyone tries to create a world he can live in," Augie says, "and what he can't use, he often can't see. But the real world is already created . . ." (p.378). In spite of Thea's fury,

Caligula will not correspond to her idea of what an eagle should be any more than the dogs Augie works with will conform to his boss's conception of a dog. And when Augie begins to question the utopian philosophers he has been reading, he says, "in those utopias, set up by hope and art, how could you overlook the part of nature or be sure you could keep the feelings up?" (p.359). In Schlossberg's terms, the utopians expected a man to be "more than human."

To make the real world conform to one's version of it requires work. Mrs. Renling works—the development in her muscles, Augie says, must come from her "covert labor" (p.152). To convince oneself that one matters, that one is right and justified, is not easy. For a moment near the end of the novel Augie is at peace. He tells the reader:

> It takes a time like this for you to find out how sore your heart has been, and, moreover, all the while you thought you were going around idle, terrible hard work was taking place. . . . It's internally done. It happens because you are powerless and unable to get anywhere, to obtain justice or have requital, and therefore in yourself you labor, you wage and combat, settle scores, remember insults, fight, reply, deny, blab, denounce, triumph, outwit, overcome, vindicate, cry, persist, absolve, die and rise again. All by yourself! Where is everybody? Inside your breast and skin, the entire cast.
>
> Lying in the bath, Stella was performing labor. It was obvious to me. And generally I was doing hard work too. And what for?
>
> Everybody gives me a line about Paris being a place of ease and mentions *calme, ordre, luxe, et volupté,* and yet there is this toil being done. Every precious personality framed dramatically and doing the indispensable work. (p.523)

Bellow makes the reader feel the foolishiness of lovely Stella and handsome Augie, well-to-do, living in the City of Man and yet struggling to create the world each can live in; fighting imaginary enemies, proclaiming, or trying to proclaim, the self.

One passage in the novel fully sums up the problem the individual faces in confronting all the forces opposing him. It sums up the inadequate solution—the creation of a version of reality which can justify and protect the individual. It is an analysis, at once, of both the personal and the political.

. . . With everyone going around so capable and purposeful in his strong handsome case, can you let yourself limp in feeble and poor, some silly creature, laughing and harmless? No, you have to plot in your heart to come out differently. External life being so mighty, the instruments so huge and terrible, the performances so great, the thoughts so great and threatening, you produce a someone who can exist before it. You invent a man who can stand before the terrible appearances. This way he can't get justice and he can't give justice, but he can live. And this is what mere humanity always does. It's made up of these inventors or artists, millions and millions of them, each in his own way trying to recruit other people to play a supporting role and sustain him in his make-believe. The great chiefs and leaders recruit the greatest number, and that's what their power is. There's one image that gets out in front to lead the rest and can impose its claim to being genuine with more force than others, or one voice enlarged to thunder is heard above the others. Then a huge invention, which is the invention maybe of the world itself, and of nature, becomes the actual world—with cities, factories, public buildings . . . becomes the reality. That's the struggle of humanity, to recruit others to your version of what's real. Then even the flowers and the moss on the stones become the moss and the flowers of a version. (pp. 401–02)

If one invents a man, a self, strong enough to face the Darkness, he can't give justice because he "must appear better and stronger than anyone else. . . ." He can't get justice because he "feels no real strength in himself" (p.401); it is not he himself who is strong but the created version of himself. In this analysis of the creation of a self and of the illusion of a world, we are strongly reminded of Genet's *The Balcony* and *The Blacks*. But for Bellow, unlike Genet, there *is* a reality underneath all the versions. Is it possible to reach it? Can one be neither a victim like Mama nor a great man fighting to protect his precious personality?

In *Seize the Day* Bellow does not emphasize the creation of Self and of World. Yet the theme is there. It is there in the office

of Maurice Venice, the talent scout, who suggests that Tommy
take a screen test. "They met and shook hands and sat down.
Together these two big men dwarfed the tiny Broadway office
and made the furnishings look like toys" (*SD*, p.17). These
images symbolize the attempt of both men to be more than
human. Tommy's world is one of ideal constructions. He lives at
the Hotel Gloriana; down the street is the Ansonia, which "looks
like a baroque palace from Prague or Munich enlarged a hundred times." Rubin, the man at the newsstand, wears a Countess
Mara painted necktie. Tommy's father, Dr. Adler, boasts about
his son, hiking his income up till he can bask in its reflected glory;
then he despises his son for not living up to the image he has
created. His indifference, his non-humanity, is the result of his
need to be a certain kind of Self and his need to make the world
one which will glorify this Self. Everyone lives in this world, as
does Robey, the millionaire insect-flitter of *Augie March*, in a
relation of power: Power-as-Money. The investment office is like
a hideous communal nightmare of Self imposed on reality. It is as
fundamentally unreal as the Ansonia Hotel, which, under the
changes of weather, may "look like marble or like sea water,
blank as slate in the fog, white as tufa in sunlight" (p.5). But the
clearest expression of the creation of a more-than-human person
living in an ideal construction occurs at the novel's end. Tommy
sees a stranger in a coffin:

Now at last he was with it, after the end of all distractions, and when
his flesh was no longer flesh. . . . He stepped out of line and remained
beside the coffin; his eyes filled silently and through his still tears he
studied the man as the line of visitors moved with veiled looks past the
satin coffin toward the standing bank of lilies, lilacs, roses. With great
stifling sorrow, almost admiration, Wilhelm nodded and nodded. On
the surface, the dead man with his formal shirt and tie and silk lapels
and his powdered skin looked so proper; only a little beneath so—
black, Wilhelm thought, so fallen in the eyes. (p.117)

Here is the ultimate image of frozen unreality, of a created
image: a tuxedoed corpse. Bellow implies that to be more than

human, to be beyond mortality and pain, is to be dead. Further-more, this is a feasible choice; it is not that Tommy finally makes this choice—no, but he feels "almost admiration" for this "fin-ished" perfection in the satin coffin. Like the Police Chief in Genet's *The Balcony,* he has become an eternal image, he has escaped into history.

The tuxedoed corpse in the satin coffin is very much like what Dr. Tamkin calls the "pretender soul." "In here, the human bosom—mine, yours, everybody's," Tamkin says in his usual grandiose manner, "there isn't just one soul. There's a lot of souls. But there are two main ones, the real soul and a pretender soul" (p.70). The pretender soul—the "presentation self"—is the be-trayer, who makes a man work to appease its need for social approval. The love it gives forth is not real love but disguised vanity. The true soul wishes to "kill the pretender" (p.71). "Therefore, all suicide is murder [i.e., murder of the pretender soul], and all murder is suicide [i.e., a projection of the hatred felt for the pretender soul]."

Tommy sees the problem as still more complex. "Tommy," the charming, affable part of him that wants to be independent of his father, is a pretender soul. So too is "Wilky," the cringing, infantile masochist. He wonders if the name his grandfather called him, "Velvel," might not be the name of his true soul (p.72). But, to simplify, it is the pretender soul which is destroy-ing Tommy Wilhelm, and it is this pretender soul which Tommy Wilhelm must destroy in order that he, as representative man, may shine forth in glory, power, beauty—and that Bellow may affirm the beauty and greatness of man.

We have seen the pretender soul in *Dangling Man* as the ideal pictures which the characters have of themselves; we have seen it in *Augie March* in the characters' romantic, overblown versions of themselves. In *Seize the Day,* Venice the talent scout pampers this pretender soul: in direct contradiction to Schlossberg, who says that to be a good actor is to be "exactly human," Venice says, "Don't be afraid [during the screen test] to make faces and be emotional. Shoot the works. Because when you start to act you're no more an ordinary person, and those things don't apply to you" (p.22). Venice's prescription for escape from the self does not work. For Tommy Wilhelm to represent the greatness and beauty of the human race, he must paradoxically become exactly what Venice says he can escape being: an "ordinary person," he must become human; to do so, he must destroy his pretender soul.

In speaking of the presentation self in a lecture in 1961, Bellow called it a "painted millstone," a "burden which [the civilized individual] . . . believes gives him distinction. . . ."[3] This description of the civilized self as a burden is similar to Tommy's description of his "characteristic self." He speaks (with the self-hatred of a Joseph) of "this Wilky, or Tommy Wilhelm, forty-four years old, at present living in the Hotel Gloriana, [who] was assigned to be the carrier of a load which was his own self . . ." (p.39). This load is physically analogous to his bulk—he compares himself to enormous animals and, when with his father, eats like one. Spiritually, it is the burden of his selfhood, which he must throw off.

This metaphor of burdens is employed again and again in the novel. Tommy's father wants "nobody on my back. Get off! And I give you the same advice, Wilky. Carry nobody on your back" (p.55). Tommy, indeed, believes that he is a burden to his father, and, lacking money, writes him a note, *"Dear Dad, Please carry me this month, Yours, W."* In the steam room his father refuses the burden: "I am not going to pick up a cross" (p.110). Just as he believes that he is on his father's back, he believes that he is also a burden for his substitute father, Tamkin. Tamkin's manipulation of his money "made him feel that he had virtually left the ground and was riding upon the other man" (p.96). But he is only half right. Actually—and this is the chief point—"I was the man beneath; Tamkin was on my back, and I thought I was on his. He made me carry him too, besides Margaret" (p.105). Thus, Tamkin and Margaret are projections of his burden, the Self he needs to unload. And his father, too, is a projection of this burden. In *Augie March* Augie carries Einhorn like an Anchises to and from the brothel; here Dr. Adler is Anchises, the father-on-one's-back, the weight of the past, the piled-up guilt, anxieties, unreal needs. It is more than anything else this (internalized) father which Tommy must get off his back.

The past, the present, and the future—all these are Tommy's own constructions. Or, rather, Tommy has introjected the world of the Others. This false world, represented by his father and by the investment office, is his burden. His need is to live in the here-and-now, the world that *is*; to be not someone else's ideal image but simply human.

CHAPTER FIVE

The Darkness

Bellow's heroes are moral masochists, cut off by despair and self-hatred from those they love, cut off from humanity by their need to go beyond human life—to be more than human. They create ideal versions of themselves, and then, unable to live in these images, they only hate themselves more, and create a version of reality in which they can live. A self and a world: but the "real" human being and the "real" world don't go away.

More important than the construction of ideal selves and worlds is the *need* for such constructions. Here again Bellow's analysis is close to that of Sartre and Heidegger. Sartre's man, for example, runs from the terror of a world of pure existence, a world not in relation to human constructs but beyond categories; he runs into a safe ego, an *en-soi*, and refashions the world into his likeness. Bellow's characters do the same. They cannot face the terror of pure being; they cannot face the terror of their own being or of the death they feel they deserve.

Joseph, in *Dangling Man,* is fenced in by his ego. Already we have seen that his ego hides a great deal of self-hatred. Ego and self-hatred may seem incongruous, but indeed the other side of a sense of greatness which separates a man from his neighbors is a sense of evil—which has the same results. In a Romantic like Byron, we find both at once. Joseph as a child believed that underneath his pleasant exterior he concealed something rotten.

One incident reinforces this sense. Joseph was visiting Will Harascha; when Will's mother introduced Joseph to her husband, Mr. Harascha said "Er ist schoen." She answered, "Mephisto war auch schoen," and Joseph, certain she had seen through him to his core of pure evil, avoided Will Harascha and his family (p.77). Although Joseph now believes that the only devil was "poor devil," the scene seems an analogue—certainly conscious on Bellow's part—of Joseph's behavior now. Thus he meets Iva's cousin on the street, is sure the man is condemning him for not supporting Iva, and so insults and leaves him. Guilt leads to alienation.

This scene at the Haraschas is connected in Joseph's mind with something deeper, more significant. Joseph remembers how, when he was four and his aunt took him for a haircut, his mother cried over his lost curls, and later when he was about fourteen he discovered the envelope with his curls together with a picture of his dead grandfather.

> Then, studying the picture, it seemed to me that this skull of my grandfather's would in time overtake me, curls, Buster Brown, and all. Still later I came to believe (and this was no longer an impression but a dogma) that the picture was a proof of my mortality. I was upright on my grandfather's bones, and . . . through the years he would reclaim me bit by bit, till my own fists withered and my eyes stared. This was a somber but not a frightening thought. And it had a corrective effect on my vanity.

Remembering, Joseph thinks of his vanity, " 'There's something wrong.' I meant there was a falseness about it" (p.76). These sentences connect the two scenes—that of the curls and the grandfather and that of the Haraschas. The relationship *under prettiness is death* is parallel to the relationship *under affability is evil*. Joseph is hiding something he does not want uncovered: that he is going to die, that he is evil; or, more accurately, that he is evil and is therefore going to die. Under the child's locks is the grandfather's skull. In order not to be found out, he must fence himself in, must reject any knowledge of his own evil—tantamount to a knowledge of his own death—and avoid those who might find him out.

Perhaps anxiety over death isn't so important as Bellow thinks, but what matters is that he sees it as central to his characters' psychology. And the result of this anxiety is an armoring which leads to alienation, evident in Joseph's concern that he and Eta may look alike. Why is he concerned? Because he wishes to see others as evil and separate from him; he wishes to blame Eta, for instance, for a vanity they actually share, and wishes to see Dolly as evil: "I have been considering Dolly. Of course I knew that she was no saint; but now reviewing her part in last night's affair, I find her farther on the hellward side than ever" (p.78). If we remember his own fear that he was secretly like Mephistopheles, we understand that what he has done is to project his evil onto others and then reject those others, so getting rid of the evil.

For evil leads in Joseph's mind to death: "The Lord will discover their secret parts. Fearing divine retribution against his own "secret parts," Joseph separates himself from the evil even though he longs for union with other people.

Very often Bellow, like Dostoyevsky, tells important truths about a character in a dream. Such are the dreams Joseph tells about just after experiencing his only moment of peace and openness. The first dream occurs in "an atmosphere of terror such as my father many years ago could conjure for me, describing Gehenna and the damned until I shrieked and begged him to stop. . . ." He has come to a vault to reclaim the body of someone killed in a massacre. He tells his guide that he did not personally know the deceased; the guide smiles as if to say " 'It's well to put oneself in the clear in something like this.' " Joseph avoids involvement with death and with those who die: in other words, with all humanity. The reason is clear: the atmosphere of the dream is of Gehenna—of death and the punishment of sin; anxiety over *his* death and damnation as the punishment for *his* sins. Again, alienation does not derive from the hostility and inhumanity of society. It derives from Joseph's fleeing those who (are evil and hence will) die; it derives from Joseph's fleeing his own death. But in doing so, Bellow indicates, Joseph also flees from himself: the bodies of the victims lie in "large cribs or wicker bassinets" and are "remarkably infantile." This description, coupled with the atmosphere of terror deriving from his childhood, leads us to associate the body he seeks with his own childhood self, his original self, which has died, and with his childhood anxieties—his father's implied threat has been realized, the guilty boy is dead. The guilty man runs. Joseph says that when the figure of death comes, "who, after childhood, thinks of flight or resistance . . ." (p.122). Yet Joseph runs. This throws new light on the incident with the chicken feather in the orange juice: "the half-cleaned chicken, its yellow claws rigid, its head bent as though to examine its entrails which raveled over the soppy draining board and splattered the enamel with blood. Beside it stood the orange juice, a brown feather floating in it. I poured it down the drain" (p.24). Understanding his rejection of death, we are not surprised. And we understand better his *amour propre* and why he is unable to give up selfhood.

The second dream is a comment on the first. The dreamer is a sapper with the Army in North Africa. As he crawls through the window of a house, he sees a grenade wired to the door. His time limited, he shoots at the grenade, only afterward realizing that if he had hit the grenade, he would have killed himself. Put most simply, the message becomes: try to preserve your life and you lose it. Once again, then, if Joseph begins by defending the self, he ends by seriously qualifying the defense. Joseph must lose his selfhood: to be fully human he must reconcile himself to humanity; he is unable to do so until he can reconcile himself to death; fleeing from his own death he flees from other people, flees the recognition of his own moral humanity, flees a recognition of personal evil which would be punished by death and hell. Yet his mortality and attendant sense of personal evil cannot be completely rejected; hence his masochism—his failure and indulgence in suffering—a way of placating the figure of death, his father (for it was his father who threatened the boy with Gehenna) and at the same time a way of separating himself by "nobility" from the rest of humanity and hence from death.

Nor is it only in dreams that we find the root terror of death. While walking home, Joseph sees a man fall down as if with a stroke: "At once I was in the center of a large crowd and, from a distance that could not have been as great as it seemed, a mounted policeman was gazing down" (*DM*, p.114). We sense immediately Joseph's identification with the fallen man: it is Joseph who is in the center of the crowd. A symbol of authority and punishment stands over them both. The scene is a perfect analogue for Joseph's terror of deserved death. Then one more clue: the policeman "bent and reached into the fallen man's pockets and produced an old-fashioned strap-fastened wallet like my father's" (p.115). The scene is an omen of his own death. Indeed, at this moment he touches a spot on his forehead which had begun to smart: he is physically reminded of the night of his mother's death when he was scratched by his Aunt Dina. The spot of blood brings back to him the mortality he has been fleeing. As he says, "To many in the fascinated crowd the figure of the man on the ground must have been what it was to me—a prevision. Without warning, down" (p.116).

Bellow's defense of Man is related to this fear of death. The fallen man is analogous to Fallen Man. Bellow's heroes must defend Man because they have the guilty need to defend themselves. It is because they feel worthy of death that they must proclaim possibilities for the life of Man.

Joseph's sense of guilt is specifically sexual. Sexual offence leads to deserved death.

At one point Joseph visits Kitty Daumler after a quarrel with his wife, Iva. He had once had an affair with Kitty, but broke it off, believing it to be an example of man's avidity, man's refusal to accept limits. Now he returns for solace. It seems clear from the scene that his philosophical reasons for rejecting Kitty are merely rationalization.

Joseph walks out into a wet, filthy night:

I moved toward the corner, inhaling the odors of wet clothes and of wet coal, wet paper, wet earth, drifting with the puffs of fog. Low, far out, a horn uttered a dull cry, subsided; again. The street lamp bent over the curb like a woman who cannot turn homeward until she has found the ring or the coin she dropped in the ice and gutter silt. I heard behind me the clicking of a feminine stride and, for a moment, thought that Iva had come after me, but it was a stranger who passed at the awning of the corner store, her face made bleary by the woolly light and the shadowy fur-piece at her throat. The awning heaved; twists of water ran through its rents. Once more the horn bawled over the water, warning the lake tugs from the headlands. It was not hard to imagine that there was no city here at all, and not even a lake but, instead, a swamp and that despairing bawl crossing it; wasting trees instead of dwellings, and runners of vine instead of telephone wires. The bell of an approaching streetcar drove this vision off. I hailed it and, paying my fare, remained on the platform. It was not far to Kitty's. If my shoes had been watertight, I would have walked. (pp. 95–96)

Kitty is home—but in bed with another man. Joseph has no right to be annoyed; he realizes that it is his own fault that someone else's shirt is hanging on her chair. But he is annoyed. He returns home:

Fog and rain had gone, abolished by a high wind, and, in place of that imagined swamp where death waited in the thickened water, his lizard jaws open, there was a clean path of street and thrashing trees. Through the clouds the wind had sunk a hole in which a few stars dipped. I ran to the corner, jumping over puddles. A streetcar was in sight, crashing forward, rocking on its tracks from side to side and nicking sparks from the waving cable. I caught it while it was in motion and stood on the platform, panting; the conductor was saying that it was bad business to flip a car in the wet, you wanted to be careful about such tricks. We were swept off with quaking windows, blinking through floods of air, the noise of the gong drowning under the horn of the wind.
"Reg'lar gale," said the conductor, gripping the hand rail.
A young soldier and a girl got on, both drunk; an elderly woman

with a pointed, wolfish face; a seedy policeman, who stood with his
hands buried in his pockets so that he seemed to be holding his belly,
his chin lowered on the flap of his collar; a woman in a short skirt and
fur chubby, her stockings wrinkling over her knees, her eyes watering,
and her teeth set.

"You'd think," said the conductor pityingly as she worked her way
through the car, "that a woman like that, who ain't no youngster,
would stay home close to the steam on a night like this, instead of
knockin' around on late cars. Unless," he added to the policeman and
me, "she's out on business," and showed his yellow teeth in a smile.

"Do'ch'ster next. Do'ch'ster!"

I jumped off and struggled homeward against the wind, stopping
for a while under the corner awning to catch my breath. The clouds
were sheared back from a mass of stars chattering in the hemispheric
blackness—the universe, this windy midnight, out on its eternal
business.

I found Iva waiting up for me. . . . In the morning we had a short
talk and were reconciled. (pp.105–06)

These are unusual passages for *Dangling Man*. The style of
most of the book is terse, sardonic, reportorial. Here there is
powerful figurative language (the lizard jaws in the swamp) and
a metaphysical referent (the universe's eternal business). Something important is going on. Now we notice the figures of the
deadly swamp and the woman which begin and end the scene;
we notice the somber ugliness of nearly everything.

The figures have changed. The dirty wet night has cleared; the
presentiment of death—the lizard jaws—has vanished. As Joseph
walks out, his guilt, in the shape of Iva, pursues him. Then it
turns out to be not Iva but a bleary-faced woman with a furpiece
—a figure we can associate with cheap sexuality (the animality of
the shadowy fur, associated with prostitutes, the disgusted look).
He follows her, in spite of the warning horns of the tugs, into the
swamp. At the end we are not surprised to discover that the
"swamp" was a place of death. But Joseph has escaped, because,
indeed, he has *not* gone into the swamp. We remember that the
first time Joseph made love to Kitty she had been in bed with a

cold caught on a wet day; and he too had been soaked that day. This time he takes the streetcar and when he gets to Kitty's he finds her with someone else. He has escaped. The streetcar conductor warns him again of death, but he is already safe—for the time being. And instead of being the object of condemnation and disgust he takes part in looking at such an object—another figure of a woman, again likened to a prostitute. Just as Herzog's guilty sexuality is projected onto the figure of the male prostitute in the courtroom, so, too, is Joseph's guilty sexuality projected onto this figure. *He* is clean, *she* is like Kitty, degenerate and decaying, something to be pitied.

Even incidental elements play a part in Joseph's fantasy. The yellow teeth of the conductor remind one of the yellow which plays so important a part in *The Victim:* it is the color of The Darkness, the terror that underlies life and cares nothing about the human. The policeman is again the figure of authority and punishment, but he is not a powerful figure now that Joseph is safe; the wolfish-faced old woman, like Augie March's Grandma Lausch, like Herzog's Aunt Zipporah, is also a figure of condemnation. The night itself broods above him, waiting: a hemispheric blackness like the Darkness Augie faces.

Often Bellow uses the same imagery to objectify the state of terror and guilt. For example, here is the description of the rape in *Herzog:*

The man clapped his hand over his mouth from the back. He hissed something to him as he drew down his pants. His teeth were rotten and his face stubbled. And between the boy's thighs this red skinless horrible thing passed back and forth, back and forth, until it burst out foaming. The dogs in the back yards jumped against the fences, they barked and snarled, choking on their saliva—the shrieking dogs, while Moses was held at the throat by the crook of the man's arm. He knew he might be killed. The man might strangle him. (p.288)

The brutal man with the stubbled face; the terrible mixture of sexuality and death; the raging dogs. Here is a similar scene from

Dangling Man; Joseph says that the scene describes his first encounter with death:

Our first encounter was in a muddy back lane. By day it was a wagon thoroughfare, but at this evening hour only a goat wandered over the cold ruts that had become as hard as the steel rims that made them. Suddenly I heard another set of footsteps added to mine, heavier and grittier, and my premonitions leaped into one fear even before I felt a touch on my back and turned. Then that swollen face that came rapidly toward mine until I felt its bristles and the cold pressure of its nose; the lips kissed me on the temple with a laugh and a groan. Blindly I ran, hearing again the gritting boots. The roused dogs behind the snaggled boards of the fences abandoned themselves to the wildest rage of barking. I ran, stumbling through drifts of ashes, into the street. (pp.121–22)

Again sexuality and death, again the wild dogs. Looking back at *Dangling Man* with a knowledge of *Herzog,* we may apply Herzog's sexual guilt to Joseph, and we may see this guilt as underlying his terror of death.

To summarize, then: Joseph's masochism and alienation, his desire to see himself as unique, stem from a terror of the death which he feels he deserves because of sexual guilt. He runs from this terror, but he knows that he will not escape.

We have already seen Tommy Wilhelm's masochism—like Joseph's—to be partly a result of guilt and self-hatred. Let me go further. Tommy, like Joseph, fears that he deserves to die because of his wrong against his father. Deserving death, he has constructed a masochistic posture which enables him to feel safe. Essentially his sin is both sexual and aggressive: it is oedipal. His oedipal feelings are hinted at in a number of ways: his loving remembrance of his mother and his disgust that his father had forgotten the year of her death; his perception of his mother as soft and yielding, of his father as harsh and judging; his father acting in the restaurant as judge of his son's sexual life; Tommy's submerged wish that his father die. It is the typical oedipal situation of Yiddish and Jewish-American literature (e.g., *Call It Sleep*). Clearly Tommy is filled with aggressive impulses against his father which he turns in upon himself. This inversion is part of the meaning of the display in the restaurant: in choking himself to show his father what Margaret is doing to him, he is choking his father as well. He is aware that his father's death will end his financial problems as well as remove a cold, tyrannical judge, and he is guilty over his awareness. Thus, *Tommy* wants to die first—or at least needs to *plan* to die first. He needs to be unaware of his own feelings, needs to say, "I don't feel like a murderer. I always try to lay off. It's the others who get me" (p.73). Tommy finds it safer to live as a little, persecuted child, to live within a masochistic construction.

The very title of *Seize the Day* indicates how Tommy, like Joseph, has run from reality. Dr. Tamkin tells Tommy, "The spiritual compensation is what I look for. Bringing people into the here-and-now. The real universe. That's the present moment. The past is no good to us. The future is full of anxiety. Only the present is real—the here-and-now. Seize the day" (p.66). To seize the day, to live in the here-and-now, is to live outside a masochistic construct. It is only at the end of the novel, when all Tommy's defenses against reality have been stripped away—Margaret has been unmerciful, his pills are nearly gone, his father has wished him dead, his money, the very symbol of the false world of living death, is at an end—that he begins to face reality. Stripped bare, he confronts reality for the first time in the novel, a reality which includes his own death, in the corpse in the coffin. As Augie would say, the "social sugars" have begun to dissolve. But until they do, Tommy hides from his guilt within a masochistic construct.

Bellow's fullest and most universal description, of the need to flee reality, to flee pure existence, to flee death, comes in *Augie March*. It is the center of the novel. For *Augie March* is not simply about pride and selfhood; as in *The Victim*, as in *Dangling Man*, Bellow is concerned with the *need* for selfhood; he wants to show the desperate desire of an individual to separate himself from the masses which suffocate his uniqueness, from the city which negates his importance, from the natural world which is indifferent to him (we remember the spot of yellow in the eye of the lion in *The Victim*) from death which finally cancels him as a "simple separate person."

This analysis is typical of Bellow. Joseph keeps aloof because of a fear of death; Tommy hides from death within a masochistic construction. In *Augie March* the conflict between groping individuality and "the darkness"—Bellow's term for all those forces beyond human encompassing which impinge upon man—is what the novel is about; the incidents in *Augie March* demonstrate this conflict nearly as much as the incidents in a *conte philosophique*.

Near the end of the novel the unlucky Italian woman whom Augie meets complains bitterly, "This is happening to *me!*" Augie comments: "This ancient lady was right, too, and there always is a *me* it happens to. Death is going to take the boundaries away from us, that we should no more be persons. That is what death is about. When that is what life also wants to be about, how can you feel except rebellious?" (p.519). To be dead is to lose one's individual existence. If in life one is no more than another inmate, another sufferer among millions, another swimmer in the municipal swimming pool, one fights back and tries to protect his ultimately unprotectable individuality. Ultimately, even Grandma Lausch, a "hard fighter," lies in a casket, "with her face covered and weight thrown on her, silent" (p.177). Even the "great" man, the Mussolini, is "slung up dead by the legs with shirt tails drooped off his naked belly . . ." (p.345). The sailors on the ship all have their secrets, their private dreams, plans and theories; but—and this is the point—the ship sinks. Augie listens to "hard luck stories, personal histories, gripes . . ." (p.492). A hip Negro lets him read this poem:

How much, you ask me, do I suffer.
Now, baby, listen, I am not a good bluffer.

> My ambitions and aspirations don't leave me no rest;
> I am born with a high mind and aim for the best. (p.494)

The poem is a parody on Augie and on Bellow's own nature. Here is the striving Self which will be full-blown in Henderson. Then the torpedo comes and the water covers them all.

Death is the core terror and the ultimate cancel stamp on the "separate Self" that Bellow defends in his address before the Library of Congress and in all his fiction. Death is the ground of all that Bellow calls the "darkness," underlying the inhuman in nature and in the social world.

Augie speaks of "the dark of this West Side [police] station! It was very dark. It was spoiled, diseased, sore and running" (p.229). Here he sees "the surplus and superabundance of human material." He sees, that is, the crowds at the municipal swimming pool—but here all the swimmers have given up; none is saying, "You, Hymie Bateshaw, *stupor mundi!*" These are victims of the Darkness, worse victims than Augie's own mother. It is partly from this darkness that the individual tries to escape. Just after Augie speaks of Mussolini's death, he speaks of another "great man," Thea's father, shown in a photograph in a rickshaw. "And I thought what there was to being picked for special distinction. . . . Around him spectators from the millions gowping at him famine marks, louse vehicles, the supply of wars, the living fringe of a great number sunk in the ground, dead, and buzzing or jumping over Asia like diatoms of the vast bath of the ocean in the pins of the sun" (pp.345–46). This is an ambiguous image. On the one hand it points to the audacity of one fat man singling himself out. Why he? In conjunction with the image of the fly-eaten Mussolini it is a picture of contemptible *vanitas* and contains an implied threat. In addition, while the "millions" are compared to insects, they dazzle like water plankton in the sun— there is a beauty to them. These humans like sea plankton remind us of Whitman's "Sea Drift." But they remind us even more of the vision of De Quincey quoted as an epigraph to *The*

Victim: the human face, the innumerable faces arising out of the sea, each one *wanting*; it is an image of despair, a despair which makes understandable the white suit, the fine shoes of Thea's father in the rickshaw. This Asian multitude out of which the individual tries to arise brings to mind another image of the Darkness: Augie speaks of a gray day at the coal yard as indicating a "middle-of-Asia darkness . . ." (p.273). A man runs from this darkness, runs even from knowledge of it; so that when Simon sees Augie sitting in a dark room looking over the dumb beast of Chicago, Simon yells, "Hey, what the hell are you doing in a dark room for Chrissake?" (p.425).

The metaphor comparing the mass of humanity to plankton brings together two forms of the opposition to human individuality—the social mass and the inhuman in nature. Not only is man an insignificant entity among the billions of his kind, he is a matter of no concern in the universe as a whole. "I wonder where in the creation there would be much of a doubletake at the cry '*Homo sum!*'" Again the language of a human-centered classicism confronts the comic, slang "doubletake" at such pretension. For Bellow, although he fights hard against this conclusion, the universe is not man's. Indeed, if one is quiet, he realizes "that wherever it was dark there was this sound of insects, continental and hemispheric, again and again, like surf, and continuous and dense as stars" (p.326). Insects, like those humans "buzzing or jumping over Asia," symbolize what Hymie Bateshaw, Machiavelli, and Mussolini have to fight in order to attain recognition of their importance or, rather, symbolize what they have to fight in order to *create* their own importance. When Mussolini is dead, "the flies, on whom he had also declared war, walked on his empty face relaxed of its wide-jawed grimace, upside down" (p.345). The flies, unconcerned with human aspirations, are the winners of the war.

So Bellow creates a mesh of metaphors for the forces which are indifferent to human aspirations, to human individuality: the *darkness, stars, insects, water or the sea.* Here, for example,

Bellow connects images of *darkness* and *water* to convey a sense
of both man-made and natural opposition to the individual:

> However, as I felt on entering Erie, Pennsylvania, there is a dark-
> ness. It is for everyone. You don't, as perhaps some imagine, try it, one
> foot into it like a barbershop "September Morn." Nor are lowered into
> it with visitor's curiosity, as the old Eastern monarch was let down
> into the weeds inside a glass ball to observe the fishes. . . . Only
> some Greeks and admirers of theirs, in their liquid noon, where the
> friendship of beauty to human things was perfect, thought they were
> clearly divided from this darkness. And these Greeks too were in it.
> (p.175)

Underlying both the natural and human darkness-liquid is death.
Bellow is showing that most of life is not under human control
and order, that in spite of the system creators, it is the irrational
which is ultimately victorious.

A related group of metaphors concerns *energy*, an inhuman
energy which is at the core of both nature and the man-made but
which defies the orderliness of the man-made—an analysis which
connects Bellow very closely to Ionesco, who, in such plays as
The Killer, shows that the irrational can never be eliminated from
man's world, that even in the splendid city of the future, the mad
killer waits with his knife. Early in the novel Augie speaks of the
splendid store in which he works:

> The place was a salon, with Frenchy torches held by human-arm
> brackets out from the walls, furled drapes, and Chinese furniture—
> such corners as are softened, sheltered from the outside air, even from
> the air of the Rue de Rivoli, by oriental rugs that swallow sounds in
> their nap, and hangings that make whispers and protocol unavoidable.
> Differences of inside and outside hard to reconcile; for up to the
> threshold of a salon like this there was a tremendous high tension and
> antagonistic energy asked to lie still that couldn't lie still; and trying to
> contain it caused worry and shivers, the kind of thing that could erupt
> in raging, bloody Gordon or Chartist riots and shoot up fire like the
> burning of a mountain of egg crates. This unknown, superfluous free
> power streaming around a cold, wet, blackened Chicago day, from
> things laid out to be still, incapable, however, of being still. (p.127)

The salon is the epitome of the human-controlled hidden away from the irrational, from the Darkness, from terror. The implication is that its very function *is* to hide and so reassure the clientele: you are important, you matter, you will not be negated. But the power waits just outside—a power seen as both social (riots) and more than social (free power), like Reichian orgone energy. Later in the novel, Augie, upon returning, sees Chicago again in terms of inhuman energy:

. . . this gray snarled city with the hard black straps of rails, enormous industry cooking and its vapor shuddering to the air, the climb and fall of its stages in construction or demolition like mesas, and on these the different powers and sub-powers crouched and watched like sphinxes. Terrible dumbness covered it, like a judgment that would never find its word. (p.425)

Snarled, cooking, shuddering, climb and fall, powers and sub-powers, crouched . . . like sphinxes: in these images we again sense the terror facing the separate Self. And we recall Yeats' rough beast of the desert "slouching towards Bethlehem to be born." Augie also speaks in awe and half-despair of a "mysterious tremor" from the "caldron of wrath" that is Chicago. "As before the work of Egypt and Assyria, as before a sea, *you're Nothing here.* Nothing." (p.459, italics mine.)

Nor is it different in nature. Bellow's nature is like his city, full of secret power and not meant for man. The sky of Mexico "held back an element too strong for life." Looking at Caligula soaring, like human hopes, under the sky, "I sometimes wondered what connection he made with this element of nearly too great strength that was dammed back of the old spouts of craters" (p.338). At other times Caligula himself represents the terror, the power—but insofar as he is Augie's bird, an analogue of the human, he represents uncomprehending humanity trying to rise out of the darkness, the irrational.

Kayo Obermark speaks of those forces which are in conflict with human plans, theories, desires, as *moha*—opposition of the finite (p.450). The most obvious of these are the forces of circumstance. We find Jimmy Klein giving money to prevent Augie from being swallowed by circumstances as Jimmy himself was—the marriage trap. Mimi refuses to let circumstances direct her life: "You can't let your life be decided for you by any old thing that comes up" (p.272). Yet she understands the force of circumstances, understands that Einhorn is presumptuous to expect to remain wealthy in the depression. Why did he deserve a fate better than anyone else? War, too, takes away one's possibility for an individual fate (as in *Dangling Man*): "The time is in the hands of mighty men to whom you are like the single item in the mind of the chief of a great Sears, Roebuck Company, and here come you, wishing to do right and not lead a disappointed life (sic!)" (p.468). Here is the eternal joke—human striving the irresistible force, *moha* the immovable object.

But the darkness is greater than the opposition of circumstances. It is the root terror Ahab felt below the surface of life. It is Job's Voice in the Whirlwind. It is Jonathan Edwards' God dangling us like insects over the fire; or still worse, it is that God without love or mercy. In other words, it is a magnified projection of the Terrible Father: Joseph's Father, Asa's Father, Tommy's Father, Henderson's Father, Herzog's Father. Augie's Father would seem to be the inhuman universe itself. Still, this is not to say that Bellow's perception of reality is distorted by fantasy. If reality is finally beautiful, it is also terrible, like Atti the lioness in *Henderson*, like Siva, Preserver-Destroyer of life. Is it possible, then, to live in reality, in touch with the Darkness yet in touch with beauty as well?

CHAPTER SIX

Transformation

Bellow's heroes are not perfectly transformed. But they are capable of salvation; they are touched with truth; they do learn to confront the Darkness, to cease, at least for a moment, construction of a world and a self to keep them safe.

The hero is crippled by the very defenses he uses against the Darkness, against guilt and the threat of death. He is unable to love, his relationships are false and incomplete; they are expressions of a child who needs the assurance he will not be destroyed. But this posture is intolerable to the true soul of the hero. And so he lives a half life, somehow knowing the truth but unable to live it. As Allbee says in *The Victim*:

"Repent! That's John the Baptist coming out of the desert. Change yourself, that's what he's saying, and be another man. . . . There's another thing behind that 'repent'; it's that we know what to repent. How?" His unsmiling face compelled Leventhal's attention. "*I* know. Everybody knows. But you've got to take away the fear of admitting by a still greater fear. I understand that doctors are beginning to give their patients electric shocks. They tear all hell out of them, and then they won't trifle. You see, you have to get yourself so that you can't stand to keep on in the old way. When you reach that stage—" he knotted his wrists. "It takes a long time before you're ready to quit dodging. Meanwhile the pain is horrible." (p.227)

At the beginning of the hero's transformation the pain is particularly horrible. New conditions—a kind of shock therapy—will not

allow him to employ his old defenses successfully. The crippled
hero can no longer use his crutches.

In *Dangling Man* the situation is the period of "freedom" while
Joseph waits for the draft to take him. Dorothy Lee, the linguistic
anthropologist, has shown how freedom is seen in America as a
vacancy to be filled, an emptiness without positive value. As
Herzog says, "People can be free now, but the freedom doesn't
have any content. It's like a howling emptiness" (*H*, p.39).
Perhaps this is true throughout the West today. In Camus, in
Sartre, in Ionesco, it is routine which helps mask the absurd.
Joseph's routine is gone, and he has to face himself.

Augie March is meant to be a picaresque novel rather than a
novel in which the hero changes. But there *are* hints of change,
and again they rise out of a new condition. The condition is his
near-death and his loss of Thea. It is the first time he loses his
larkiness. It tells Augie, as a similar shadow of death tells
Henderson, that he is living in a world which is not human,
which cares nothing for the human.

In *Seize the Day* the new situation is Tommy's financial
collapse. It is as if the charlatan-guru Tamkin intentionally
brought him to his knees. Certainly Tommy would not give up
his pseudo needs, his presentation self, while he had money in the
bank. "I'm stripped and kicked out," Tommy groans (p.117), and
we agree. But it is only now that we see him as savable. He must
stand naked on the heath before he is worthy of being decked
with flowers.

Sometimes—particularly in *The Victim, Augie March, Seize
the Day,* and *Henderson*—the hero is helped toward his transformation by a savior. In *Augie March* the only significant savior is
Mintouchian, who teaches Augie to face himself:

"Here several years ago I was sitting on the toilet figuring a big deal
mentally when suddenly the Angel of Death plucked me by the nose.
My mind turned black. I fell on my face. . . . Then by and by the
spark of life came back to me. My mind filled again with the typical
thought and light of Mintouchian. Now, I reflected, you're Min-

touchian again. As if I had an option. Do I have to come back Mintouchian, including the distressing parts? Yes, because to live is to be Mintouchian, my dear man." (pp. 479–80)

And Augie tells him:

"You will understand, Mr. Mintouchian, if I tell you that I have always tried to become what I am. But it's a frightening thing. Because what if what I am by nature isn't good enough?" I was close to tears as I said it to him. "I suppose I better, anyway, give in and be it. I will never force the hand of fate to create a better Augie March. . . ."

And he tells Mintouchian, "I owe you much for this explanation" (p.485). Mintouchian is one of Bellow's beloved eccentrics; he has the word.

And so too has Dr. Tamkin, half fake, half wise man. He tells Tommy that he is one of the "small percentage who want to live." Tamkin's ideas are healing ideas. It is Tamkin who tells Tommy of his real soul and his pretender soul. It is Tamkin whom Tommy thinks he sees outside the funeral parlor at the end of the novel; it is as if Tamkin has served as guide; now he disappears that Tommy may find himself.

The process of transformation is amazingly similar in all of Bellow's novels. The hero must enter the world that *is* as a simple human creature, giving up his constructed reality and his constructed self. These are, indeed, his burdens. He has to put them down.

If we look carefully at *Dangling Man*, we do not find a novel in defense of individuality and we do not find a novel ending in mere resignation of freedom. The novel concludes in partial hope of new life—a life based on a loss of selfhood.

For Bellow attacks the self as strongly as does Sartre in *Nausea*. Both writers move in their novels toward a new idea of human life without selfhood. Not that their conclusions are the same: Sartre's book moves toward a man aware of his freedom, aware that he has no self which can protect him from choosing and from the world of existence; Bellow's novel works toward selflessness of a different, more traditional sort—closer to religious brotherhood and the mystical death of the self. Nevertheless, in both, the individual ego is put in question. In his Library of Congress address Bellow, as pointed out earlier, deplores the face that in recent fiction "the Self is asked to prepare itself for sacrifice. . . ."[1] Yet this is precisely what he himself is asking in *Dangling Man.* In *Nausea* Roquentin gives up the illusion of a fixed ego and submits instead to existence, an existence as free and superfluous as that of a tree. But "this freedom," says Roquentin, "is rather like death" (*N*, p.209). And he plans to "outlive himself" (p.204)—simply to exist.

Bellow, too, questions the value of the self. As just another 1-A waiting to be called, a petit bourgeois subject, like Kafka's victim-heroes, to an incomprehensible bureaucracy, his "self" seems pretty unimportant. "Who can be the earnest huntsman of himself when he knows he is in turn a quarry? Or nothing so distinctive as a quarry, but one of the shoal, driven towards the weirs" (*DM*, p.119). Does he then, have a separate personal destiny? Certainly he wants to think so, as does Rogin in "A Father-to-Be" and Grebe in "Looking for Mr. Green," wanting to regard the war as "only an incident." But Joseph—and Bellow—have strong doubts. Indeed, at what seems one of Joseph's moments of insight he says that "if the quest is the same . . ."; if "we are all drawn toward the same craters of the spirit—to know what we are and what we are for, to know our purpose, to seek grace"—if so, then "the differences in our personal histories, which hitherto meant so much to us, become of minor importance" (p.154). *Our* purpose, not *my* purpose; what *we* are, not what *I* am. Therefore: it is not only that war and the death of millions make it unfortunately impossible to uphold individuality; it is not desirable to do so. Joseph may long to keep "intact and free from encumbrance a sense of his own being, its importance" (p.27), but he has very different longings too: "While we seem so intently and even desperately to be holding onto ourselves, we would rather give ourselves away. We do not know how. So, at times, we throw ourselves away. When what we really want is to stop living so exclusively and vainly for our own sake, impure and unknowing, turning inward and self-fastened" (p.154). The distinction between giving ourselves and throwing ourselves away is important: to become a mass man, to join, to belong to a movement in which you can eschew personal choice, in which you can avoid thinking and feeling for yourself—this is throwing yourself away; it is partly what Joseph is doing by putting himself up for immediate induction: "Long live . . . the supervision of the spirit!" But a different loss of selfhood—a giving yourself away, joining the human brotherhood, longing for such a loss of selfhood, is also implicit in Joseph's giving himself to the army. Certainly Joseph doesn't keep to this truth (as Asa Leventhal will gain similar understanding in his sleep and lose it the next day), but it is truth; certainly he becomes "sick" when his fictional alter ego suggests: "Then only one question remains. . . . Whether you have a separate destiny" (p.168)—but the question is asked. Joseph may begin by defending individuality, but he ends by seriously qualifying it.

Certainly on one level, Joseph ends his journal in failure. As the value of his life decreases for him "it was impossible to resist any longer. I must give myself up" (p.183). He does; he asks his draft board to call him at once. He believes "I had not done well alone" and hopes the war "could teach me by violence, what I had been unable to learn during those months in the room" (pp.190–91). Then come the ironic final lines ending "Long live regimentation!" Joseph has thrown himself away.

He gives up the freedom he has not learned to use. And as the army means loss of choice and as "the more choice is limited the closer we are to death" (p.148), the novel moves toward various hints of Joseph's death. The Spirit of Alternatives says during their second "dialogue": "The vastest experience of your time doesn't have much to do with living. Have you thought of preparing yourself for that?" (p.165). There is a preparation for death

during the rest of the novel. First, Mrs. Kiefer dies; an analogy to
his own case, she had been isolated in her room for a long while.
There is an analogy between Mrs. Kiefer's nurse Mrs. Bartlett
and Iva—both are freed by the absence of the one they take care
of. Because of Mrs. Kiefer's death Marie the maid visits Joseph in
black. "She gloomily wiped her cheeks with a black-edged hand-
kerchief" (p.187). Then Vaneker, the old man who all through
the novel serves as a Dostoyevskian double for Joseph—isolate,
thief, guilty offender generally—moves, leaving a box of junk,
like the drift of a man's life: like the trunk Joseph packs immediately thereafter. Then Joseph sees in his father's house "a
Persian print of a woman dropping a flower on her interred
lover" (p.187). There are also many plays on the idea of death:
Iva refers to the waiting period as "your last week" (p.185),
Almstadt says "since I had to go, it was better to go and get it
over with" (p.187), the postman who gives him his notice draws
a finger across his throat. Finally, Joseph's father (a figure who
recalls the threat of death) gives Joseph a watch.

But death has, as we saw in the last chapter, a special meaning
in this novel. Joseph, terrified of death, has closed his eyes to
mortality and humanity. But the approach of death is not purely
negative. First, the metaphorical death is partly the death of the
old self—of the egocentric individual who must die before
Joseph can become human. Second, it is representative of the
physical death Joseph must face. By approaching death Joseph
can be reconciled to humanity. And, as a matter of fact, we find
that the novel does move toward a shaky unity between Joseph
and other people. True, a metaphor is not the basis for psychological change, and we do not find Joseph directly confronting
the fact of his own death; likewise, the change in Joseph can be
seen simply as a relief from the insecurity of freedom. But the
metaphor seems to hold promise of Joseph's redeeming potentiality—of the possibility of future reconciliation with society.

At any rate Joseph moves away (again, shakily) from selfhood
and toward union, not merely submission: toward giving as well

as throwing himself away. He is struck by his own arrogance; he finds himself closer to Iva (p.152). He feels a communion between himself and John Pearl, who is unhappy in Brooklyn (p.153). He wants to be free from himself—which represents for him a new idea of freedom (p.168). He tells the Spirit of Alternative, "I would be denying my inmost feelings if I said I wanted to be by-passed and spared from knowing what the rest of my generation is undergoing" (p.166). The streetcar conductor who takes him to the induction center treats him like one of the boys. And all this occurs in an atmosphere of partial regeneration: spring with warm rains and new green. Joseph says: "This atmosphere, I say, was one of an impossible hope, the hope of an impossible regeneration" (p.172).

Joseph even cleans up for supper; and doing so, he notices "new folds near my mouth and, around my eyes and the root of my nose, marks that had not been there a year before. It is not pleasant to find such changes. But, tying my tie, I shrugged them off as inevitable, the price of experience, an outlay that had better be made ungrudgingly, since it was bound in any case to be collected" (p.173). Joseph does not confront directly the fact of his death, but here he comes close to acknowledging the skull under the curls. Of course, typically for Bellow, this comes just before a vicious fight with Iva; but it comes. Then, on the next to last page of the novel, he reflects, "Recently I had begun to feel old, and it occurred to me that I might be concerned with age merely because I might never attain any great age and that there might be a mechanism in us that tried to give us all of life when there was danger of being cut off." The ending of the novel is not happy; it is complex and ambiguous, partially hopeful, pointing to a future Joseph, if he lives, who is not an individual but (in Buber's sense) a person, again in touch with his childhood self. Joseph is joining not only the army but the human race.

To return to my comparison with Sartre: I have shown that *Dangling Man* is close both superficially and significantly to *Nausea,* and even more important, that both books attack the separate ego. Marcus Klein is incorrect when he says that the problems of Bellow's heroes come to this: meeting "with a strong sense of self the sacrifice of self demanded by social circumstances."[2] The sacrifice of self is demanded by Bellow, as it is demanded by Sartre, in the interest of creating a more human person. Richard Lehan, in "Existentialism in Recent American Fiction: The Demonic Quest," is, however, mistaken when he tries to make *Dangling Man* a work of existentialist fiction. Lehan does not develop his idea, but he believes Joseph to grow "from philosophical innocence to a state where he questions the nature of creation and human existence. In sum, *Dangling Man* follows the dramatic pattern of *The Stranger* and *Nausea*—reveals an innocent mind coming in contact with the absurd and portrays the effect this has."[3]

There is support for this view; Joseph does say, "To be pushed upon oneself entirely puts the very facts of simple existence in doubt" (pp.190–91). He is subject to the social absurdity of officialdom, and he sees the world as real by human agreement: "The room, delusively, dwindled and became a tiny square, swiftly drawn back, myself and all the objects in it growing smaller. This was not a mere visual trick. I understood it to be a revelation of the ephemeral agreements by which we live and pace ourselves" (p.190). Like the existentialists, he contrasts the concrete man to the ideal constructor and agrees that the ego is a created object defending the person from reality. With them, Bellow sees the necessity of confronting one's own death in order to become authentic. Finally, as Glicksberg describes the existential hero, he could be referring to Joseph: "The existential heroes, despite their manifest desire for commitment, are handicapped by a radical inability to act. Though they search for authenticity, they are without a self they can call their own; they are a potentiality without content, a freedom without form or direction. Their besetting vice is their indulgence in introspection, which leads them to distrust their own motives as well as the words in which they are clothed."[4] But it would be unwise to exaggerate these similarities between *Dangling Man* and such an existentialist novel as *Nausea,* for there are essential differences.

First, the two writers attack the self from different perspectives: Sartre's is metaphysical, Bellow's is moral. Sartre denies the reality of a self. Bellow may agree but is not concerned: rather, he is concerned with denying the importance and moral worth of the self cut off from other people. Sartre is less concerned with community, the relationship of person to person. "I don't want any communion of souls, I haven't fallen so low," says Roquentin. But Bellow's novel points to communion as the place of salvation. Both heroes lose themselves in contemplation of a piece of music—jazz or Haydn. But whereas for Roquentin this is a moment outside the world of existence, a point of metaphysical freedom, for Joseph it is an experience from which he can learn how to live as a whole human being.

Second, Joseph is not a hero of the void. At the very center of Sartre's novel is Roquentin's awareness of pure existence. "Existence had suddenly unveiled itself. . . . The diversity of things, their individuality, were only an appearance, a veneer. This veneer had melted, leaving soft, monstrous masses, all in disorder —naked, in a frightful, obscene nakedness" (pp.171–72). Awareness of existence produces nausea because the existents have no meaningful relation to the subject. Underlying existence is nothingness, the void. Life, grounded on this void, is fundamentally absurd. Joseph, too, touches, for a moment, pure existence, but with very different results (pp.118–19). This occurs at a still point in the storm of the book—Joseph is in bed with a cold; Iva comes home early and they doze off together. "I gazed up at the comfortable room and heard the slight, mixed rhythm of her breathing and mine. This endeared her to me more than any favor could." He is mild, gentle, open. Then:

The light gave an air of innocence to some of the common objects in the room, liberating them from ugliness. I lost the aversion I had hitherto felt for the red oblong of rug at the foot of the bed, the scrap of tapestry on the radiator seat, the bubbles of paint on the white lintel, the six knobs on the dresser I had formerly compared to the ugly noses of as many dwarf brothers. In the middle of the floor, like an accidental device of serenity, lay a piece of red string.

The passage reminds one of the moment of blessing in Coleridge's *Rime of the Ancient Mariner*. Like Roquentin, Joseph faces pure existence. But the contact produces not nausea but serenity. Bellow does not point to a void at the heart of life, but to mysterious beauty. It is like the "spontaneous mysterious proof" for the justification of life's continuation that Bellow speaks of in "The Writer as a Moralist," a proof that has no need to argue with despair (p.62).

Finally, although Bellow attacks individuality in *Dangling Man*, he does so through a character who is no automaton, no Jacob Horner (Barth, *End of the Road*), but a complex human being with a rich inner life. Bellow himself has called Meursault in *The Stranger* a "shallow creature."[5] Joseph certainly is not. He is a creature capable of salvation.

There is a basic contradiction inherent in *Augie March*. If life is to be seen as a struggle against the Darkness, how can the picaresque form be appropriate? On the one hand is a belief that the individual is rigidly bounded by *moha* and is faced with an incomprehensible Terror underlying things; on the other hand is Augie, free, unbounded, and larky. Do the Laws hold for everyone but Augie? If so, is the ebullience false, the affirmation only the result of wishing?

Partly it is false. But partly—though rather unsuccessfully—Bellow accounts for this contradiction by having Augie change, or learn, during the course of his life. Since Augie tells the novel from the vantage point of the present, he can hint throughout of his change. Writing of the time when he is rejected by Simon and forced out on his own, Augie tells us: "You do all you can to humanize and familiarize the world, and suddenly it becomes more strange than ever. The living are not what they were, the dead die again and again, and at last for good." He adds, "I see this now. At that time, not" (p.285). Not seeing, he begins in larkiness, and he hopes to retain his innocence and happiness. He hears the "consent to death" in his brother's voice but is sure he himself can escape. Not wishing to admit the inhuman into his world, he feels sorry for the lizards which Caligula is to devour, and Thea tells him (as the wife tells the husband in "By the Rock Wall"), "Oh, you screwball! You get human affection mixed up with everything, like a savage." Augie wants Wordsworthian Nature, and he is secretly pleased that Caligula has cowardly, human instincts and wishes for a "fierce nature." Like Caligula, Augie runs from pain, runs toward meat that is offered him freely. "You want people to pour love on you, and you soak it up and swallow it" (p.317). So he sits comfortably in a bullhide chair—that is, comfortably on the skin of the dead—reading his utopian writers. As he writes from a future vantage point:

It takes some of us a long time to find out what the price is of being in nature, and what the facts are about your tenure. How long it takes depends on how swiftly the social sugars dissolve. But when at last they do dissolve there's a different taste in your mouth, bringing different news which registers with dark astonishment and fills your eyes. And this different news is that from vast existence in some way you rise up and at any moment you may go back. Any moment; the very next, maybe. (p.362)

He knows this now, but at that time he was anxious for "crystal-sugar esteem." We know—and Augie now knows—what lies under the sugar.

It is in Mexico that he begins really to touch inhuman energy, to plunge into the Darkness, to find what lies under the sugar. He is kicked unconscious by a horse, and this touch of death is significant. Afterward his cheeks sink, his bones seem larger, his eyes grow sleepy, he sprouts a kind of Indian mustache; he becomes more like a native, more like those who know the Darkness and inhuman power at first hand; he attunes himself to the landscape. Later Augie meets Mintouchian, who tells him of his own near-death. In the merchant marine, Augie experiences near-death on his own; in his terror, "All the consciousness there was to me seemed a hairlash in the crushing water universe" (p.495). But his sense of the frailty of individual consciousness does not lead him to despair; it leads him to a balanced sense of the comedy of existence—of the human being struggling for importance and the forces of life resisting but never quenching the individual's hope. Even though he recognizes this joke, Augie still tries, on the final page of the novel, to "beat the dark to Bruges . . . [to] see the green canals and ancient palaces." He still wishes, escaping the Darkness, to comfort himself with creations of human order. At the same time, as a voyager on this raw day, he sees himself as a kind of explorer in the "terra incognita"—the world not under human system or control.

Many of the incidents have this duality: Bellow gives with one hand while he takes with the other. If going off to Mexico to train an eagle is a proposition of human freedom, of the world as romance, yet it is in Mexico that Augie first strongly encounters that part of reality not under human control. Augie can do anything, but in doing so, it becomes apparent that death and the inhuman surround him.

I am not convinced that these two poles are part of one world and that Bellow successfully blends freedom and necessity. I am suspicious of Augie's ingenuousness and larkiness and ability to slip through. And, on the other hand, given Augie's freedom, I can't believe that the Darkness is so all-pervading as Bellow has Augie tell us: for Augie himself, it is not.

Augie's learning to confront the Darkness is an important part of his search for salvation, for to confront the Darkness is to stop construction on one's private Tower of Babel; it is to enter the *shared condition*. At one point, speaking of the metaphorical Darkness, Augie says that rain, "an emblem of the shared condition of all," indicates perhaps that what is needed to redeem us is also "superbundantly about" (p.201). "With the dark," Augie explains, "the solvent is in this way offered until the time when one thing is determined and the offers, mercies, and opportunities are finished" (p.201). We think of the hope that begins Henderson's quest: "The forgiveness of sins is perpetual. . . ." Bellow believes in personal redemption, and this redemption, this alternative to *victim* and *precious personality*, is always the same: the loss of selfhood and its replacement by humility; a humble person who is part of humanity does not struggle to protect his individuality, but lives in the here-and-now. Thus, although Bellow claims to be, as a writer, dedicated to the defense of "individual being," he sees redemption as precisely a redemption from the defense of individual being.

You can, of course, attack Napoleonic egos and at the same time attack the swallowing up of the individual by the masses; indeed, the drive for power is no assurance that the driver is truly an individual, nor is humility any indication that one is not an individual. But Bellow goes further both in his defense of individuality and in his rejection of it. Clearly Bellow loves the noble figure, the great man; clearly he wants to defend the search for a personal destiny; but just as clearly he condemns the noble figure and not only laughs at the notion of a personal destiny but sees the search as destructive. By desiring individuality Bellow's characters make redemption impossible. In their moments of truth (Bellow's characters can never hold onto the truth fully) they merge, they stop striving to be individuals, they admit that they are part of humanity. For Joseph the moment comes in peaceful apprehension of the piece of red string while he lies in wordless communion with his wife; for Asa it comes in his half-sleeping recognition that all events occurred as if in a single person; and when Augie speaks of redemption the image he uses—of *rain*—is an emblem of the oneness of the many. Indeed, this rain is one of the metaphors—water—symbolizing the forces against which the individual strives. It is poetically right, then, that to be redeemed one must stop striving and must enter the "shared condition of all." And this is the third possibility, the way of being neither victim nor "precious personality."

In *Augie March* this possibility emerges in Edenic terms: as a kind of Wordsworthian innocence. Thus, when Trotsky in exile arrives in the little Mexican town with his entourage, Augie is excited to see this great man; but the kitten Augie pets was simply "nuzzling and kneading under my arm with her paws" (p.373). This opposition of innocent animal world to power-hungry human world is made many times. Augie, who often speaks of his joy in simply soaking in the day, feels able to live "almost like birds or dogs that have no human condition but are always living in the same age, the same at Charlemagne's feet as on a Missouri scow or in a Chicago junkyard" (p.327). One of the loveliest passages in the novel is about Augie's lovemaking with Thea under some pines, while "the clouds, birds, cattle in the water, things, stayed at their distance, and there was no need to herd, account for, hold them in the head, but it was enough to be among them, released on the ground as they were in their brook or in their air" (p.330). Clearly Bellow is less innocent than Augie, who seems to have forgotten about the terrible in nature. But these passages are not meant ironically; they represent a way of life opposed to individualism. Instead of a man controlling the world of nature, he lives in it, one creature among others. He is an entity as much as any other creature—but not an individual.

Here is the answer to the irreconcilability of human striving and the forces surrounding man: stop striving. It is not a comforting answer to Hymie Bateshaw in the municipal swimming pool; it is a difficult answer for a man aware of all the forces—death, mass life, nature, the city—opposing his separate being. But it is Bellow's answer. Augie speaks a number of times late in the novel of "the axial lines of life with respect to which you must be straight" (p.454). And how does one become straight?

When striving stops, there they are as a gift. . . . And I believe that any man at any time can come back to these axial lines, even if an unfortunate bastard, if he will be quiet and wait it out. *The ambition of something special and outstanding I have always had is only a boast that distorts this knowledge from its origin,* which is the oldest knowledge, older than the Euphrates, older than the Ganges. At any time life can come together and man be regenerated. . . . He will live with true joy. . . . *Death will not be terrible to him if life is not.* The embrace of other true people will take away his dread of fast change and short life. (pp. 454–55, italics mine)

The quest for a special fate is self-deceptive; it hides one from his true humanity, which requires a loss of the desire for prestige, power, independence. Yet when he stops striving, nothing will take him away from himself: "Even wandering will not take him away from himself. . . ." Thus this loss of Self is a gain of a truer Self. The individual is gone, but the human being underneath remains.

Augie adds, "And this is not imaginary stuff, Clem, because I bring my entire life to the test" (p.455). He does not, in fact. Bellow's answer never really becomes Augie's; Augie ends as a Columbus looking for his personal America although he knows that his very striving makes his goal impossible: "I have trouble being still, and . . . my hope is based upon getting to be still so that the axial lines can be found" (p.514). Augie remains an individual, although Bellow's answer is not individuality.

One of Augie's dreams throws further light on Bellow's solution to the conflict between the individual and the forces against him. In this dream a pug-nosed old woman panhandles Augie. First he laughs at her, " 'Why you old guzzler, I can hear the beer cans clinking in your shopping bag.' 'No, them ain't beer cans' she said, 'it's my window-washer stuff, my squeegee and Bon Ami and such, and for the love of God, must I wash my forty-fifty windows every day of my life?' " He gives her not the price of a beer as she expects, but one of each kind of coin: ninety-one cents. "And Ugly Face, she thanked me; she was almost like a dwarf, with a wide behind. 'Well, there's a few windows free,' I said. 'I haven't got one I can call my own.' 'Come,' said she warmly, 'and let me treat you to a beer.' 'No thanks, mother, I've got to go. Thanks all the same.' In kindness, I touched her on the crown of her old head and a great thrill passed through me from it. 'Why, old woman,' I said, 'you've got the hair of an angel!' 'Why shouldn't I have,' she said gently, 'like other daughters of men?' " (pp.506–507).

In the beginning of the dream Augie separates himself from this old, ugly wreck. She is one of the coolies, he the man in the rickshaw. But as in *The Victim*, sympathy leads to identification: he, too, is out of luck, homeless. The closeness between them is reinforced by the word *mother*. And then, just as Joseph feels spontaneous love for the things around him, in Ancient Mariner fashion Augie feels kindness inside him and he touches the crown of her head—she is, surprisingly, noble—and is thrilled to discover that Ugly Face has angelic beauty, a lesson the Mariner learns as "the thousand thousand slimy things" become "happy living things." She drives the lesson home: this beauty is universal, belonging not to the special individual but to Everyman.

It is the beauty and nobility of the simple human being, then, rather than the individual with a special destiny, that is Bellow's standard. A holy brotherhood of people who do not try to remove themselves from the swimming pool—this holy brotherhood is what is desired. Besides, humanity is not a swarm of swimmers, not a mass of insects, but a band of near-angels. Augie is not able, anymore than Asa, to live with this new wisdom; in the dream he has to wander on, the lonely orphan; awake, the next day, "instead of bosom fraternity, what took place . . . [in the lifeboat] was a battle"—but it *is* wisdom. "God send you truth," the washerwoman says. For Augie, as for Asa and Joseph, truth comes in a dream. Here truth comes in the figure of the washerwoman: the baptizer, redeeming with water. Augie may not be redeemed, but he is touched with truth.

Seize the Day does not end in Tommy's masochistic acceptance of his role as victim; it ends in hope for a new life. For if, on the one hand, Tommy is heading toward defeat, acceptance of suffering, perhaps literal death by suicide or heart attack, on the other hand, he is also committed to life. And if the final scene is a symbolic drowning, it is also a symbolic rebirth out of water.

Throughout the novel there are moments of serenity when striving has stopped. Just as Joseph lies at peace for a moment and sees "In the middle of the floor, like an accidental device of serenity, . . . a piece of red string" (*DM*, p.119); just as Augie, lying for a moment with Thea, comes in touch with the axial lines in the same way, Tommy has found peace momentarily in the past. He has been in touch with his axial lines, has stopped striving and taken truth as a gift:

When he was with the Rojax Corporation Wilhelm had kept a small apartment in Roxbury, two rooms in a large house with a small porch and garden, and on mornings of leisure, in late spring weather like this, he used to sit expanded in a wicker chair with the sunlight pouring through the weave, and sunlight through the slug-eaten holes of the young hollyhocks and as deeply as the grass allowed into small flowers. (pp.42–43)

It is as if the sunlight were pouring through Tommy, a simple living thing among other living things. Today again, remembering, in the whirring of the shining numbers on the commodities' board the birds of Roxbury:

He breathed in the sugar of the pure morning.
He heard the long phrases of the birds.
No enemy wanted his life.
Wilhelm thought, I will get out of here. I don't belong in New York anymore. And he sighed like a sleeper. (p.82)

Always it is the sleeper in Bellow who is possessed of truth. Earlier he had said that to suffer in New York felt like "real life"; but if *"he doesn't belong in New York,"* the place of suffering, perhaps this means that he may be able to redeem himself from his impostor soul. These moments are few and brief, but in the materialistic atmosphere of the Hotel Gloriana and the commodities' market, they point the way toward Tommy's salvation. (One of the beauties in this novel is the picture of this gross man seeking salvation—a search distinct from that for self-justification —in the Hotel Gloriana and amid the whirring machines at the market.)

Just after his memory of Roxbury, Tommy thinks of how difficult it is in New York to communicate the simple need of a glass of water. "Every other man spoke a language entirely his own" (p.83). Here is a favorite theme of Bellow's—the tower of Babel (see Chapter Four), or more generally, the lack of community. But this picture of alienation, Tommy thinks, finally does not matter:

A queer look came over Wilhelm's face with its eyes turned up and his silent mouth with its high upper lip. He went several degrees further —when you are like this, dreaming that everybody is outcast, you realize that this must be one of the small matters. There is a larger body, and from this you cannot be separated. The glass of water fades out. You do not go from simple *a* and simple *b* to the great *x* and *y*, nor does it matter whether you agree about the glass but, far beneath such details, what Tamkin would call the real soul says plain and understandable things to everyone. There sons and fathers are themselves, and a glass of water is only an ornament; it makes a hoop of brightness on the cloth; it is an angel's mouth. There truth for everybody may be found, and confusion is only—only temporary, thought Wilhelm. (p.84)

In tone and spirit this passage is like the conclusion of Isaac Singer's Yiddish story, "Gimpel the Fool," translated by Saul Bellow thus:

Another *schnorrer* is waiting to inherit my bed of straw. When the time comes I will go joyfully. Whatever may be there, it will be real, without complications, without ridicule, without deception. God be praised: there even Gimpel cannot be deceived.[6]

But the *there* is quite different. Gimpel refers to redemption in another world, Tommy to a redemption always at hand, found eternally in the here-and-now. If the false soul, the presentation self, is the individual, uncommunicating ego, the true soul is the common human soul which tells everyone the same message and which reveals the glory of the most common thing: a glass of water, Tommy Wilhelm.

And so the moment of truth is not isolating to the individual—quite the contrary. He feels himself part of a larger body. He feels love, as he did in the subway on his way to the Polo Grounds, when "a general love for all these imperfect and lurid-looking people burst out in Wilhelm's breast. He loved them. One and all, he passionately loved them. They were his brothers and sisters. He was imperfect and disfigured himself, but what difference did that make if he was united with them by this blaze of love? And as he walked he began to say, 'Oh my brothers—my brothers and sisters,' blessing them all as well as himself" (pp. 84–85). In this moment of love Tommy, like Asa, is able to forgive himself. This is not the false love of the impostor soul but the true love which can rid Tommy of his burden. As Augie understands in his dream about the beggar-woman, instead of striving for individuality, one is to merge, to unite. At another time, acting with the impostor soul of his father, Tommy rejects an old fiddler begging for money—the figure comparable here to Augie's begging washerwoman—even though the "old bearded man with his bandaged beggar face and his tiny ragged feet and the old press clippings on his fiddle case to prove he had once been a concert violinist, pointed his bow at Wilhelm, saying 'You' " (p.100). Tommy refuses the identification, denies the omen. Or rather, seeing himself in the beggar who was once, as he himself was, a success, he rejects his common humanity with the beggar. And although he helps blind Mr. Rappaport to cross the street, he does it begrudgingly, out of duty, not love. The blaze of love passes; yet it is the center of the novel.

By the end of the novel Tommy is stripped bare. His lard and rye have no future; both his doctors have given him up. His unfinished telephone call to Margaret seems his final break in communication. She hangs up and he tries to rip the phone from the wall. He is cut apart from the world—without position, money, human contact.

But if he has lost his place in the world, he has also lost his artifices, his roles, his defenses. He is, like Lear, stripped bare. Perhaps now he will have to be reborn, have to love. Thus, if Tommy is symbolically the corpse in the funeral home, perhaps this death can be seen (as for Joseph in *Dangling Man*) as a release from the burden of selfhood, the death of the presentation self, the impostor soul. The real soul, according to Tamkin, tries constantly to kill the impostor soul, and unless it succeeds, "The pretender soul takes away the energy of the true soul and makes it feeble, like a parasite" (p.71). When Tommy thinks, standing at the coffin, "If you want [my life] . . . then kill me. Take, take it, take it from me," is this resignation a moment in which by humility he is at least temporarily saved from his pretender soul? Is it Tommy's real or his pretender soul which is symbolically lying in the coffin? Since the defeats he suffers are at the expense of the pretender soul, it would seem to be this soul which is wounded. Although such defeats can be turned into victories by the masochist, it seems that this exhaustion and breakdown are not masochistic.

Bellow has learned a good deal from Reichian therapy; indeed, many of his friends, in particular the late Isaac Rosenfeld, have been Reichian devotees. Throughout the novel many of Tommy's physical symptoms are very much the kinds of symptoms dealt with by Reich in his discussions of "armoring"—in particular, the knot in Tommy's chest and his feeling of choking. "In certain patients," Reich reports, "we meet a syndrome stemming from the armoring of the chest which produces a particularly complicated system of difficulties. These patients complain, typically, of a 'knot' in the chest. . . . The lives of such patients are characterized by a general lack of initiative and by work disturbances based on the inability to use their hands freely." The condition cannot be changed "without the previous dissolution of the chest armor and without liberating the emotions of raving rage, of longing and genuine crying."[7] Tommy's attempt to rip the phone from the wall is such rage, his weeping at the funeral, for Tommy such crying; thus, in Reichian terms, the end of the novel represents a healing release, a healing surrender of the armored self.

The moment before the coffin is very much like the moment of love in the subway—it is an expression of Tommy's true soul, his love for all men, and his acknowledgment of their common humanity. For if the corpse represents his father, himself, and (according to Klein) Dr. Tamkin, it is also simply a stranger, "another human creature."

> "It must be somebody real close to carry on so." . . .
> "The man's brother, maybe?" (p.118)

Maybe the man's brother. And if so, insofar as this *is* so, the "consummation of his heart's ultimate need" is not death and the acceptance of his status as victim but, rather love, and if love, life for the true soul within Tommy.

This interpretation is supported by the passage immediately preceding the funeral, in which Tommy sees "the great, great crowd . . . on every face the refinement of one particular motive or essence—*I labor, I spend, I strive, I design, I love, I cling, I uphold, I give way, I envy, I long, I scorn, I die, I hide, I want.* Faster, much faster than any man could make the tally" (p.115). It is like the municipal swimming pool in *Augie March*, like the sea of faces in the epigraph to *The Victim*, like the hunger of Eugene Henderson. It is out of this grasping crowd that the corpse appears to Tommy. Thus the corpse, "with his formal shirt and his tie and silk lapels and his powdered skin [which] looked so proper" is like Tommy's striving, inauthentic soul, his presentation self, and the man's corpse represents the death of this false soul and the possibility of new life, liberated from this soul.

The image of death-by-drowning offers hope. Tommy, who "dies" amid sea-like music, sinking "deeper than sorrow," has quoted, "Sunk though he be beneath the wat'ry floor." If in the death of Edward King, Milton expressed not only anxiety for his own life but also hope for the future ("Tomorrow to fresh woods and pastures new"), then by analogy the image of death-by-drowning hints at Tommy's rededication to life and to the living, his at least partial redemption from Selfhood. Further:

> Lycidas your sorrow is not dead,
> Sunk though he be beneath the wat'ry floor
> So sinks the day star in the ocean bed
> And yet anon repairs his drooping head. . . .
> So Lycidas sunk low but mounted high. . . .

and if Lycidas mounted high, perhaps so can Tommy Wilhelm.

This hope is sustained by the image of the fish under the water which began the argument of this chapter. The fish is analogous to Tommy's true soul, "a mysterious being beneath the water, driven by hunger" (p.92). Tommy is fishing *in* himself *for* himself. And if this fish is an image of his soul, his soul seems safe: fish don't drown in water.

Finally, this is, as Klein notes, a moment of *Angst:* "At the point of death, he realizes existence, the 'true self,' the vitality which all men share, and which defines men."[8] The confrontation of one's own death is always, in Bellow's novels, the beginning of new life within an admission of one's humanity.

It seems likely, then, that the "drowning" at the end is not an accession to masochistic failure, as Weiss believes, but a hint of new life for Tommy's true soul, an image of spiritual hope like that of the fisherman at the end of Eliot's *Waste Land.* If the final breakdown of Tommy's armoring signifies despair, more crucially it signifies hope. It is the wail of a baby at his birth. And if this ambiguous ending points toward possible redemption, it also affirms the beauty and dignity of Tommy Wilhelm and of all men.

It seems strange that a writer who is defending the individual sees human redemption possible only by discarding individuality. Yet this is Bellow's answer. It is not merely that Bellow looks for a new kind of individuality, one freed from pride, from false, traditional ideals of greatness. It is not only that Bellow points to a self more real than the presentation self, a "core" self. He does these things, but besides, he indicates that beneath the presentation self and the "core" self lies a mystery which is not personal but transpersonal; further, as each novel fulfills its essential rhythm, we find that Bellow points toward a loss of selfhood—a loss of Self and discovery of the transpersonal mystery—as the way the burdened hero can redeem his humanity. It is an answer quite contrary to his love of nobility, his love of the individualist; it is an answer which goes beyond simple goodness to a kind of sainthood, a spiritual condition like that of the Jewish *zaddik* or the Zen monk. Bellow is not satisfied with this loss of Self; he cannot rest in this answer, for he is fiercely individualistic. Yet his fiction shows that the only redemption is through a loss of individuality and a cessation of striving, an absorption into reality rather than an imposition of Self on reality. "When striving stops," Augie says, "the truth comes as a gift." He cannot stop striving any more than Joseph can. Henderson and Herzog *say* they have stopped, but the endings are in doubt. What is not in doubt, however, is that the only way to remove the burden of Self is to remove Self. This elimination of Self is an answer more oriental than Jewish. Bellow's heroes, when they achieve their moments of grace, free of striving and free of Self, are similar to the sainted fool or holy *zaddik* of Jewish folk and literary tradition—Herzog painting the piano green, Henderson dancing *zaddik*-like around the plane—but Judaism does not emphasize a personal salvation into a sainted life, the self absent. A Jew is saved as a Jew among Jews. The answer is peculiarly in agreement with the very book which Bellow, in his Library of Congress address, chose as an indication that something is wrong with our literary culture: Wylie Sypher's *Loss of the Self in Modern Literature and Art*. Sypher writes, "The sacrifice of the self in 'brutal' art and in Zen implies a belief that [quoting Dubuffet] 'the universe is more important than our recognition of the universe.' When we believe this deeply, we lose the self in a silence before things. . . ."[9]

Thus (1) Bellow wants to be able to affirm the possibilities

136   SAUL BELLOW: *In Defense of Man*

for the individual to live a meaningful life in our civilization, and so (2) he attacks the literary tradition of despair and alienation and the negation of Self. But (3) he himself despairs, both because of what he sees in the culture and because of his own temperament. (4) We find his characters weighed down by guilt, masochism, and the burden of themselves imposed upon reality. They fear the Darkness and set up a world in which they can live, a self to sustain them. But this strategy is crippling; it is a terrible burden. And so (5) Bellow sees elimination of selfhood as the way to redemption of the individual. As Herzog says, "Everything of intensest significance. Especially if divested of me" (*H*, p.326). Henderson tells Lily, "I should move from the states that I myself make into the states which are of themselves. Like if I stopped making such a noise I might hear something nice" (*HRK*, p.284). (6) The state of grace which Bellows arrives at as a solution is an anonymous state in opposition to the individuality he loves and would like to defend; but it is a state which allows him to keep faith in the value of the human being and link him spiritually with others.

I add one point: Bellow never fully completes this "rhythm." He is too strongly individualistic to believe or make believable to his readers the possibility of a new life free of Self. Rather, the hero's transformation is only partial or he deceives himself into believing it complete, as did Bummidge in *The Last Analysis:* "I have attained rebirth" and "I am ready for the sublime" (p.97). Bellow is too much a Jew, too much an American, and too much a Westerner ever to rest in the "sublime": it is only a still point in a turning world.

- 3 -

Studies of Individual Works

CHAPTER SEVEN

The Victim

Like Joseph, Asa Leventhal is a solitary with few friends, and a depressive. He feels burdened by a constant struggle against the world, because of a difficulty which is at once psychological and moral, as in the case of Joseph. The theme of this book is the casting-off of his self-imposed burdens by learning to accept himself and others rather than to judge and blame, by learning to have an open heart. Asa's chief burden, like Joseph's, is his pride, which is the very antithesis of true dignity. Bellow wishes to reveal the true beauty and dignity of the human being; but this beauty and dignity can be realized only by admitting that you are merely human, by accepting rather than blaming yourself and others.

The Victim also concerns the obligation of the human being to others. The book has two epigraphs. The first tells of a merchant who is confronted with a huge Ifrit brandishing a sword. " 'Stand up that I may slay thee even as thou slayest my son!' Asked the merchant, 'How have I slain thy son?' and he answered, 'When thou atest dates and threwest away the stones they struck my son full in the breast as he was walking by, so that he died forthwith.' " What are the limits of human responsibility? Is a man guilty for what he does not intend? The second epigraph is not about individual suffering but about the suffering of humanity at large. It is a passage out of De Quincey—a vision of an ocean turning into a human face, then a multitude of faces "upturned to the heavens; faces, imploring, wrathful, despairing; faces that

surged upwards by thousands, by myriads, by generations. . . ."
Partly this is the question of *Dangling Man*—the relationship of
the individual and the mass. Partly it is an image of the futility,
the immensity, the helplessness of humanity's suffering. What
can you do to stop all this suffering? Many are called, few are
chosen; why one and not another? These precisely are the
problems raised in *The Victim*.

Asa Leventhal, a city Jew of guilts and duties—the city, his
job, his brother's family are all weights on his back—blames
everyone and assumes that everyone is blaming him. Kirby
Allbee, another "victim" and anti-Semite, does indeed blame him,
accusing Asa of having intentionally cost him his job years before,
the loss of which led to poverty, his wife's death, and his
degeneration.

Two plot strands develop. In the first, guilty Asa tries to deal
with Allbee, to get rid of him, to understand him, to help him, to
beat him up. Allbee, not revealing what he is after, insinuates
himself more and more deeply into Asa's life—visiting him,
following him, living with him, locking him out of his own house
while Allbee has sexual relations with a pick-up, finally trying to
kill Asa and himself. Asa begins by refusing to acknowledge
responsibility, moves toward helping Allbee, and ends by expel-
ling him, no longer quite so afraid of Allbee as an image of his
own possible failure and a projection of his own self-hatred. As in
Malamud's "Last of the Mohicans," a stranger forces the hero to
see his own spiritual failings—and departs. Now Asa can call his
wife, who has been South with her mother, and ask her to come
home.

If Asa is healed, it is due partly to the second plot strand. Out
of a sense of duty, he takes charge of his brother's family when
Max is away. Partly on Asa's responsibility, Max's son Mickey is
sent to the hospital, where he dies. Asa's emotional involvement
here—his change from blame of Max for being away from his
family to love of Max, and from duty to concern—helps make

Asa aware that a man is not flawless, that in humility he must take responsibility even for what he (like the merchant in the epigraph) is hardly responsible.

The last chapter of the novel occurs years later. Asa, however, looks younger. The burden of guilt and so of struggle is lighter now. Meeting Allbee, Asa no longer sees him as the Persecutor. They have both changed: Allbee is now externally happy and semi-successful but essentially the same; Asa is externally the same but essentially changed, owing to an "expansion of the heart" and a recognition of his merely human status.

Saul Bellow's only dramatic plot—dramatic in that it is founded on an active conflict between individuals—is based directly on a novella by Dostoyevsky, *The Eternal Husband.* (What better shows that Bellow is a monologuist who longs to become a dialoguist?) This derivation has been noted by a number of critics, though none has developed the relationship in detail.[1] Bellow himself says that the parallel is obvious to him now, although not at the time he wrote the novel.[2] I shall not compare the two works in depth; but I will point to a number of similarities and differences which show clearly the influence of Dostoyevsky on Bellow's early fiction—how much he was working in the Russian's moral-psychological mode—and, more important, the changes Bellow makes, changes which significantly aid him in celebrating the dignity of the human being.

The theme of Dostoyevsky's novella is the dignity of a man. Like Asa Leventhal, Alexey Velchaninov is unwell physically and burdened with guilt. To each comes a "double"—a projection of his guilty nature—whom Leventhal and Velchaninov have hurt in the past. The heroes reject these doubles as wild animals, as less than human. The "victims"—Trusotsky and Allbee—prey on the guilt-ridden heroes with a combined hatred and love. Trusotsky tells Velchaninov that he had loved him and looked up to him; he begs Velchaninov to drink with him; he kisses his hand

and begs for a kiss on the lips; he cares for Velchaninov like a mother when Velchaninov is sick. Allbee wants to rub his fingers through Asa's kinky "Jew" hair (an act more homoerotic than anti-Semitic), he feels hurt that Asa is not intimate with him; finally he brings a woman into Asa's bed, not only, it seems to take Asa's place but to bind himself to Asa. Fiedler says, "Allbee . . . is Leventhal's beloved as well as his nightmare; just as Leventhal is Allbee's beloved as well as his nightmare. . . ."[3] Nightmare: for at the same time, each victim hates enough to kill; not only do Trusotsky and Allbee wish to kill their enemies, but Leventhal and Velchaninov also threaten a number of times to kill their persecutors; at the end, both antagonists indeed *try* to kill. In each case this attempt cuts the cord between the doubles. The hero is freed. But the process of becoming free is in each case more complex than this—and nearly the same: Velchaninov and Leventhal must draw close to their enemies, identify with them, pity them. Asa acknowledges his responsibility, offers help, and understands that Allbee is a suffering human, not merely his persecutor; Alexy acknowledges his kinship with Trusotsky—"We are both vicious, underground, loathsome people"[4]—and then, in humility, tells him, "You are better than I am! I understand it all; all. . . ."(*EH*, p.455). But in both cases there is the need for the attempted murder, the physical scuffle, the expulsion. Afterward each hero is healed. Velchaninov is no longer sick, no longer depressive; Leventhal's health is also improved, and he is happier, less burdened. Both encounter their doubles again, but greet them now as whole men who have regained their dignity.

In incidentals, too, the two works are alike. Both heroes are temporarily alone, deserted by a maid, a wife. It is the purgatory of summer in a great city, the first paragraph of each novel telling of the intense heat. And with the lifting of the psychological burden of each hero comes autumn coolness; each hero goes to the window for a breath of cool air. The dream figures of Allbee and Trusotsky are introduced the same way: the heroes fall asleep and are awakened by a bell: no one is there. Both show at this point evidence of guilt—Velchaninov dreams of an unknown accusation, Leventhal thinks he sees mice darting along the walls. The "victims" have been spying on, scrutinizing the heroes for some time. They wear the signs of their loss—Trusotsky a black crepe indicating the death of his wife and indicating, too, the loss of her faithfulness; Allbee the seedy clothes and disarranged look of a Bowery drunk, indicating how low he has fallen since Leventhal cost him his job. Like Trusotsky, Allbee has lost his wife, and he considers Leventhal responsible for this since she left him (and was killed in a car crash) after he ran out of money. Both pairs are complementary: Allbee is the anti-Semite Leventhal needs to justify his sense of persecution and feed his guilt, while Leventhal is the persecutor Allbee needs to be able to believe that not he but the world is responsible for his fall; similarly, Trusotsky is the projection of Velchaninov's self-accusation, Velchaninov the cuckold whom the eternal husband can't do without. Both "victims" act with aristocratic pride alternating with degenerate drinking, wild displays, and threats to a small child. Yet the heroes are doubles of the victims in the simplest sense: Velchaninov and Leventhal become drunk and sloppy, and they parallel, in imagination at least, the sexual behavior they condemn in the widowers (Trusotsky's engagement to a teenaged girl, Allbee's pick-up of the woman). In each novel a young child dies, having been taken from home on the insistence of the hero: in *Eternal Husband* it is Velchaninov's own child, in *The Victim*, the child of his brother. Each novel, finally, ends in an epilogue with a bell which calls the victim-figure back to his new life.

Yet in spite of all these similarities, Bellow has written his own novel, not only in its creation of an American urban environment —where else is there so brilliant an evocation of the deadly weight of a metropolis in summer?—or in its added complexity and integration of material (the substitution of his brother's

family for Velchaninov's friends in the country is a fine move)—
but especially in its development of the theme of human dignity.

The theme has its central expression in the two-page speech of
the old Yiddish journalist, Schlossberg. It is a speech which has
no parallel in *The Eternal Husband* and, like most of Bellow's
important choral speeches, has no function in the plot. It is,
perhaps, the central speech of Bellow's fiction.

"I try to give everybody credit," declared the old man. "I am not a
knocker. I am not too good for this world."

No one contradicted him.

"Well," he said. "And what am I kicking for?" He checked their
smiles, holding them all with his serious, worn, blue gaze. "I'll tell you.
It's bad to be less than human and it's bad to be more than human.
What's more than human? Our friend—" he meant Leventhal, "was
talking about it before. Caesar, if you remember, in the play wanted to
be like a god. Can a god have diseases? So this is a sick man's idea of
God. Does a statue have wax in its ears? Naturally not. It doesn't
sweat, either, except maybe blood on holidays. If I can talk myself into
it that I never sweat and make everybody else act as if it was true,
maybe I can fix it up about dying, too. We only know what it is to die
because some people die, and, if we make ourselves different from
them, maybe we don't have to? Less than human is the other side of it.
I'll come to it. So here is the whole thing, then. Good acting is what is
exactly human. And if you say I am a tough critic, you mean I have a
high opinion of what is human. This is my whole idea. More than
human, can you have any use for life? Less than human, you don't
either."

He made a pause—and it was not one that invited interruption—
and went on.

"This girl Livia in *The Tigress*. What's the matter with her? She
commits a murder. What are her feelings? No love, no hate, no fear,
no lungs, no heart. I'm ashamed to mention what else is missing.
Nothing! The poor husband. Nothing is killing him, less than human.
A blank. And it should be so awful the whole audience should be
afraid positively to look in her face. But I don't know if she's too pretty
or what to have feelings. You see right away she has no idea what is
human because her husband's death doesn't mean to her a thing. It's
all in packages, and first the package is breathing and then it isn't

breathing, and you insured the package so you can marry another
package and go to Florida for the winter. Now maybe somebody will
answer me. 'This sounds very interesting. You say less than human,
more than human. Tell me, please, what is human?' And really we
study people so much now that after we look and look at human
nature—I write science articles myself—after you look at it and weigh
it and turn it over and put it under a microscope, you might say,
'What is all the shouting about? A man is nothing, his life is nothing.
Or it is even lousy and cheap. But this your royal highness doesn't like,
so he chokes it up. With what? With greatness and beauty. Beauty and
greatness? Black and white I know; I didn't make it up. But greatness
and beauty?' But I say, 'What do you know? No, tell me, what do you
know? You shut one eye and look at a thing, and it is one way to you.
You shut the other one and it is different. I am as sure about greatness
and beauty as you are about black and white. If a human life is a
great thing to me, it *is* a great thing. Do you know better? I'm entitled
as much as you. And why be measly. Do you have to be? Is somebody
holding you by the neck? Have dignity, you understand me? Choose
dignity. Nobody knows enough to turn it down'. . . ."

"Bravo!" said Harkavy. (*V*, pp.133–35)

Notice first the authority figure: an *alte jude* who speaks in
slightly Yiddish constructions (*I'm entitled as much as you*) and
rhetorical expressions like those in the fiction of Sholem Aleichem
and Peretz, although these are mixed with an American idiom. So
he speaks with the weight of Jewish tradition and sets this tradition, implied in the tone, against the cheapening or fraudulent
ennobling of human life current in America. Again and again in
Bellow, wisdom comes from the Jewish past, or at least a non-
American past, often spoken by a *meshugenah*, an eccentric. In
The Victim Schlossberg and the old lady Harkavy serve this
function. Then, too, this authority figure is from the common life,
and his speech is the conscious opposite of polished rhetoric. The
responses at the end of the speech—Harkavy's "Bravo!" and
Shifcart the talent scout's "Amen and amen!"—thus establish the
quasi-comic-dramatic, quasi-religious quality of the speech. Then
Shifcart offers the old man a card—and a screen test: that is,
Schlossberg himself is an actor and, according to his definition,

"exactly human." The card falls near Leventhal: that is, he is on his way to becoming human—to understanding the wisdom of Schlossberg.

The wisdom of Schlossberg is that human life has dignity; human life has greatness and beauty—but only on condition that it is *human* life, not subhuman or more than human. Schlossberg's attack on the "more than human" was seen earlier in Bellow's assault on greatness and ideal constructions in *Dangling Man:* man tries to make himself into a god, dehumanizing himself to remove himself from humanity and hence from mortality. It is a perfect description of the roots of Joseph's alienation. If this is wisdom that Asa Leventhal already possesses (it was he who pointed to Caesar as a false ideal of greatness), he must learn how it applies to him, for, like Caesar, he rejects his human weakness and projects it onto others. Asa lacks still more the complementary wisdom that to be human means to feel human concern; that to be human means to be responsive to the suffering of others.

Less-than-human, human, more-than-human is not one continuum; a man who is more than human will also be less than human. Both deviations involve a detachment from humanity, a refusal to admit that one is like other men. But while there is not one continuum, the philosophy of Schlossberg does see man as occupying a middle state traditional in Judeo-Christian theology. Being human rests on the admission of this middle state: "I am not too good for this world," Schlossberg says. I am reminded of Peretz' short story, "If Not Higher," in which Litvak, mistrustful of the rabbi of Nemirov, who disappears every Friday morning at the time of the Penitential Prayers, hides under the rabbi's bed. Early he hears the rabbi's groans of suffering for all Israel; then he sees the rabbi dress in peasant clothes and go anonymously to help a sick woman. The rabbi brings her firewood, kindles it, in spite of her objection that she cannot pay, and as the fire burns recites the prayers. The Litvak becomes the rabbi's disciple, "and ever after, when another disciple tells how the Rabbi of Nemirov ascends to heaven at the time of the Penitential Prayers, the Litvak does not laugh. He only adds quietly, 'If not higher'" (*Treasury*, p.233). Higher not by leaving the earth but by involving himself with it; he does not remove himself from humanity but enters it, listening to and heeding its groans.

Here is the standard old Schlossberg—and Bellow—apply. By the end of this morality-novel Asa has largely succeeded in meeting it. And so, the novel is affirmative in spite of its dark tone, much more completely than *Dangling Man*. But a man has difficulties in becoming "exactly human" and thereby choosing dignity.

First, Asa, like Allbee, feels he is a victim. He is afraid that his boss, his brother's wife and mother-in-law, even his friend Williston, are against him because he is a Jew. Actually, he is never injured on these grounds; indeed, he is never persecuted at all. He fears a blacklist—there is none; he fears an attack by Elena's mother—it doesn't come. This book is not about victims. Mickey dies in the hospital, but Bellow does not inveigh against metaphysical injustice. Subtly he introduces a quick snapshot of a *real* victim of the city: "A Filipino busboy came to clear the table. He was an old man and frail looking, and his hands and forearms were whitened by immersion in hot water. The cart loaded, he bent his back low over it, receiving the handlebar in his chest, and pushed away slowly" (p.130). Here is a victim, not Asa, eating with Harkavy, Shifcart, and Schlossberg.

It is rather Asa's sense of being a victim that we should look at—his and Allbee's too. For Allbee, the gentile and anti-Semite, feels society has become anti-gentile. "Sometimes I feel . . . as if I were in a sort of Egyptian darkness. You know, Moses punished the Egyptians with darkness. . . . When I was a boy, everything was different. We thought it would be daylight forever. Do you know, one of my ancestors was Governor Winthrop. . . . The old breeds are out. . . . It's as if the children of Caliban were running everything" (pp.144–45). His life has been ruined and it is none of his doing—he is a victim. "You're the one that's responsible. You did it to me deliberately, out of hate. Out of pure hate!" (p.78).

To be a self-created victim is to lose greatness and beauty. It is to hit back, as Asa wanted to in the movie when a woman made an anti-Semitic remark. Therefore, as Opdahl says, playing the victim leads to playing the very image that the victimizer hates: Asa is in danger of becoming Allbee's *kike*.[5] Allbee, in turn, by submitting to the role of victim, has degenerated into the drunken, irrational anti-Semitic *goy* of Asa's dreams and *shtetl* tradition.

Obviously, to be a "victim" is to reject dignity. The "victim" despises himself: "I feel worthless. I know what I am. Worthless," Allbee weeps (p.195). And Asa recognizes that he had fought with Allbee's boss (and so cost Allbee his job) not only because the man had been abusive: "No, he, he himself had begun to fear that the lowest price he put on himself was too high and he could scarcely understand why anyone should want to pay for his services. And under Rudiger's influence he had felt this. 'He made me believe what I was afraid of,' Leventhal thought" (p.120). Again, as in *Dangling Man*, the *amour-propre* is greater the less one loves himself; self-hatred leads to ugly defensive pride. Williston tells Asa that when unemployed, "you were fighting everybody, those days. You were worst with Rudiger, but I heard of others. . . . You should have had better judgment than to blow up."

"What, wipe the spit off my face and leave like a gentleman? I wouldn't think much of myself if I did."
"That's just it."
"What is? What I think of myself? Well. . . ." (p.118)

Bellow does not fully go into the causes of Asa's sense of worthlessness. We know the insecurity of Asa's childhood— economic and psychological. We know his father's philosophy:

Ruf mir Yoshke, ruf mir Moshke
Aber gib mir die groschke.

(Call me Ikey, call me Moe
but give me the dough.) (p.111)

His father walled himself off with contempt; to this extent he
was less than human. Although Asa "rejected, and recoiled" from
this view (p.111), he was strongly influenced by it. "And who
were his enemies?" he asks about his father. "The world, everyone. They were imaginary." Asa recognizes this about his father,
but not about himself. Asa's mother, too, is another source of his
insecurity, and the loss of her sanity makes him fear for his own;
the loss of a home makes him fear he will never have a permanent place.

Asa's self-hatred and his role as a victim also come from
present failures to live up to what he wants to be or to accept
himself as he is. This is also found in the guilty Velchaninov, but
Bellow greatly enlarges on the theme. Asa himself knows the
process—in other people. Asa says of Allbee that he was
"haunted in his mind by wrongs or faults of his own which he
turned into wrongs against himself" (p.38). And he is right:
Allbee, hating himself for his degeneration and his wife's death,
puts the blame first on the world or chance, and secondly on Asa.
But this is just as true for Asa himself: he uses Allbee as a
vindication of his picture of the anti-Semite—the anti-Semite who
must hate him since he hates himself. Also, Asa uses Allbee and
others as scapegoats for his self-hatred: thus, Asa is sloppy and
fears sloppiness as a sign of (1) failure—the failure he could
have fallen into; (2) the insecurity of a house that, unlike
Williston's, is not ordered and traditional; (3) a disordered mind
(his mother's madness). So, fearing sloppiness, he condemns it in
Allbee and Elena but "disregards" it in himself.

A better example of his refusal to accept himself is his fear of
sexual indulgence. Throughout the novel, with his wife away,
Asa has sexual temptations, although he never allows them to
become conscious. First, there is Elena, his brother's wife. Asa
tries to keep contact between them at a minimum: "He hesitated
to tell her that Mary had gone South for a few weeks to be with

her mother. Elena would have insisted that he stay" (p.11). Bellow symbolizes his vaguely sexual feelings by having Asa knock his wedding ring against a bedpost when he and Elena are alone in a hot room; later, before he remembers to call Elena, he clicks his wedding ring on his shirt buttons. Once, awakened from a nap by thunder, he looks across the street into a window: "A woman lay on a sofa, one arm bent over her eyes. At the next sound of the retreating thunder she moved her legs" (p.138). This dreamlike sexual image is immediately followed by a call to Elena.

More important than Elena is Mrs. Nunez, the superintendent's wife. There are a number of hints of Asa's sexual feelings. Returning home one night, he sees her on the stoop—small, Indian face, full-hipped figure, high bosom, parted lips. "Mary, whom nothing escaped, had once said about Mrs. Nunez' suits, 'I don't see why she wears them. She could look very pretty in silk prints.' Till then Leventhal had scarcely noticed her. Now, when she said good evening and he nodded to her, he remembered this and had a moment of intense longing for his wife." She asks about his wife:

"Coming soon?"
"I don't think so." . . .
"Too bad," she repeated, and Leventhal, with a glance of surmise at her small face under the white brim, wondered what hint her sympathy might contain. There was a burst of music above them; a window was thrown open. (p.150)

He tells her he will be a bachelor for another month; he goes inside. The Nunez' dog rubs up against him and Mr. Nunez tells Asa, "'she's crazy about you'" (p.151). Again he remembers to call Elena. The reader is aware that Asa has projected his own desires onto Mrs. Nunez. Then, music—and an open window—symbolizing the rush of passion and the hint of possibility. An association is made between Mrs. Nunez and her dog, who is "crazy about" Asa. Mr. Nunez says not "the dog" but "she." This animal is clearly a sexual image and, leading as it does to the call to Elena, reminds the reader of the sexual images Asa sees through the window at Elena's. "In one of the other flats, a girl in a parlor chair was brushing a dog that yawned and tried to lick her hand. She pushed its muzzle down" (p.57). In this way, Asa's unconscious feelings for Elena and Mrs. Nunez, both Mediterranean types, are tied together.

The point is not that Asa has sexual desires of which he is unconscious or only dimly aware, but that he gets rid of his guilt by projecting these desires onto Kirby Allbee. Here again, Bellow expands on hints in Dostoyevsky. It is Allbee who should be ashamed of looking at girls near Asa's office when "Last night he was crying for his wife" (p.200). It is Allbee who is "nasty, twisted, bitching dirty" for reading the intimate postcard from Mary (p.207). "A lot a dirty drunk like that would know about a woman like Mary" (p.208), Asa grumbles. On the final night of their relationship, Asa comes home to find the door locked and chained: Allbee is with a woman. He smashes his way in. "There Allbee, naked and ungainly, stood beside a woman who was dressing in great haste. . . . Her hair covered her face; nevertheless Leventhal thought he recognized her. Mrs. Nunez! Was it Mrs. Nunez? The horror of it bristled on him, and the outcry he had been about to make was choked down" (p.269). The horror bristled because he was seeing a projection of his own unconscious desires—seeing the scene he wanted to act out. Soon we discover how completely it was projection: "She was a stranger, not Mrs. Nunez; simply a woman." And Asa feels "enormously lightened." Then, when the woman is gone, Asa yells, " 'You hypocrite! I thought you couldn't get over your wife' " (p.271). Seeing the image of his desires, he condemns it in Allbee—" 'You're not even human, if you ask me' "—and throws him out. Before he does, Allbee says, "Don't you people claim that you're the same as everybody else? That's your way of saying that you're above everybody else' " (p.272). He is referring to Asa as a Jew, but in his twisted way he is correct about Asa as a man. And this is the point: by denying guilt, by hating in Allbee what he cannot admit in himself, Asa separates himself from others—becomes less than human in his lack of compassion because he demands to be more than human, perfect, pure. Kirby Allbee is right when he tells Asa, speaking of adultery, " 'Nature is too violent for human ideals, sometimes, and ideals ought to leave it plenty of room' " (p.203).

To be human, then, means you have to confront elements inside yourself you do not wish to see; it means you have to confront the inhuman within and without. This idea of the *Dangling Man's* fear of the "unhuman in the all too human city" is vastly expanded in *Augie March* and in *Henderson* as the negative side of the affirmative joy of these novels. Here in *The Victim* the *unhuman* is an important motif. After seeing a tanker seabound on a terribly hot day and feeling the suffering of the men in the shaft alley by the keel, Asa imagines that the light over the towers on the shore and water

was akin to the yellow revealed in the slit of the eye of a wild animal, say a lion, something unhuman that didn't care about anything human and yet was implanted in every human being too, one speck of it, and formed a part of him that responded to the heat and the glare, exhausting as these were, or even to freezing, salty things, harsh things, all things difficult to stand. The Jersey shore, yellow, tawny, and flat, appeared on the right. (p.51)

One of the reasons we read Bellow is his ability to connect the external environment with the heart and mind; the spot of yellow is on the Jersey shore, in the eye of a lion (looking forward to Henderson), and within human beings. It is this unhuman quality that engulfs the city in summer heat; it is this quality he finds in the brutal scene he sees late at night between husband and adulterous wife; when Allbee is caught with a woman and thrown out, "a yellowish hot tinge came over his bloodshot eyes" (p.271). It is what Asa rejects in himself and fears being engulfed in.

This yellow is also in the eyes of Mr. Benjamin, the insurance broker, who argues about death with Harkavy at Libbey

Harkavy's birthday party. Death is the ground of the unhuman, and it, like the passion and violence within each of us, must be confronted and accepted. This truth is emphasized less here than in *Dangling Man,* but it is present, and it has no counterpart in Dostoyevsky. We have heard Schlossberg explain that men try to be more than human in order to avoid death, and speaking at the birthday party he says:

> Here I'm sitting here, and my mind can go around the world. . . . But in another minute I can be dead, on this spot. There's a limit to me. But I have to be myself in full. Which is somebody who dies, isn't it? That's what I was from the beginning. I'm not three people, four people. I was born once and I will die once. You want to be two people? More than human? Maybe it's because you don't know how to be one. (p.255)

To accept your self you must accept the end of yourself. To avoid facing death is to avoid being human, to turn yourself into an abstract entity, a "corporation" as Schlossberg puts it, and to cut yourself off from the rest of humanity. Schlossberg has just told of the paper grass which covered the dirt at the last funeral he attended. Now he says: "Paper grass in the grave makes all the grass paper" (p.256).That is, if you try to expunge death from consciousness, you are implicitly making life something other than what it is. But Schlossberg means more than that the denial of death is a denial of reality—"makes all the grass *paper*"— denial of death makes life less significant by taking away its existential seriousness. It is a concept similar to Fernando Molina's interpretation of Heidegger's *Sein und Zeit:* "Only the awareness of one's finitude extricates the person from the endless whirl of pleasing himself, taking things lightly, and shirking tasks that fill much of everyday living."[6] Confrontation of death results in living as an "I," a particular subject, instead of living as a "they"; and it results in acknowledging yourself as a member of humanity.

"I am not too good for this world," says Schlossberg. And it is by admitting this that one becomes good enough for it, that one becomes human. The theme of humble acceptance of oneself is repeated again and again in the novel. Harkavy tells Asa of a girl who found fault with him: "All I can say is, 'Lady, God bless you, we all have our faults and are what we are. I have to take myself as I am or push off. I am all I have in this world. And with all my shortcomings my life is precious to me'" (p.88). In this easygoing character, a Jew who isn't bothered by other people's anti-Semitic remarks, we hear the music of Augie March—these are precisely Augie's speech patterns: the world is possibility. This self-acceptance is echoed by Asa's brother, Max. When he is attacked by Asa for having left his family, Max simply agrees. "'Yes,' he said. 'I should have been here.'" And speaking of the death of his son, he admits, "We must have made mistakes, too. But what can you do? It's not like with God, you know, in the Bible, where he blows his breath into Adam or whoever." He is only human (pp.237–43).

If a man cannot accept the darkness in himself, he cannot fulfill Schlossberg's criteria, for (1) he wishes to be more than human, and (2) he is less, cutting himself off from other people. As Allbee says, apologizing for having attempted to kill them both, "When you turn against yourself, nobody else means anything to you either" (p.293). Conversely, accepting yourself, you can accept other people. Thus Max says of his mother-in-law when Asa tells him to get rid of her, "I know she doesn't like me. So what? A worn-out old woman. I feel sad, sometimes, when I look at her" (p.241). And Max tells Asa of walking into the hospital and finding his son dead. "'Those fools!' Leventhal exclaimed. 'Not to have somebody posted there.'" But "Max excused them with a downward wave of the hand. 'All the nurses didn't know. It's a big place'" (pp.241–42).

Asa cannot accept what he sees in himself; no more can Allbee. Despising himself for having caused the death of his wife, Allbee uses her insurance money for drink to destroy himself, feeling that to advance himself with the money would be immoral (just

as Joseph preferred to be victim rather than beneficiary). Asa too
feels unworthy, largely because of guilt, afraid he has stolen his
place in life and that he may end up like his brother, a common
workman, or like Allbee, a derelict. He had seen bad days
himself, had clerked in a hotel for "transients" on lower Broadway, and so Allbee's status was always a possibility for him. Asa
dreams one night of missing a train; trying to reach a second
section of it through a new gate, he is pushed out into an alley
(p.168). The anxiety that he has no right to succeed, that he has
stolen his place, that he has "gotten away with it" (as a child
Joseph was anxious to be found out—that the evil under his mask
would be uncovered) is reinforced by the double, Allbee, to
whom the Jew is an interloper, an intruder into American society.
Of course Asa may reject the idea that he has taken another's
place. " 'Why me?' he thought, frowning." It is the problem of the
merchant and the Ifrit. "In a general way, anyone could see that
there was great unfairness in one man's having all the comforts of
life while another had nothing. . . . Admittedly there was a
wrong, a general wrong. Allbee, on the other hand, came along
and said 'You!' " (p.79). But Allbee is a menace only because Asa
sees himself as interloper. Who knows? One false move and he
might be fired by Beard as Allbee was by Rudiger.

Asa's belief that he is lucky and his guilt over success make up
part of a larger theme, that of causality, responsibility, and the
benefit from disaster. As the bell rings to return Asa and Allbee
to their seats, Asa asks, " 'Wait a minute, what's your idea of who
runs things?' " (p.294). In one way or other, this question is
asked again and again. Asa wonders about Mickey's disease,
"Did medicine have any idea how a thing like that singled out a
child in Staten Island rather than, say, St. Louis or Denver?"
(p.64). Allbee alternates between blaming Asa and blaming
chance. In the latter mode he says " 'the day of succeeding by
your own efforts is past. Now it's all blind movement, vast
movement, as the individual is shuttled back and forth' " (p.70).

Asa doesn't agree: he wants to deserve. Mrs. Harkavy, with comic incongruity, points up the difficulty of determining the cause of success or failure: " 'Influence is a good thing. . . . You mustn't forget it. If you don't use it, you're left behind in the race of the swift' " (pp.83–84). Luck, swiftness, influence: in any event, the Harkavys can accept what comes to them without having to deserve it. A rug of theirs comes from "the estate of a broker who committed suicide on Black Friday" (p.257). And although Mrs. Harkavy says "Asa, sometimes I feel wicked still to be here at my age when children die," she adds. "But I'm not taking it away from anybody" (p.246). Accepting herself, she accepts what comes to her.

At the beginning of the novel Asa, because he feels unworthy, is in a continual struggle to keep his place. We see him shoving through the closing subway doors, pushing into the bus. But by the end of *The Victim,* Asa is more comfortable. "The consciousness of an unremitting daily fight, though still present, was fainter, less troubling. . . . As time went on he lost the feeling that he had, as he used to say, 'got away with it,' his guilty relief, and the accompanying sense of infringement" (p.285). Better able to accept himself, Asa is better able to accept what comes to him, whatever it be—"this was not even a true injustice, for how could you call anything so haphazard an injustice? It was a shuffle, all, all accidental and haphazard" (p.285).

Before speaking of how this change takes place, I want to point out that Asa's categories of perception are at fault. He sees nearly everything with regard to whether it does or does not deserve blame. Elena is to blame, Allbee is to blame, Max is to blame. Complementary to this blame is the expectation of being blamed, as when Asa attends Mickey's funeral. Asa's task is to learn to see outside the categories of moral judgment, for if it is true that hatred of oneself leads to hatred of others, conversely, judgment of others leads to judgment of oneself.

This is true in Dostoyevsky's novel, in which Velchaninov is split between his "higher" and "lower" ideas, split between slandering others and being slandered by them, and it is even truer in *The Victim*. Chizhevsky shows that the elimination of abstract moral judgment and its replacement by the perception of individuals, of "I"s, is integral to Dostoyevsky.

> In Dostoyevsky's opinion, "not to judge" is the main condition of the specific relation to people through which they become our neighbors. For Alyosha Karamazov "not judging" is the inescapable norm of ethics. . . . Precisely because of this unwillingness to judge, Alyosha appears everywhere loving, near, and familiar; for him everybody is a neighbor in the genuine Christian sense of the word. His place—his "sphere of freedom"—is the whole moral world.[7]

Asa must move from an attitude of duty to an attitude of love in his relationship with others; he must cease perceiving people as measurable by abstract ethics and approach them instead as unique, as "thous."

But to do so means to renounce his secure isolation. To keep himself detached from Allbee and Max enables him to detach himself from failure potentially his own and from guilt. Furthermore, as Schlossberg's female counterpart Mrs. Harkavy explains, "People are bound not to take things too much to heart, for their own protection" (p.84). One important movement in the book is his learning, in both plot strands (with Max and with Allbee), to take things to heart, to perceive others outside an abstract ethical system, to grow close to them.

Asa's relationship with his brother Max begins, naturally, in blame. Why wasn't Max here to take care of his family? Does he think he has fulfilled the duties of a father by sending home money? He decides to send Max a night letter, "the harsher the better" (p.62). Then he becomes more and more emotionally involved with Max's family, growing to love his nephew Philip. But this closeness isn't enough to stop him from roaring out, when he learns of Mickey's death, "Where is my damned brother!" (p.176), and he intends to meet Max in anger: "his very first word was to have been a rebuke." But seeing his actual brother rather than an abstract family-deserter,

instead of speaking, he took in his brother's appearance, the darkness and soreness of his swollen face, the scar at the corner of his mouth from a cut received in a street fight years ago in Hartford. Outdoor work had weathered him; the loss of several teeth made his jaw longer. His suit—it was a suit such as laborers used to buy in his father's store. His new black shoes were dusty.

"I didn't make it in time," he said.

"I heard, Max." (p.181)

He pities and supports his brother the rest of the afternoon. And if Asa begins by blaming Max when his brother comes to see him, he ends in love.

"I'm going south with the idea of a new start. I paid a deposit and so on. But to tell the truth, I don't expect much. I feel half burned out already."

Leventhal felt his heart shaken. "Half burned?" he said. "I'm older than you and I don't say that."

Max did not reply. His large trunk was ungainly in the double-breasted jacket.

"There have been times when I felt like that too," Leventhal went on. "That's a feeling that comes and goes." His brother turned his crude, dark face up to him and his voice died. (p.242)

Asa's heart is "shaken," but more important is that in separating himself from what his brother feels ("I'm older than you and I don't say that") he reverses himself and identifies: "There are times when I felt like that too." Bellow writes in "Distractions of a Fiction Writer": "Between the radically unlike there is no love" (p.12). Here there is an admission of alikeness, and there is love. Asa is becoming, according to Schlossberg's standards, "exactly human." Then he takes Max to the subway:

"If you need me for anything . . ." Leventhal said.

"Thanks."

"I mean it."

"Thank you." He extended his hand. Leventhal clumsily spread his arms wide and clasped him. (p.243)

Leaving the subway, "he felt faint with the expansion of his heart." Exactly—for it had expanded, and so had Asa. (We remember Mrs. Harkavy's warning about the danger of such expansion). "Buttoning his coat, he raised the collar, and his eyes moved from the glare of the cars ahead, *not quite steady in the immense blackness*" (italics mine). Identifying with his brother, Asa gets a taste of the darkness he has been avoiding.

In Asa's relation with Allbee, too, blame gives way to perception of a person and finally to identification. In the beginning Asa will not acknowledge his affinity with Allbee. Allbee is a bum, a drunk; Asa pigeonholes Allbee as "not a normal person, someone you would have to reckon with" (p.37). Allbee has fallen because of his own character, different from Asa's (although Asa acknowledges that he himself might have fallen "in another way," p.38). Later, during the conversation with Williston, he acknowledges "it was necessary . . . to accept some of the blame for Allbee's comedown" (pp.119–20). But this legalism does not bring about Asa's transformation; what does is his growing sense of closeness to Allbee, his sense of almost physical oneness. He feels this first at the zoo where he has taken Philip.

Leventhal, in speaking to Philip, or smoking, or smiling, was so conscious of Allbee, so certain he was being scrutinized, that he was able to see himself as if through a strange pair of eyes: the side of his face, the palpitation in his throat, the seams of his skin, the shape of his body and of his feet in their white shoes. Changed in this way into his own observer, he was able to see Allbee, too, and imagined himself standing so near behind him that he could see the weave of his coat, his raggedly overgrown neck, the bulge of his cheek, the color of the blood in his ear; he could even evoke the odor of his hair and skin. The acuteness and intimacy of it astounded him, oppressed and intoxicated him. (p.107) [8]

Momentarily Asa becomes the other; momentarily he sees himself from the point of view of the other. And he sees the other intimately. Later, during Allbee's visit, this strange perception comes to Asa again—"a feeling of intimate nearness." He is able to enter Allbee: "He could feel the weight of his body and the contact of his clothes." And he senses that "the look of recognition Allbee bent on him duplicated the look in his own" (p.160). Even if Asa tries to "keep alive in his mind the thought that Allbee hated him," he gives him a place to stay, lets him come to live with him. In Dostoyevsky's novella, Velchaninov *forces* Trusotsky to stay over one night to be sure he will be able to bring him to Lisa in the morning. Here Asa *offers*—not without pressure, it is true—to let this man who hates him move in. And he offers help; he feel tied to Allbee in a way that extends beyond duty and repayment. As with Max, Asa finds himself regarding Allbee "with a look of dismayed pity" (p.196), makes coffee for him, carries him to bed, and, finally, feels himself "singularly drawn with a kind of affection. It oppressed him, it was repellent. He did not know what to make of it. Still, he welcomed it, too. He was remotely disturbed to see himself so changeable. However, it did not seem just then to be a serious fault" (p.224). Immediately after this, Asa becomes furious when Allbee runs his fingers through his wiry, "Jew" hair. The anger may be seen as directed against the intimacy of contact as much as against the threat of anti-Semitism.

This intimate contact is hinted at by Asa's perception of the relation between Allbee and Yvonne Crane, whom he escorts to the theater where Asa meets him years later. When Allbee, true to form, quarrels with the driver for having cheated them, Yvonne Crane throws the driver a bill and they go inside; this is all Asa sees, but as he interprets the scene :"he's got that woman under his thumb" (p.290). In other words, he projects the relationship that, as Harkavy said, Asa had had with Allbee. *He* had been under Allbee's thumb. This identification of himself with Allbee's mistress indicates the intimate nature of the relationship.

The identification which Asa comes to make between himself

and Allbee is largely added to what Bellow found in Dostoyevsky; there the essential relationship was complementary—cuckold to cuckolder; here it is essentially parallel—the polarity of anti-Semite/Jew merely lends irony to their similarity. And it is a similarity which grows stronger as the relationship develops. Asa becomes more slovenly; he gets drunk at the Harkavys'; he camps out, like Allbee, at another man's house. It is this new closeness that leads Asa to reject with otherwise inexplicable fury Harkavy's suggestion that Allbee is insane; Asa fears for his own sanity.

There is little intimacy in the final scene with Allbee. Perhaps the danger wrought by the closeness between them is partly responsible: Asa is no longer able to detach himself from Allbee; the awareness *I could do what he has done* is too close to consciousness. At any rate, Asa recognizes that the act of bringing in a woman to have sexual relations on Asa's bed is an act of symbolic closeness with Asa himself. Fiedler is correct in speaking of "a kind of rejection scarcely distinguishable from rape."[9] It seems that only when Asa and Allbee are wedded by the two scenes of final violence can they divorce. Asa must enter the irrational world Allbee represents to him. "He felt dimly that this disorder and upheaval was part of the price he was obliged to pay for his release" (p.274). Then he considers the scene again, this time from the point of view of Allbee and the woman. He realizes that "Both of them . . . moved or swam toward him out of a depth of life in which he himself would be lost, choked, ended. There lay horror, evil, all that he had kept himself from" (p.279). The point is that Asa is forced to meet the darkness from which he had kept himself. He has seen Allbee's swollen feet, he has remembered the smell of disinfectant used in hotels for transients. He is no longer protected from taking things "too much to heart." Particularly when Allbee returns to kill them both with gas, Asa is forced to confront the irrational, the something-akin-to-the-yellow-of-a-lion's-eyes: death.

Norman Podhoretz, although essentially correct, exaggerates

SAUL BELLOW: In Defense of Man

when he writes that Asa "has not ventured into the 'depths' that he once feared would drown him; he has merely (like a successfully analyzed patient) learned something about himself that has helped him come to terms with the world and make a settlement."[10] Perhaps it is more accurate to say that because he understands that the depths he fears are within him, he does not have to be destroyed by them.

Through the growing sense of the reality of others, through his growing awareness of their kinship with him, Asa has become, in Schlossberg's terms, "human." Now he can call his wife home; he is ready for her. That he has changed permanently we know by the final chapter, which finds him healthier, happier, and a father-to-be. His burdens, unlike those of Rogin's ("A Father-to-Be") are cast off. Surely it is incorrect to say that Asa's change "grows out of the healing power of time rather than the plot itself."[11] Rather, as we have seen, it grows subtly out of Asa's experiences: subtly, as in life. But like *Dangling Man*, *The Victim* moves toward a redefinition of what *human* is, a definition which goes beyond Schlossberg's wisdom. In the middle of the novel Asa's dream of expulsion from the railroad station leads to an overwhelming sense of truth-found. "Yes, I do know it, positively. Will I know it in the morning? I do now" (p.169). Typically for Bellow, Asa does not hold onto it; he oversleeps, wakes up irritated. But for a moment, he knew.

To retell the dream in greater detail: the dreamer is in a terribly crowded station trying to get to the second section of a train he has missed. Pushed into a corridor, he tries to go down through a newly constructed gate to the tracks. But a contractor in a fedora stops him—the other man, a workman, is not able to interfere with his boss—and pushes him out into the alley; his face is covered with tears.

There is no simple relationship between this dream and the truth that eludes Asa. It is like Asa's strange pain on awaking after the birthday party at the Harkavys':

He had the strange feeling that there was not a single part of him on which the whole world did not press with full weight, on his body, on his soul, pushing upward in his breast and downward in his bowels. He concentrated, moving his lips like someone about to speak, and blew a tormented breath through his nose. What he meanwhile sensed was that this interruption of the customary motions he went through unthinkingly on rising, despite the pain it was causing, was a disguised opportunity to discover something of great importance. He tried to seize the opportunity. He put out all his strength to collect himself, beginning with the primary certainty that the world pressed on him and passed through him. Beyond this he could not go, hard though he drove himself. He was bewilderingly moved. . . . And then the cramp and the enigmatic opportunity ended together. (p.258)

Again truth approaches out of sleep. Again there is the reaching out for some ultimate truth about the self, a truth just out of reach. Here it is seen as a kind of birth (hence the significance of the "birthday party")—Asa himself newborn: doubled over, unable to breathe or cry; at the same time it is Asa *giving* birth, giving birth to the elusive truth. Often in Bellow (as in "A Father-to-Be" or *Seize the Day*) we find this un-Jewish imagery of personal rebirth, redemption into a new life.

The dream of the missed train is another moment of such transfiguration. On the surface the dream represents the defeat of the anguished dreamer by the reality principle (in business suit and fedora), a defeat analogous to death—there is no way out; one cannot cheat the rules. But far more important, Asa is able to identify himself with the runner unable to catch his train (or with Allbee, who often asks for a place on "the train"), with the rigid enforcer of the "rules" who prevents him from succeeding, and with the helpless workman (Asa's self-righteousness and conscience, his pity and sense of helpless responsibility). All are inside Asa, and thus this truth is formed: "It was supremely plain to him that everything, without exception, took place as if within a single soul or person" (p.169). This is not solipsism but its opposite. It is a sense—a vision—of the unity of all persons, the essential alikeness of all persons, each mysteriously containing all. This is where the movement toward perception of the other as real, toward identification with others, and toward acceptance of self, of others, and of death, has been leading: toward a submergence of individuality in a transpersonal, anonymous self. It is the vision of victim and victimizer as one.

This is a truth not found in Dostoyevsky's novella, although indeed Trusotsy and Velchaninov are bound tightly together and Dostoyevsky does believe every man is responsible for every other (e.g., *Brothers Karamazov*), but this truth of unity is essential here. It is Bellow's way of reconciling the individual and the community, analogous to Whitman's magic:

> I celebrate myself and sing myself,
> And what I assume you shall assume,
> For every atom belonging to me as good belongs to you.

Now it is clear that the continual presence of crowds in the summer heat is not mere background. Maxwell Geismar speaks of "those Dreiserian and Whitmanesque masses that this highly sensitive and withdrawn artist has always yearned to link himself with."[12] Clearly, Bellow wants us to see *all* men as if they were *one* and *each* man as if he were *all*. It is his way of answering Allbee's quandary:

> The world's a crowded place, damned if it isn't. It's an overcrowded place. There's room enough for the dead. . . . because they don't want anything. But the living. . . . Do you want anything? Is there anything you want? There are a hundred million others who want that very same thing. . . . It's hard to believe that my life is necessary. I guess you wouldn't be familiar with the Catholic catechism where it asks, 'For whom was the world made?' Something along that line. And the answer is, 'For man.' For every man? Yes, for every last mother's son. . . . For everybody who repeats 'For man' it means 'For me.' 'The world was created for me, and I am absolutely required, not only now, but forever'. (pp.193–94)

How can the human being possess dignity among so many, all wanting as he wants? The answer: each man is everyman. All-Be:

in touching Allbee, Asa touches all of humanity; indeed, he *becomes* all of humanity. Returning to the epigraphs, then, we can answer their riddles: De Quincey's vision of the human face upon the ocean is first a single face, then "innumerable faces," as the individual is at the same time all individuals, possessing the dignity not of the exceptional man but of everyman. What can a man do, looking upon this ocean, confronting all those who want? He can recognize the humanity in common between himself and the others; and he can answer one want—in this he will have responded to all.

Is he responsible to them? This brings up the parable of the slaying of the Ifrit's son. Considering the complexities of causality, one cannot say "You are guilty", but one must answer, "I am responsible." These are not the same—Asa, feeling guilt, rejects responsibility; accepting responsibility, he feels less guilt. One responds, to relieve the other's suffering. And if all are one, the other's suffering is one's own, too.

To what extent does Asa live with this truth? Bellow emphasizes that (unlike Velchaninov's complete change) Asa's change is partial. But far more successfully than Joseph the Dangling Man, Asa ends his alienation. Beginning, like Joseph, as a solitary, separated from his wife and hostile to the few friends he has, he goes much farther than Joseph in joining humanity without surrendering to society. His success heralds the over-eager affirmation of Bellow's next novel, *The Adventures of Augie March.*

CHAPTER EIGHT

Henderson the Rain King

Henderson the Rain King is the thousandth retelling of *Don Quixote:* the dissatisfied idealist, the bourgeois longing to fulfill his life, to transform himself and the world into something more noble. The hero's dream of glory meets with reality and the hero is transformed or defeated.

The theme of *Henderson*, like that of *Augie March*, is this twofold comedy of life: the individual moaning or shouting "I want," reality replying, "I am." "Ages of longing and willing, willing and longing, and how have they ended? In a draw, dust and dust." Henderson wants to break out of the cycle and its pessimism; he refuses to die, he demands redemption. But his "I want," as always in Bellow's fiction, alienates Henderson from community and makes impossible the redemption he seeks.

Henderson's quest for redemption, for salvation, is similar to Tommy Wilhelm's. Both heroes begin as alienatees, both are prepared during the progress of the novel for a partial return to community. Both have to learn to plunge into the here-and-now, to seize reality as it is. But *Henderson the Rain King* is a comic version of the quest, a romance-satire on the American quixotic self who rebels against life's terms and, like Augie, demands a special fate.

Eugene Henderson, a middle-aged millionaire who feels like a displaced person, flees from the piled-up burden of his life and from the unredeemed death he sees before him. He decides to find salvation not in civilization but in the primal, savage state:

he leaves his wife and goes to Africa. Trekking deep into the country with a guide, Romilayu, Henderson comes upon two tribes. The first, the meek, cattle-loving Arnewi he tries to impress by his deeds; he tells Itelo he will singlehandedly kill the frogs which are desecrating the cattle's drinking water; but in doing so, he also blows out the wall of the cistern and loses all the water. Before this disaster he gains "wisdom" from Queen Willatale, who tells him "Grun-tu-molani"—man wants to live. With this ambiguous truth he goes on to the Wariri, a dangerous tribe dealing in death—"chillen dahkness," as Romilayu says. By lifting up the wooden idol Mummah at rain ceremonies, Henderson becomes Rain King. He and the king, Dahfu (who learned English at Beirut with Itelo of the Arnewi), become friends. Dahfu promises he can redeem Henderson by teaching him to appreciate and imitate a lioness. Henderson roars, Henderson walks on all fours, and he claims that his spirit's sleep is being burst. But Dahfu is killed trying to capture another lion, supposed to contain the spirit of his father, and Henderson has to run from the tribe to avoid being made king and husband to sixty-seven wives. He brings back with him to civilization a lion cub, containing the spirit of Dahfu. Reconciled to reality, Henderson is now returning home, to be a better husband and to start belated medical training. In a moment of holy joy when the plane stops to refuel at Newfoundland, he runs and leaps around the plane in the snow, holding an orphan in his arms.

QUESTION: "Which of your characters is most like you?"
BELLOW: "Henderson—the absurd seeker of high qualities."[1]

In a sense Eugene Henderson is a caricature of all Bellow's characters who seek salvation. Through him Bellow can laugh at his own questing spirit.

Critics have not understood how comically this spirit is treated. Henderson's search is generally taken too seriously—it is not seen as a parody search. Among the critics, Alter is an exception:

"*Henderson*," he writes, "is a composite parody of all the memorable twentieth century novels of personal or mythic quest into dark regions."[2] Instead of plunging into undiscovered country, Henderson finds two university-bred, English-speaking chiefs, one believing that to wrestle is "invaluable," the other having (it would seem) read Wilhelm Reich; instead of feeling "the horror, the horror," Henderson "lay with eyes open, bathed in high feelings" (*HRK*, p.99). Instead of being killed by the chief when, like Lord Jim, he makes a terrible mistake, he goes off to the next tribe already deciding to make use of his trouble (p.114). I am reminded of Bellow's discussion of Harold Rosenberg's idea that the middle class mind always converts every loss to a profit—that even while tripping on a sidewalk crack, the bourgeois is collecting the insurance money.[3] Fiedler has pointed out that Eugene Henderson's initials are those of another "absurd seeker after high qualities"—Ernest Hemingway.[4] Both, fed up with civilized hypocrisy, go to Africa to find essential truth from essential things. But Henderson's beautiful 375 Magnum is taken from him before he can arrive at his moment of truth. He brings home no lion but only a tiny cub. Finally, if Dahfu is like a Laurentian genital hero or a Faulknerian wisdom teacher, he is also a crackpot (Dahfu = daffy)—like Dr. Tamkin.

This is the comedy of a Self beating itself on the chest and thinking "this is going to be one of my greatest days" before he destroys the Arnewi's cistern—a Self roaring to a stadium full of villagers and lifting their heavy wooden idol Mummah, only to find himself stuck with the job of Rain King. Fulfillment, self-transcendence! cries Henderson's heart, as have so many romantic hearts. Childe Harold seeks his lost innocence, better and more guilty than other men, striving and questioning the value of striving. "If I couldn't have my soul it would cost the earth a castastrophe," says Henderson-Raskolnikov (p.282). Klein may be correct that Bellow intended a parallel between Henderson's conversion and Zarathustra's: as Zarathustra goes through three stages—camel, lion, child—so Henderson goes from pigs and cattle to lion to child, ending in the holy joy Nietzsche sees as the goal of self-transcendence.[5] But Klein seems to miss the humor of the parallel: Henderson, the bulky millionaire, is not Zara-thustra; his quest is a parody of the nineteenth century struggle (and Bellow's own struggle) for self-transcendence. *Henderson* also parodies such contemporary novels as Kerouac's *Big Sur*, in which his King of the Beatniks tries (with only slight irony) to find his salvation in a Thoreau-like Eden on the California coast; or *Deer Park*, in which Sergius O'Shaughnessy tries to transcend the artificial, impure society in which he finds himself. Like Southern's *Candy*, Bellow's novel is a parody of the questing bourgeois self speaking of love but more concerned with its own improvement and fulfillment. We are to laugh at Henderson's quest. It is not merely the contrast of gross millionaire and airy quest which is funny ("The Kingdon of Heaven is for children of the spirit. But who is this nosy, gross phantom?"); the humor lies in the quest itself—the egoistic quest for personal fulfillment.

Just one week before *Henderson* was published Bellow warned in the *New York Times*, "Deep Readers of the World, Beware"; novels should not be read with constant attention to symbols.[6] Important symbols are obvious (the whale in *Moby Dick*); others should be ignored. Readers can lose the novel in a search for symbols. But if so, then why does Bellow write a novel as filled with symbolism as *Henderson*? Is he unaware of how symbolic a novel he has written? Critics have tried to apologize for Bellow, not seeing that the symbolism of the novel is a put-on. Of course the novel is symbolic. Of course there are patterns out of Freud, Jung, Frazer; but we should see the patterns as parody, just as *The Last Analysis* is a parody of psychoanalysis and the style of psychoanalytic patients. Of course Henderson is the mythic hero who enters the dangerous kingdom, marries the god-dess, reconciles himself with the father, and takes a boon back to the tribe. But the pattern is parodic. Bellow is making fun of mod-ern literary pretentiousness: as if he were saying, "You want a symbolic novel? I'll give you the most symbolic novel you ever wrote a critical article about." More important, in *Henderson* as in *The Last Analysis*, Bellow is making fun of his own propensity for self-examination and his own longings for rebirth. Indeed, he is making fun of these traits in the culture at large.

Bellow has said, "*My* welfare, *my* development, *my* advancement, *my* earnestness, *my* adjustment, *my* marriage, *my* family—all that will make the modern reader laugh heartily."[7] This remark, although in context it defends the individual, applies directly to *Henderson the Rain King*. "I want, I want," says the voice inside Henderson, and so Henderson does not concern himself with the sick children of his landlord in France (p.14). When he first sees the Arnewi, he says, "I have a hunch this spot is going to be very good for me" (p.47). Then, burning a bush with a cigarette lighter (the Burning Bush, Henderson cast as God), he makes a "brilliant manifestation" (p.48). Seeing tears, he assumes *he* has caused them. Seeing a brilliant dawn, he assumes that the world gave him "a kind of go-ahead sign" (p.100). When he asks for wisdom and finds that he has won the heart of Mtalba, he snaps, "Hell with her heart." Stupendous Henderson will annihilate the frogs (we recall Robey with the flit gun in *Augie March*) and then modestly refuse a high position: "The thing is up to me alone" (p.97). When he fails, he mourns, "Why for once, just once! couldn't I get my heart's desire?" (p.111). The heart's desire is more important than the thirsty Arnewians. We are reminded of the destructive egotism of Goethe's *Faust*, making the world after his image at the cost of slave labor and of the lives of Baucis and Philemon. Even with the Wariri, Henderson thinks, as he goes to pick up the idol, Mummah, "I still couldn't pass up this opportunity to do, and to distinguish myself . . ." (p.186). "Here comes Henderson" (p.186).

But Henderson is not a Candy—we respect his quest a good deal more. Marcus Klein says that what Henderson seeks is reality: "He goes to Africa to discover Reality, Reality as an idea. That is what the voice within him that says 'I want' ultimately wants."[8] This view is incorrect. Reality is what Henderson says he wants, and perhaps it is what he finds, but it is not what he really wants. Instead, he wants reality to fulfill his hope that "chaos doesn't run the whole show. That this is not a sick and hasty ride, helpless, through a dream into oblivion" (p.175). Henderson wants to affirm, like Joseph, Augie, Herzog, and other Bellow characters, the meaningfulness of human life, to show that a human life is not like a stone falling from life to death— "exactly like a stone, straight into deafness, and till the last repeating *I want, I want, I want,* then striking the earth and entering it forever" (p.297). At the end these negative assertions turn into a positive one: "But there is justice. I believe there is justice and that much is promised" (p.328). The affirmation comes in fever (as Asa's in half-sleep) in the midst of an absurd Africa by a comic character, but it is made. It is Henderson's affirmation; it is Bellow's.

This affirmation of the human being rests, as it did in *Seize the Day,* on the salvation of one man: here, Eugene Henderson. He begins his quest with the hope of personal redemption; he reads, this gross millionaire, "the forgiveness of sins is perpetual and righteousness first is not required" (p.3). And so he runs to Africa, hoping to be spiritually transformed into one worthy of redemption. Seeing himself with his father's eyes, like Tommy Wilhelm and Moses Herzog, he despises this "pig" who seems to have lived by accident, wrongfully, when his loved older brother drowned. He feels like the interloper, the displaced person, waiting, trembling, for the "rightful one." Unable to live in the joy of the here-and-now, he says, "When the rightful one appeareth we shall all stand and file out, glad at heart and greatly relieved, and saying, Welcome back, Bud. It's all yours. Barns and houses are yours. Autumn beauty is yours. Take it, take it, take it'" (p.34). He must run to Africa to escape his sense of intrusion, asking "who shall abide the day of his coming?" Henderson sees himself as sinful and unworthy of his place.

Having stolen his brother's place, he runs to Africa as on the day of his brother's funeral he ran to Canada to avoid his own father-fed guilt. In Henderson's unconscious as in Joseph's, personal sin is punished by death; he must run from his infringement and from his death. His quest is not for reality but for release from mortality.

In his interview in *Show* Bellow says:

What Henderson is really seeking is a remedy to the anxiety over death. What he can't endure is this continuing anxiety: the indeterminate and indefinite anxiety, which most of us accept as the condition of life which he is foolhardy enough to resist.

He tells the King that he is a 'Becomer' and that the King is a 'Beer.' I believe I meant him to say that human life is intolerable if we must endure endless doubt. That is really what I feel is motivating Henderson. All his efforts are a satire on the attempts people make to answer the enigma by movement and random action or even by conscious effort.[9]

Finally, then, Henderson wants not to die. Grun-tu-molani—man-want-to-live—can be taken partly in this simple sense: man-want-not-to-die. When he tells Romilayu, "I wouldn't agree to the death of my soul" (p.277), he means he wouldn't agree to the death of his *self*.

It is specifically from this death that he flees. His quarrel with Lily at the beginning of the book comes because she tells a friend that Henderson is "unkillable" (p.6). He wants to believe so and says it himself later, but her introduction of the subject invokes anxiety. In retrospect, he recalls how in France he got rid of Lily. Unable or unwilling to have intercourse with her, he becomes furious at her for trying, sends her off, saying, "You'll never kill me, I'm too rugged!"—and weeps. That same afternoon he sees something which rebuffs his boast:

I looked in at an octopus, and the creature seemed also to look at me and press its soft head to the glass, flat, the flesh becoming pale and granular—blanched, speckled. The eyes spoke to me coldly. But even more speaking, even more cold, was the soft head with its speckles, a cosmic coldness in which I felt I was dying. The tentacles throbbed and motioned through the glass, the bubbles sped upward, and I thought, "This is my last day. Death is giving me notice." (p.19)

This cosmic coldness, this absolute Inhuman, is like the darkness Asa and Augie found at the ground of being—an Other which is totally unconcerned with human longing and human life. Instead of submitting to this moment of *Angst* as Tommy Wilhelm does at the end of *Seize the Day*, Henderson runs. He runs from the absoluteness of death, playing the violin in order to reach his dead father, "for it so happens that I have never been able to convince myself the dead are utterly dead" (p.30). Then, the very last link in the chain which leads him to Africa is again the fact of death: Miss Lenox, the Hendersons' maid, dies in the kitchen (perhaps in response to Henderson's yelling) and Henderson, going to the woman's cottage, is shocked by the hoards of ancient claptrap she kept as a means of cheating death And he thinks, "You, too, will die of pestilence. Death will annihilate you and nothing will remain, and there will be nothing left but junk" (p.40). He goes off for the plane ticket, and although he says, "having dreamed at the clouds from both sides as no other generation of men has done, one should be able to accept his death very easily" (p.42); yet *he* cannot accept—and he postures in a variety of ways so as to keep off the fact of death. When Queen Willatale tells him "world is strange to a child," Henderson agrees that he plays the child—that the grown man, fearing death, lets himself be abducted, like a child, by "the strangeness of life, which makes death more remote" (p.84). We are reminded of the psychic bargain Herzog makes: pretended innocence to keep death away. As in *Dangling Man* and *Augie March*, the desire for individual greatness directly results from the desire for immortality: ordinary humans die, not the magnificent Henderson, who can lift Mummah.

Henderson continues to run from death. Dahfu calls him an "avoider." He is. He throws the ex-sungo's corpse into the ravine but returns to the hut to find the corpse already there; that is, he

will not be able to avoid death. His terror of the octopus is repeated with the lion. The composition of the base of the walls
outside the lion's cave "recalled to me the speckled vision of twi-
light at Banyules-sur-Mer in that Aquarium, where I saw the
creature, the octopus, pressing its head against the glass" (p.220).
The lion itself provokes terror: "The animal's face is pure fire to
me. Every day. I have to close my eyes" (p.283). Thinking of the
death that awaits him from one slap of the lion's paw, he writes,
"One stroke, one dizzy moment, the mind fills with might. Ah,
God! No stars in that night. There is nothing" (pp.263–64). Again,
when he sees the shrivelled skull of an executed "sorceress," "it
spoke to me as that creature had done in Banyules at the Aquarium after I had put Lily on the train. I thought as I had then, in
the dim watery stony room, 'This is it! The end!'" (p.252).

This death he fears is imaged in a number of ways: skulls,
corpses, octopi and other creatures of the sea (like the images of
drowning in *Seize the Day*); blood and the color red, as in
Dahfu's lips, his wound, and Henderson's beard; black (like the
darkness in *The Victim* and *Augie March*) and white. For
instance, we find the image of the white octopus in Willatale's
defective eye, "with a cataract, blueish white" (p.72). Again,
Henderson's own face, like the octopus, "is always undergoing
transformations making it as busy, as strange and changeful, as a
creature of the tropical sea lying under a reef . . ." (p.131). The
rocks of the landscape of the death-dealing Wariri are white—a
white limestone which originated, like the octopus, in water. The
white rocks in front of the palace, "about the size of Pacific man-
eating clams, held fierce flowers, of a very red color" (p.119):
Death as blank unhumanness and bloody fierceness. The hut in
which a Wariri king is strangled (the hut in which Henderson is
locked up) is of the same stone, and in it he feels as if he were
drifting away. The white of the octopus and stones is also the
color of the lion's belly and the color of the chalk worn by the
Bunam's man, the executioner, as an omen of Dahfu's death. In

terror for Dahfu, Henderson groans: "a sob came out of me . . . like a great sea bubble from the Atlantic floor" (p.298).

Running from death, Henderson runs from reality. For reality, the given, is composed of beauty and terror—beauty built on a substructure of terror (the lion beneath Dahfu's palace)—and refusing to confront the terror, Henderson must refuse the beauty. The purest example is the lioness, to whose beauty Henderson, from fear, cannot respond. He also rejects a beauty which he feels comes to him through another's death. Feeling guilt, like Joseph, Asa, and Tommy, at being a beneficiary, he cannot accept the beauty of his estate—the moment of serenity that comes to him as to Joseph (the red string), to Asa (the moment of awareness in bed), to Augie (the moments of Edenic peace and love amid nature), to Tommy (the moment of love in the subway:

It's one of those velvety days of early autumn when the sun is shining on the pines and the air has a spice of cold and stings your lungs with pleasure. I see a large pine tree on my property, and in the green darkness underneath, which somehow the pigs never got into, red tuberous begonias grow, and a broken stone inscription put in by my mother says, "Goe happy rose . . ." That's all it says. There must be more fragments beneath the needles. The sun is like a great roller and flattens the grass. Beneath this grass the earth may be filled with carcasses, yet that detracts nothing from a day like this, for they have become humus and the grass is thriving. When the air moves the brilliant flowers move too in the dark green beneath the trees. They brush against my open spirit because I am in the midst of this in the red velvet dressing gown from the Rue de Rivoli bought on the day that Frances spoke the word divorce. I am there and am looking for trouble. The crimson begonias, and the dark green and the radiant green and the spice that pierces and the sweet gold and the dead transformed, the brushing of the flowers on my undersurface are just misery to me. They make me crazy with misery. To somebody these things may have been given, but that somebody is not me in the red velvet robe. So what am I doing here? (pp.28–29)

In contrast to Henderson, who is guilty, unable to take the here-and-now, Queen Willatale pays the cost of beauty; she, like the lioness, manifests reality: "The queen expressed stability in every part of her body. Her head was white and her face broad and solid and she was wrapped in a lion's skin" (p.72). Her white head is linked to the bleached skulls tossed in ritual by Dahfu: she lives in the presence of death. And she is at peace with the fruits of death: the skin of the lion.

Henderson believes that he accepts reality. He tells us over and over,. "I am on damned good terms with reality, and don't you forget it" (p.36). He begs for reality, asking, in rebuttal of Eliot, "But how much unreality can [humankind] . . . stand?" (p.105). And he boasts:

I have always argued that Lily neither knows nor likes reality. Me? I love the old bitch just the way she is and I like to think I am always prepared for even the very worst she has to show me. I am a true adorer of life, and if I can't reach as high as the face of it, I plant my kiss somewhere lower down. (p.150)

But Henderson lies to himself. The reality he loves is *his* reality, his (to quote Augie) "version," his (to quote Joseph) "ideal constructions." He believes: "It's you who makes the world what it is. Reality is *you*" (p.123).[10] Travel is "mental travel"; the Arnewi are *his* savages, and the rosy dawn speaks to *him*. Putting his personal stamp on the world, like Thea in *Augie March*, he prepares the bomb to kill the Arnewi's frogs: "Poor little bastards was what I said, but in actual fact I was gloating—yuck-yuck-yuck! My heart was already fattening in anticipation of their death. We hate death, we fear death, but when you get right down to cases, there's nothing like it" (p.89). There is nothing like death, that is, when *he* dispenses it: death under his control.

Reality in the novel is "the old bitch"—a female figure: the lioness and, especially, Willatale. Henderson is invited to kiss Willatale on the belly. A great heat emanates from her and he feels "contact with a certain power—unmistakable!" (p.74). This reality is joyful, for these "women of Bittahness" are, in spite of death and sorrow, joyful; they possess, like the figures in Yeats' "Lapis Lazuli," an *amor fati* which Henderson does not yet have. "There was no anxious care in her, and she was sustained. Why, nothing bad happened! On the contrary, it all seemed good" (p.79). Henderson would like to imitate her, to stop striving and be redeemed. But given his fears and his "ego emphasis" (as Dahfu calls it), it is impossible.

Later, understanding more, he writes Lily: "This king here . . . tells me I should move from the states that I myself make into the states which are of themselves. Like if I stopped making such a noise all the time I might hear something nice" (p.284).

Just as Augie longs to live in reality rather than in his version of reality, so Henderson needs to learn to "stop making such a noise." To enter into the given, into reality as it is, he must accept death as well as beauty. Then he can be redeemed and Man's life affirmed. How does he progress toward these possibilities?

According to legend, the Arnewi and Wariri were once one tribe but split on the issue of luck: the Wariri are "ibai," *lucky*, the Arnewi, "nibai," unlucky. Often in Bellow it is personality that influences luck. The Wariri seem to make their luck: they beat their wooden gods to produce rain; the Arnewi simply suffer and seem to offer up this suffering like a sacrifice to propitiate the gods. The Arnewi are professional victims; the Wariri Machiavellians. In other words, the Arnewi are like Joseph, Mama March, Tommy Wilhelm, Herzog; while the Wariri are like the tough, older brother figures of Amos and Simon and the father Dr. Adler. The split between tribes projects the split within Bellow's literary personality and the split within Henderson himself. Henderson, like the Arnewi in some ways, the Wariri in others, must choose a third possibility (while drawing from both): must be neither victim nor executioner.

If the Arnewi—not including the gay "women of Bittahness"—offer up their suffering like a sacrifice, so does Henderson. "Who can suffer like me? I am to suffering what Gary is to smoke. One of the world's biggest operations" (p.260). The purpose of the operation is propitiation of the gods—in this case, his dead father, to whom he plays on the violin—so that his life will be spared. "Suffering was the closest thing to worship that I knew anything about" (pp.303–304). The Arewi, weeping guiltily and futilely over their dying cattle as Henderson over his dying (and animal-like) body, are likewise trying to propitiate the gods by their suffering. As they weep out their guilt, he, afraid he has done something wrong by burning a bush, begins to berate himself in front of them, a delightfully funny, parallel self-castigation.

But Henderson is not pure Arnewi. He is also, once again, a bumbling parody on Western man, the achiever, the American Faust. He fails (in his attempt to aid the Arnewi); but this side of Henderson is picked up in the following adventure by the Wariri. Instead of coming to Henderson in tears, the Wariri approach with guns; they use *his* tactics. Like Henderson, they give orders to reality, whipping their gods. If Henderson enjoys dispensing death, the Wariri enjoy it more.

However, the essential function of the Wariri and of their chief Dahfu is to change Henderson by shattering his ego and forcing him to confront the Real. He must go beyond "man-want-to-live" to the understanding of how to die, an understanding which permits life.

There is, for instance, the night with the corpse: Henderson is treated as intruder, not honored guest, and is made to touch death. Then, in the arena, he is not permitted simply to feel heroic (as with the Arnewi) when he caries away Mummah; he is forced to realize the consequences: life is not a game nor he a child. His clothes are ripped from him, he is coated with mud, he is whipped until he partakes of the inhuman and himself whips the gods. Naked to reality, he is covered with it and is forced to confront its underside: only then does the fertilizing rain fall. Frenzied, in a miniature version of his whole transformation, he must try "to remember who I was. *Me*" (p.199). His identity, his very selfhood, is shaken, and he yells "Not my will, but Thy will!" (p.199). Truth, as Henderson tells us, comes in blows.

With his new partial identity of the Sungo or Rain King, he is continually made to confront death: the executed victims, the sorceress' skull, the penalty for impotence, the presence of the executioner, the threat to his own life. But more important, it is through the person of King Dahfu that Henderson confronts death and the Real, loses his selfhood, and enters the given.

Dahfu is to Henderson what Tamkin is to Tommy—healer, teacher, and quack. If Henderson, fed up with civilization, is seeking wisdom in the Savage, Dahfu the savage paradoxically heals him with wisdom brought back from civilization. For it is not traditional tribal teaching; it is the product of his studies at Beirut.

Dahfu's audio-visual aid, his machine for programmed instruction, is Atti, the lioness: again, reality is the female.

> You ask, what can she do for you? Many things. First, she is unavoidable. Test it, and you will find she is unavoidable. And this is what you need, as you are an avoider. Oh, you have accomplished monumentous avoidances. But she will change that. She will make consciousness to shine. She will burnish you. She will force the present moment upon you. Second, lions are experiencers. But not in haste. They experience with deliberate luxury. The poet says, 'The tigers of wrath are wiser than the horses of instruction.' Let us embrace lions also in the same view. Moreover, observe Atti. Contemplate her. How does she stride, how does she saunter, how does she lie or gaze or rest or breathe? . . . She has much to teach you. (p.260)

Like Tamkin, Dahfu tries above all to force his student to "seize the day"—the here-and-now. Henderson has been avoiding reality because, as Dahfu tells him, "You did not believe you had to perish" (p.260). You did not *want* to believe is more to the point—and not wanting, Henderson has played the child and has created his own reality. There are two necessities: one, that Henderson imitate the lion, become like a lion instead of a pig (a motif which produces a good deal of the book's humor); two, that Henderson lose his fear: "When the fear yields, a beauty is disclosed in its place. This is also said of perfect love, if I recollect, and it means that ego emphasis is removed" (p.262).

Henderson holds back out of fear of death, manifested in an emphasis on his individuality. As the Master says, "The tendency of your consciousness is to isolate self" (p.264). By becoming the beast Henderson is to shake off this isolated self and so submit to reality: "I should move from the states that I myself make into the states which are of themselves" (p.284).

The process is difficult; he feels the "old self" more as it dies. " 'I feel it all the time. It's got a terrific grip on me.' I began to cough and grunt, and I was in despair. As if I were carrying an eight-hundred-pound load—like a Galapagos turtle. On my back (p.275). If Tommy Wilhelm's old self is felt as a hippopotamus, Henderson's is felt as a pig (grunt); both are felt as physical burdens. The image of the Galapagos turtle is not found in *Seize the Day*, and it is significant here. A sea animal like the octopus, it is a symbol of death and by extension, of the self that must die. It drops off, as Henderson later recognizes, not through imitation alone but through moments of *Angst* which shock him into facing the Real.

The snarling of this animal was indeed the voice of death. And I thought how I had boasted to my dear Lily how I loved reality. "I love it more than you do," I had said. But oh, unreality! Unreality, unreality! That has been my scheme for a troubled but eternal life. But now I was blasted away from this practice by the throat of the lion. His voice was like a blow at the back of my head. (p.304)

The healing wisdom that Dahfu brings back from civilization is not only Heideggerian but Reichian. Like Wilhelm Reich—and Tamkin and Bummidge—Dahfu is "triumphantly sure" of his ideas. Each is of the category of "dreamer-doers," each "a guy with a program"; both programs are Daffy and brilliant. More concretely, Dahfu and Reich both emphasize the interrelatedness of flesh and mind. Reich began as an unusual psychoanalyst who emphasized the necessity of initially breaking down the "character armor" that a patient had constructed to defend himself from anxieties, but later he discovered that this "character armor" had its muscular components, and, like Dahfu, he tried to crack the presentation self by physical means. He asked the patient to imitate the physical component of an emotion releasing the locked-up emotion and baring the accompanying anxiety. Releasing muscular "armor segments," freeing the breathing, he then channeled the anxiety into excitement and energy.

Henderson is in need of Reichian therapy: "I stood there half deaf, half blind, with my throat closing and all the sphincters shut" (p.224). Of course, Henderson is in the presence of a ferocious lion, not a couch, but these are the kinds of symptoms— Reich would speak of "contactlessness"—that a Reichian therapist deals with, as well as "confusions between right and left, and various exaggerations and deformities of sensation" (p.246—the content of articles which Dahfu gives to Henderson to read). Both Reich and Dahfu are concerned with proper respiration:

"Observe Atti. Contemplate her. How does she stride, how does . . . she breathe? I stress the respiratory part," he said. "She does not breathe shallow. This freedom of the intercostal muscles and her abdominal flexibility . . . gives the vital continuity between her parts. It brings those brown jewel eyes their hotness." (p.260)

For Dahfu, as for Reich, the respiration creates the flow of the animal and her power. Dahfu speaks of "hotness," not orgone energy, but Henderson, describing Dahfu, speaks of the power within him—describing the hum that came through the king's high-swelled lips as "the sound you sometimes hear from a power station when you pass one in New York on a summer night . . ." (p.210). Thus Dahfu is like Reich's "genital man," emanating orgone energy. He fits this category not only because of his sixty-seven wives whom he must satisfy but because of his whole demeanor: the animal-like grace with which he lies on a couch, his combination of ease and energy.

This Reichian king is physically and spiritually an ideal for

Henderson. First, he is able to affirm the meaningfulness of human life, speaking of mankind's "noble possibilities." It is this affirmation which excites Henderson more than any other doctrine of the king's. Second, Dahfu is able to impose imagination on reality. "What *homo sapiens* imagines, he may slowly convert himself to," says Dahfu in words reminiscent of Keats. For Dahfu is immersed in reality, but he is also an idealist. Third, just as Henderson has played his violin to communicate with his father, so Dahfu, on the day he is killed, intends to be "reunited with a dear parent," as Henderson puts it (p.289). In general, Dahfu is the exceptional man Henderson desires to be. Defending the king to the Bunam, Henderson says, "he is an exceptional man and does exceptional things. Sometimes these great men have to go beyond themselves, like Caesar or Napoleon or Chaka the Zulu" (p.251).

But more important for Henderson's redemption is the fact that Dahfu lives with joy in the presence of death. "Look at all the things he has to fear, and still look at the way he lies on that sofa" (p.277). More than the lioness it is Dahfu himself who teaches Henderson how to live. After Henderson rejects Lily on the Field of France, he feels threatened by death. This connection between sexual inability and death is found again among the Wariri, for when a king is unable to satisfy his wives, he is strangled, a death which reminds us specifically of the tentacled octopus in the aquarium. Dahfu, however, is not afraid.

The essential function of Henderson's double is to die—without fear and with grace. Just as Tommy Wilhelm sees his own death in the stranger's, so Henderson lives through his castration and death in Dahfu's. It was Henderson who was terrified of castration when Atti first sniffed him; it was Henderson who was terrified of death from her claws. Dahfu receives both. But before he is clawed, he radiates *amor fati*. After he is clawed and before he dies, he is at peace. "I never took another death so hard," Henderson says. "As I tried to stop his bleeding, there was blood all over me and soon it was dry" (p.314). This is a physical manifestation of the closeness between the two, a symbol of Henderson's having confronted his own death in Dahfu's. Also, it leads Henderson to try to incorporate Dahfu, the double, within himself.

If one strong motif of this novel is that of the *Messiah*—fragments of the oratorio text are woven in, signifying not only that Henderson is a "man of sorrows" but also that he seeks a savior—there are a number of indications that Dahfu is partly the Messiah; hence, his blood is saving. It saves, for it forces the recognition that the living rest on the bones of the dead, who, often like Jesus or Henderson's brother Dick or Dahfu, are better than we. We recall Mrs. Harkavy's sigh, "Asa, sometimes I feel wicked still to be here at my age while children die," and then her recognition, "But I'm not taking it away from anybody" (V, p.246). Henderson, planning how to escape from the tomb in which he, as well as Dahfu, is contained, now remembers the death of his brother Dick without guilt. While he is also without fear, he is prepared to act the lion and murder to escape. Holding the spirit of the Messiah in the form of the lion cub, Henderson is resurrected from the tomb—certainly this symbolism is intended —and he is more than king of the Wariri; symbolically he is a king in the sense Tamkin promises to Tommy Wilhelm as a possibility: he is redeemed Man.

Even by the time of his letter to Lily, Henderson is changed. He has partially entered the given, the real as it is. He knows that the stars are "endless fire," not small gold objects as we see them (p.285). He knows that he will never "leave the body of this death." He understands that he had tried to avoid the presence of death and in so doing had avoided life: "I wanted to raise myself into another world" (p.284). No longer trying to impose himself on reality so much, he says, "I had a voice that said 'I want!' I want? I? It should have told me *she* wants, *he* wants, *they* want" (p.286). After the death of Dahfu, Henderson is at peace with reality. He kisses the earth and calls the grass his cousins. Aware that dead is dead, he tells us: "Dahfu will never be seen again, and presently I will never be seen again; but every one is given the components to see: the water, the sun, the air, the earth" (p.333). He has returned to his lost, childhood self, his true self:

> It is very early in life, and I am out in the grass. The sun flames and swells; the heat it emits is its love, too. I have this self-same vividness in my heart. There are dandelions. I try to gather up this green. I put my love-swollen cheek to the yellow of the dandelions. I try to enter into the green. (p.283)

The earth is his again. Returning now to America in the spirit of *amor fati,* a kind of holy fool coming home to do God's work, he runs in joy around the airplane, holding an alien orphan, an image of his true self, the child he had been and had become alienated from: "leaping, leaping, pounding, and tingling over the pure white lining of the gray Arctic silence" (p.341). This joy comes in spite of the cold and white—symbols of death. Henderson is like Willatale, like Dahfu. He is ready for Lily, for love, for America.

At least this is the transformation Bellow would have us accept. To show the transformation as credible—Henderson as still Henderson—Bellow has him beat his chest in the hut-tomb and roar (or grunt) at the U.S. Embassy officials. But these qualifications are not enough to dispel the doubts of the reader. The comic tone makes it difficult to take the transformation seriously: Henderson in the lion's den seems to be mugging for the cameras and groaning for the microphones: he is more like Bummidge than like Tommy Wilhelm. More important, the first person form makes any change of character difficult to portray (this difficulty is found also in *Lolita* and in *All the King's Men,* for example), for if events are being reported from a single vantage point *after* those events are over, then the speaker's tone must remain consistent. But if it does, a most valuable tool for portraying change is lost. Finally, although Bellow would have us believe that Henderson enters into the given, the style is so clearly that of the romance, so clearly not a transparent lens but a symbolic filter, that we must believe Reality is Henderson, Reality is Bellow. Henderson does not enter into *our* reality.

But aside from the tone of the novel, Bellow is still unable to bring off the change, because he cannot dramatize it. We see desire to change, symbols of change; we are told that change has occurred. But we do not see the change. Is Henderson's escape from the Wariri any evidence of his inner peace? Are his relationships with Romilayu and the stewardess on the flight home any indication of new-found ability to love? Surely not enough.

Henderson affirms. Bellow affirms. Perhaps, however, Philip Toynbee is right that "this is the book of a sad man who 'decided' to be affirmative."[11] At any rate, the affirmation is too cheaply won. Bellow says that he wrote the ending of *Henderson* in "a sort of frenzy. I was very moved. . . ."[12] We, too, are often moved, particularly watching the dance of the clumsy, bear-like man around the plane. But we cannot believe that he is fundamentally different from what he was. Bellow tells us he can confront death and be absorbed in Reality, but we have only the words. And does not the switch to the bear near the end mean that Bellow was afraid to propose too great a change? When Henderson had run from home feeling rejected by his father after his brother's death, he worked for a carnival in Canada. He was paid to ride a roller coaster with Smolak, an old trained bear. Both castaways, both orphans, they hug each other in terror as they ride; therefore Henderson "didn't come to pigs as a tabula rasa" (pp.338–39). Perhaps, by Dahfu's theory of transference from animals to people, Eugene Henderson was only a rough bear, not a crude pig. The transformation seems less extreme and makes more understandable the picture of gross Henderson, with his lionish/bearish red beard. Henderson holds the orphan on his lap and comforts him, just as he once rode with Smolak and was comforted by Smolak. Both know (as Henderson says of the bear) "that for creatures there is nothing that ever runs unmingled" (p.339). Like the bear, Henderson expresses his *amor fati,* a lyric and richly comic expression, earned or unearned.

CHAPTER NINE

Herzog

In style *Herzog* combines the two main impulses of Bellow's fiction: realism and romance. Like *Dangling Man, The Victim,* and *Seize the Day,* it conveys the sense of a real sufferer hedged in by circumstances and neurotic attitudes; like *Augie March* and *Henderson the Rain King,* it possesses an exuberance and a sense of infinite possibilities. The combination is possible because this is not the novel of a sufferer in the city but of a sufferer who contains the city within him. Moses Herzog calls himself a "prisoner of perception" (p.72), but actually perception is *his* prisoner. He sees only what he needs to see, and we see only what Herzog sees. This dependence on a distorted perceiver has caused critical misunderstanding of the novel. *Herzog* is a psychological novel: the ideas have a function in the hero's story. Herzog is not Bellow. In spite of difficulties, Bellow has maintained ironic distancing, creating a character whose development is typical of his fiction.

We have seen in each of the novels an alienated hero who wants to return to community; often, paradoxically, a depressive and masochist who wishes to defend the self and affirm the beauty and dignity of man. We have seen one character after another creating ideal constructions of reality, humanizing the world after his own image in order to impose himself on reality but, instead, submitting to it in a spirit of *amor fati.* Through this process Bellow has been able to affirm human possibilities—not the possibilities of preserving the self but of dissolving the self in a brotherhood. He does it once more in *Herzog,* this time in a more complex context and with the issue of belief in humanity more central.

Herzog begins and ends with a partially reborn hero, Moses Herzog, at peace with the world, living amid nature—nature growing up raggedly about him, the stars overhead like spiritual fires, his food shared with rats. The rest of the novel tells the process of arriving at this state, of his initial need "to explain, to have it out, to justify, to put in perspective, to clarify, to make amends" (p.2)—generally, to preserve his crumbling ego system. The novel tells of his divorce and confusion, of his thinking, compulsive thinking, ratiocinating about Mady, his ex-wife, and Gersbach, the ex-friend who was secretly cuckolding him. He thinks about the various women in his life—Daisy, his first wife, Ramona, his present lady friend, Wanda and Sono, encountered along the way; and he thinks especially about ideas, examining the wreck of our culture as he examines the wreck of himself, to see if both can be saved. *Herzog* tells of his seemingly haphazard travels to find sanity—from New York to Martha's Vineyard back to New York, then to Chicago, finally to a country house in Massachusetts; of his real quest, into his own past, especially his childhood. The meaning of this past is revealed by a series of experiences—a visit to the courthouse where he confronts a degeneracy he fears in himself; a trip to Chicago during which he considers killing Mady and Gersbach, is unable to, and in the process is purged. At the end, living like God's Humble Man, he feels ready, as did Henderson, to return to community.

Herzog has suffered from too much praise followed by too much blame—both for the wrong reasons. Critics rightly see that the novel's ideas are often Bellow's own, but are unable to perceive the ironic distance between Bellow and Herzog. Rahv defends the majesty of intelligence in *Herzog,* ignoring the internal meaning of that intelligence;[1] Poirier attacks the gap in Bellow's novels between "intellectual and historical pretensions, on one side, and the stuff of life as he so brilliantly renders it, on the other. . . ." Believing that Bellow means us to take *Herzog* at face value, Poirier says that Herzog attacks himself to "assure the reader of objectivity."[2] But what if Bellow is not after objectivity? Fiedler attacks Bellow as a sellout to middle-class optimism, not understanding the function of optimism in the novel,[3] and Mailer criticizes the intellectuality, feeling that *Herzog* "has the same relationship to ideas that a cookbook has to good eating."[4] Not only the ideas but the attitudes of Herzog are identified with those of Bellow. Thus Geismar says, foolishly, "the central figure is in effect a wailing infant, who is, I suppose, the author himself."[5] Only Jack Ludwig has realized the degree to which the reader is to be "cynical," and has understood that the real story is different from "the boring Ancient Mariner one he carries around the country with him." Ludwig does not explain the ironies, noting only that Bellow must be aware that Herzog is not much more moral than his Mady and Gersbach.[6]

The confusion of critics is easy to account for. First, the point of view, as we have noted, makes distancing difficult. We are prisoners of Herzog's perception. Second, the ideas are so profuse in the novel, and are so clearly Bellow's own, that Herzog seems merely Bellow's spokesman.

More than in any other of Bellow's novels we have been given full-blown discussions of Bellow's own essential beliefs. The defense of man, which has been central in all the novels, is more obviously so here. "Come to the point," Herzog writes in a letter attacking the Philosophy of Risk with regard to radioactivity. "But what was the point? The point was that there were people who could destroy mankind and that they were foolish and arrogant, crazy, and must be begged not to do it" (p.51). While Herzog is speaking of the possessors of atomic power, he makes a more general reference—to the cultural nihilists, the intellectual doomsters, the preachers of despair, the negators of the human spirit as well as the potential killers.

Is this the full crisis of dissolution? Has the filthy moment come when moral feeling dies, conscience disintegrates, and respect for liberty, law, public decency, all the rest, collapses in cowardice, decadence, blood? Old Proudhon's visions of darkness and evil can't be passed over. But we mustn't forget how quickly the visions of genius become the canned goods of the intellectuals. The canned sauerkraut of Spengler's "Prussian Socialism," the commonplaces of the Wasteland outlook, the cheap mental stimulants of Alienation, the cant and rant of pipsqueaks about Inauthenticity and Forlornness. I can't accept this foolish dreariness. We are talking about the whole life of mankind. The subject is too great, too deep for such weakness, cowardice—too deep, too great, Shapiro. (pp.74–75)

This rejection of "foolish dreariness," the belief that man is worth saving, is clearly Bellow's as well as his hero's. As Poirier says, "What he wants to do is nothing less than possess our minds with a portraiture alternative to the alienated Wasteland figures of earlier twentieth century literature."[7] And even Bellow, while detaching himself from Herzog ("Herzog is still a comic figure to me"), notes their general agreement: "He believes in certain virtues which have nearly disappeared. Goodness, duty, courage —I think they're just in hiding everywhere." He refuses to believe "that the human being is through." Instead, he says "we have had a bellyful of a species of wretchedness which is thoroughly pleased with itself. . . ."[8] "After absurdity, what . . . ?" he asks of Sartre, Ionesco, Beckett, Burroughs, and Ginsburg.[9]

In defending man, Herzog-Bellow attacks two complementary errors. The first is the error that *Henderson the Rain King* satirizes, the romantic overevaluation of the self: Herzog's unfinished study was to overturn "the last of the Romantic errors about the uniqueness of the self; [to revise] . . . the old, Western, Faustian ideology . . ." (p.39). It is the error of dramatizing life with *you* as the central character; of fulfilling yourself at the expense of those around you; it is the assumption by the bourgeoisie of aristocratic dignity, a dignity which gives the bourgeoisie the justification to speak of "decline" (p.76). "Asserting too much," the sovereign self ends in a second error by "suffering from self-hatred as a consequence" (p.164). This self-hatred manifests itself culturally in the belief that man is finished, the self is nonexistent or a joke, our civilization is in collapse and there is nothing for us but the void. Rejecting these errors, Herzog-Bellow believes that all of us live in possible touch with "the inspired condition" (pp.163–165)—that each man has within him possibilities of changing, and that reason "can make steady progress from disorder to harmony . . ." (p.165).

Or rather, this is what Herzog-Bellow wishes to believe. In dealing with *Augie March*, I discussed Bellow's admission of depressive tendencies, the fact that his affirmation of the human being results more from longing than from faith. *Herzog* also shows this to be true. *"Believing that reason can make steady progress from disorder to harmony and that the conquest of chaos need not be begun anew every day.* How I wish it! How I wish it were so! How Moses prayed for this!" (pp.181–82). How Bellow also prays for this! But trying not to falsify, he does not give us faith in man and in Western civilization; nor does he give us a believing character; rather he gives us a character struggling to have faith, needing faith, unable to believe completely in himself or in man. Indeed, in an unusually bitter moment, he despairs: "No true individual has existed yet, able to live, able to die. Only diseased, tragic, or dismal and ludicrous fools who sometimes hoped to achieve some ideal by fiat, by their great desire for it. But usually by bullying all mankind into believing them" (p.67). Or again, "certainly anyone who takes dignity seriously, old-fashioned individual dignity, is bound to get the business. Maybe dignity was imported from France. Louis Quatorze. . . . It all belongs in the museum now" (p.193).

Most important, Saul Bellow has not created an author-surrogate—a Frederic Henry, say—but gives us a character who, while he may be extremely similar to the author, is ironically distanced from him. Bellow recognizes Herzog's self-deception, his failings, his unconscious motivations, and he oversees

Herzog's conversions; the reader must discern from the story Herzog tells the essence of the one Bellow is telling.

The ideas in the novel must be read as the ideas of an alienatee, a self-created victim—a guilt-ridden masochist like Tommy Wilhelm. Clearly Herzog is alienated from other people. He is like the bearded Negro who blows a toy trumpet which can't be heard. He writes letter after letter, but he never mails them. Herzog is corresponding, really, with the president and the bishop of his own mind; he is in an imaginary, not actual, community. Words, words, words: Thomas Meehan, in his wonderful *New Yorker* parody "Claus," ends, "and, for the rest of that winter, to the relief of virtually everyone but Philip Rahv, he didn't write another letter. Nothing. Not a single word."[10] Until Herzog's transformation, his consciousness is composed of words; he is living in words, not in the world, and the letters, far from attaching him to other people, make them more distant and unreal. The figures dim, the ratiocination catches all the light. Waiting on her bed for sexy Ramona to appear, Herzog considers Rousseau, Kant, and Hegel (p.203). In the middle of a letter about radiation, a conductor takes Herzog's ticket. "He seemed about to say something." But Herzog, considering the fate of man, ignores this reality and continues writing, deciding also to avoid the club car, where he might have to "talk to people" (p.52). Forgetting his class, he jots down note after note—notes with fine ideas: "On the knees of your soul? Might as well be useful. Scrub the floor" (p.3)—but ideas which have little to do with his life.

Nor is it only from strangers that he is alienated. He is unable to remain with Libby and Arnold at Martha's Vineyard; he runs from Ramona's kindness. During his marriage to Mady, Herzog recalls, he ignored or fought with her, and remained aloof watching the garden when Shapiro came to visit. Of course we are to recognize the foolish ego play going on between Shapiro and Mady, but we are also to feel that Herzog's dislocation is not merely the result of the divorce but is characteristic. Even from his family, Moses, like Tommy Wilhelm, felt cut off once he had grown up. Indeed, it is his sense of separation from his childhood family world that is at the root of his alienation.

He is the outcast, the outsider, and more—he is the "victim." His sexual powers have been damaged by Madeline the Bitch. She has her heel in his groin. She wishes to do him in, she votes for his nonexistence, she (like Margaret, Tommy Wilhelm's wife) wants to bleed him, to take all his money or, symbolically, to castrate him. All these metaphors recur. And not only have she and Valentine Gersbach betrayed him; so have his lawyer, his psychiatrist, Mady's mother, Mady's aunt. Over and over, as he bitterly admits, he tells his story to whoever will listen: "like an addict struggling to kick the habit, he would tell again how he was swindled, conned, manipulated, his savings taken, driven into debt, his trust betrayed by wife, friend, physician" (p.156).

Of course, he *has* been victimized—although he asked for it—but it is his self-pity that makes Geismar call Herzog a "wailing infant . . . complaining that his life has been ruined by a woman, or by a series of women, or by his false friends, or in short by other people, never himself."[11] It is this assumption of the role of victim that makes Meehan say, "the letters did lend him claim to being, as far as self-indulgence goes, the world's long-distance champion."[12] But it is Herzog's, not Bellow's, self-indulgence. Whether Bellow is equally self-indulgent is irrelevant; what matters is that he has written his hero's self-indulgence into the novel; it is part of the book. Looking at external evidence, it seems incredible that a writer who has made a study of the "victim" his very theme, who has transcended victimization to use it as his subject in novel after novel—*Dangling Man, The Victim, Seize the Day*—would suddenly become the victim, identifying with Herzog-as-victim. Bellow has himself denied that *Herzog* is "victim literature." "I consider *Herzog* a break from victim literature," he told David Boroff.[13] But internal evidence is sufficient. Why does Bellow include Libby Vane and her new husband in the novel if not to show a necessary parallel:

Herzog helped Libby greatly when her last husband tried to kill her; he feels friendly toward her new husband. But in the main plot *he* is the wounded husband who takes revenge; Mady is a parallel to Libby. He now hates Mady, when before in a similar situation he had helped Libby; he feels persecuted and attempts to kill, when previously he had protected Libby from being killed. Clearly Bellow is using the parallel to show Herzog's lack of objectivity.

Moses Herzog is extremely clever; he recognizes his tendency to play the victim—and he laughs at "that suffering joker" (p.11), or feels *"immonde"* about his self-pity (p.157). He recognizes that he would like to be given rest in a hospital, notes "with distaste his own trick of appealing for sympathy" (p.112), and he groans, "I hate the victim bit" (p.82). Moreover, he knows that he characteristically falls "upon the thorns of life. I bleed. And then? I fall upon the thorns of life, I bleed. And what next? I get laid, I take a short holiday, but very soon after I fall upon those same thorns with gratification in pain or suffering in joy—who knows what the mixture is!" (p.207). He seems to recognize not only his posturing but his essential masochism: "What I seem to do, thought Herzog, is to inflame myself with my drama, with ridicule, failure, denunciation, distortion, to inflame myself voluptuously, esthetically, until I reach a sexual climax" (p.208). What an excellent description of a masochistic cycle! He knows that "he had asked to be beaten too, and had lent his attackers strength." He even knows that he is using his suffering as a sacrifice (p.103, p.206) and that his very self-criticism is a way of seeming valuable—look how I suffer, look how I castigate myself: *"But how charming we remain, notwithstanding"* (p.5).

Unlike Tommy Wilhelm, Herzog knows these ruses of a masochist, but he has other ruses of which he is less aware. First, he—not Bellow—is unaware that the verbalization of his neuroses makes him not only intriguing but safe—they are categorized in language, therefore under his control. Second, as it is used by Herzog, the irony is itself an example of masochistic self-hatred, just as were the galling diary entries of Joseph in *Dangling Man*. Third, stances he may at one moment recognize as masochistic, at another time he defends as not masochistic. Speaking of his submissive attitude to Madeline, he complains, "Charity, as if it didn't have enough trouble in this day and age, will always be suspected of morbidity—sado-masochism, perversity of some sort" (p.56). Remembering how he had let Madeline physically beat him, he thinks, "Herzog turned and took these blows on his back. It was necessary. She was sick" (p.57). Fourth, he doesn't recognize even verbally many of his masochistic symptoms: he says that he helped his attackers—but he does not realize *how intentionally* he helped them. Before his marriage to Madeline he lived with her long enough to know she would make him miserable. Indeed, he chose her over the gentle Sono (Sono is in the novel to show the reader that Herzog had a far different choice, a lovely one, and rejected it). Mady forced on him all her sexual guilt; he accepted it like a page taking a queen's tiara. She snapped at him, accused him, treated him with contempt: " 'No! It'll be these rules or nothing. . . . Do you hear me?' 'Oh yes,' he said. 'Yes. I do.' " After marriage, although he is not pleasant to Mady either, it is he who is the weak one in the family, letting her ride him as Leopold let Molly. She spent his money, decided when they were to move, finally shoved him out of the house. Earlier, in Ludeyville, he humbly handed to Gersbach Mady's diaphragm to take to Boston. Certainly Bellow does not mean us to believe that Herzog was unaware of what was going on. We must believe that he unconsciously needed to be the ground-under-heel cuckold.

It is not accidental that Herzog happened to fall in love with Mady. He is always attracted to the aggressive, masculine woman (p.202). "Female arrogance" excites him (p.34). Potentially a sexual as well as moral masochist, he speaks metaphorically of "writhing under this sharp elegant heel" (p.76). When he remembers the red-light district in Hamburg, the image that he retains is one which would excite a masochist: "Some of the whores, in black lace underthings, wore German military boots and rapped at you with ridingcrops on the windowpanes" (p.46). Bellow certainly understands this as an image out of a Masoch novel; Herzog simply remembers it.

The dangerous underside of the masochist is also to be found in Moses Herzog in the form of repressed sadism: "He too would get back at his enemies. *Yemach sh'mo!* Let their names be blotted out! They prepared a net for my steps. They digged a pit before me. Break their teeth, O God, in their mouth!" (pp.202–203). Or, more clearly: "What if he had knocked her down, clutched her hair, dragged her screaming and fighting around the room, flogged her until her buttocks bled. What if he had!" (p.10). Underneath Moses Herzog is Stephen Rojack (Mailer's protagonist in *An American Dream*). Leslie Fiedler has reason to wonder whether killing one's wife is not the essential American Dream![14]

Guilt is at the root of Herzog's masochism. Here the connection is made clear: "What he was about to suffer, he deserved; he had sinned long and hard; he had earned it" (pp.8–9). And what is his sin? Essentially, it is sexual.

It is not only that Moses is "a Quaker in love-making" (p.201). Sex is terribly guilt-producing. Twice during the novel—once in connection with Ramona, once with Mady—Herzog complains that he is a prisoner to sex. He remembers how he had made his wife have intercourse with him on the bathroom floor in Ludeyville: "He tried to make his lust comical, to show how absurd it all was, easily the most wretched form of human slavery" (p.219). A number of times the connection between dirt (the bathroom floor) and sex is made. In the police station, wondering why a certain prostitute is attractive, he decides it was "because she had dirty ways, that was why. Lewd knowledge" (p.297). A minute later, upon seeing Mady, he wonders "whether she still gave off those odors of feminine secretions—the dirty ways she had with her . . ." (p.298). Thus Bellow and the reader know, while Herzog does not (consciously), that he considers his wife to be as lewd as a whore, and *lewd* means for him *dirty*. Earlier, Herzog feels sorry for Daisy because her senile mother thinks that Daisy is a whore and will catch a disease. But who is the whore? Moses Herzog, who so feared that Wanda had given *him* a disease, now feels dirty and guilty himself—it was he who left Daisy, not Daisy, him—and therefore he remembers this incident between Daisy and her mother and projects his guilt onto Mady. Another time Herzog remembers his affair with Sono, and wonders, "Have all the traditions, passions, renunciations, virtues, gems, and masterpieces of Hebrew discipline and all the rest of it—rhetoric, a lot of it, but containing true facts—brought me to these untidy green sheets, and this rippled mattress?" (p.170). And this with lovely Sono!

There is here not only sexual guilt and its association with dirt, but also a conflict between illicit sexuality and his Jewish traditions. He is the *mamzer* his rabbi warned him he would become. While his children are growing up alone, he is purchasing a sports outfit. What kind of Jew is he? Recalling his affair with Mady, he wonders, "What was he doing here? He was a husband, a father. He was married, he was a Jew. Why was he in church?" (p.63). Washing up before dinner with Ramona (after which he knows he'll make love to her), he is reminded of

The word in the Haggadah, *Rachatz!* "Thou shalt wash." It was obligatory also to wash when you returned from the cemetery (*Beth Clam*—the Dwelling of the Multitude). But why think of cemeteries, of funerals, now? Unless . . . the old joke about the Shakespearean actor in the brothel. When he took off his pants, the whore in bed gave a whistle. He said, "Madam, we come to bury Caesar, not to praise him." How schoolboy jokes clung to you! (p.181)

But it is obviously more than schoolboy jokes. We have seen a number of times in Bellow's fiction the connection between sin and punishment by death—here again it is so; sex leads to death; he must wash his hands.

We understand, then, part of the reason why Moses needs to

sacrifice by suffering. He is expiating his sexual sins. And, as with Tommy Wilhelm, it is his father to whom he makes the sacrifices —his father through whose eyes he condemns his own un-Jewish behavior, the father who punished him with quick slaps as a boy, who threatened to kill him for his *goyishe* ways as a man. Mady the Bitch is then a father substitute. Just as Herzog's father was disgusted at Moishe for the disorder in his life, so Mady demands order: "It'll be these rules or nothing" (p.117). She, too, is his judge and beater, she too—and this is most important—wants him dead, at least as Herzog sees it. The female is the castrating father: Herzog remembers not only Mady examining her reflection in a knife blade (p.318); he remembers even warm, gentle Ramona as castrator: "she entered a room provocatively, swaggering slightly, one hand touching her thigh, as though she carried a knife in her garter belt" (p.16). Although he knows Ramona to be a tired woman who wants marriage and a family, he sees her as a *devoradora*.

If Herzog expects punishment from The Father it is because he has sinned against him; there is some evidence that the origin of his guilt is in an oedipal relationship. About to make love to Ramona, he remembers telling her "she would never turn an old herring into a dolphin" (p.202); that is, he could not learn to enjoy new ways of lovemaking. "Old herring" refers to his Jewish upbringing (the Jewish family traditionally eats herring)—the standard of his sexual life. But the imagery of *fish* reminds us of another scene in the novel: after a night of lovemaking for which Mady is making him feel guilty, Moses stops by the window of a fish store, "arrested by the odor."

The fish were packed together, backs arched as if they were swimming in the crushed, smoking ice, bloody bronze, slimy black-green, gray-gold—the lobsters were crowded to the glass, feelers bent. The morning was warm, gray, damp, fresh, smelling of the river. Pausing on the metal doors of the sidewalk elevator, Moses received the raised pattern of the steel through his thin soles; like braille. But he did not interpret a message. The fish were arrested, lifelike, in the white,

frothing, ground ice. The street was overcast, warm and gray, intimate, unclean, flavored by the polluted river, the sexually stirring
brackish tidal odor. (p.113)

Here again there is a connection between sex—the odor, an odor
like that of Mady herself—dirt—the polluted river, the unclean
street—and death—the fish. The image of braille indicates that
the scene contains a hidden, undecipherable meaning: a sexual
meaning, evident in the reason for his stopping—the odor—and
the quality of that odor. We recall Tommy Wilhelm also seeking
and losing some truth in the image of a fish: "My father. My
mother—" he says to Tamkin; then the fish gets away. If there
were hints of oedipal guilt in this passage from *Seize the Day*,
they are clearer here. Braille reminds us of one character in
Bellow's fiction—Augie March's blind mother. But it is unfair to
make so tenuous a connection and unnecessary: in the scene at
hand, Mady tries to hurry Herzog: " 'What were you dawdling
for?' 'Well, my mother came from Baltic provinces. She loved
fish.' " (p.113). His sexual feelings for his mother are clear. It is
his guilt over these feelings which leads him to masculine
women, to women who will punish him like a father. Only under
such conditions of punishment, only with a woman who threatens
him symbolically with the castration and death he fears from his
father, can he accept his pleasure.

But at the same time, Herzog wants love from Mady as from
his father. Ravitch, the old, drunken, self-pitying immigrant, is in
the novel to help explain Herzog's sacrifice of suffering. Ravitch
suffered and told his story; in response, Herzog's father pitied
and cared for him. In an analogous way, perhaps Herzog's
suffering will produce pity and love. Herzog's illusions are similar
to those of Tommy Wilhelm.

Mady is not only the spiked heel and the whip; she has another
function: she—and Gersbach too—are scapegoats onto which
Herzog is able to project his guilt. As I have shown, her "dirty
ways" are the ways he has fallen into; he rejects them: she is the
whore. It is not he who has betrayed father and religion;

Gersbach is the betrayer. We have seen this process most clearly in *Dangling Man* and *The Victim;* we must understand, then, that when Herzog says of Gersbach, "At moments I dislike having a face, a nose, lips, because he has them" (p.45), we are not to believe that Gersbach is living evil and Herzog living virtue. We are to remember his affair with Wanda, who introduced him to her husband. We are to remember that when Zelda accuses him of being reckless about women while still married to Mady, he does not deny it. Instead, "Herzog felt himself redden. A thick, hot, sick pressure filled his chest. His heart felt ill and his forehead instantly wet" (p.39). We are to understand, when Herzog lists and gloats over the traits of paranoia he attributes to Mady ("Pride, Anger, Excessive 'Rationality,' Homosexual inclinations, competitiveness, Mistrust of Emotion, Inability to Bear Criticism, Hostile Projections, Delusions," p.77), that he does so to free himself of guilt. He is being unnaturally self-righteous and he is seeing her traits as religious sins so that he can view himself as without sin, made clear by the way he introduces this list: "I put the scribbled paper in my wallet and studied it like the plagues of Egypt. Just like 'DOM, SFARDEYA, KINNIM' in the Haggadah" (p.77). It is not he, then, who has sinned against the Jewish faith and will be punished. It is she! Yet if we reflect on the list at all, we see that except possibly for "delusions" all the traits belong to Moses Herzog. Pride? Clearly. Anger? Enough to kill. Excessive rationality? He needs to keep everything under verbal control. Homosexual inclinations? Later we shall discuss his guilty identification with homosexuals. Inability to bear criticism? He runs from it, even when dispensed by lovely Ramona. Hostile projections? He accuses Mady and Gersbach of wanting him dead, though it is he who tries to kill them.

Projecting his guilt for sexuality, disorder, and the betrayal of his father's ways onto Gersbach, he wildly attacks him in front of Simkin the lawyer:

"When I think of Valentine [Gersbach] . . . I think of the books I devoured as a boy, on the French and Russian revolutions. And silent movies, like Mme. Sans Gene—Gloria Swanson. Or Emil Jannings as a Czarist general. Anyway, I see the mobs breaking into the palaces and churches and sacking Versailles, wallowing in cream desserts or pouring wine over their dicks and dressing in purple velvet, snatching crowns and miters and crosses. . . ." (p.215)

Simkin laughs:

"I never saw a man pour wine over his dick in any movie—when did you ever see that?" said Simkin. "At the Museum of Modern Art? Besides, in your mind, you don't identify yourself with Versailles or the Kremlin or the old regime, or anything like that, do you?"

"No, no, of course not. It's nothing but a metaphor, and probably not a good one." (p.216)

On the contrary, the metaphor is excellent. It connects depraved sexuality with revolution, the tearing down of tradition. Afraid of these things in himself, he exemplifies them in Gersbach. Thus he can satisfy the Father within him—for surely it is The Father—who demands order. *"There is someone inside me. I am in his grip. When I speak of him I feel him in my head, pounding for order"* (p.11). When he speaks of the sacking of Versailles he refers again to this order-demander: "he was again in the grip of that eccentric, dangerous force that had been capturing him." We remember Tommy Wilhelm's father, disgusted at Tommy's lack of order; we remember Asa, projecting his own sloppiness, which he fears, onto Elena and Allbee. We remember Henderson among the pigs, a gesture of self-contempt as if he were trying to act out his father's picture of him. Saul Bellow has noted that he himself needs to fight to preserve orderliness, and has also noted that he was rejected by his own father.[15] But while Bellow and Herzog may be similar, Bellow has carefully made Herzog's conflicts work in the fiction; they *are* the fiction. What, then, is the relationship between Herzog's conflicts and Herzog's ideas? Clearly, if Herzog is a backslider from his father's image of the Jewish family man; if Herzog feels himself given over to evil sexuality, indeed to debauchery, he is, on the other hand, a defender of his father's faith. In fact, he must defend tradition so strongly precisely because he feels that he has none himself. He must defend the Fathers because of his guilt before his own father. To answer Simkin, then: yes, Herzog does identify with Versailles, the Kremlin, the old regime.

Continually Herzog juxtaposes the nineteenth century with the present. He may scorn those who "have fashioned a new utopian history, an idyll, comparing the present to an imaginary past, because we hate the world as it is" (p.163); he may attack the "Christian view of history" which sees "the present moment always as some crisis, some fall from classical greatness, some corruption or evil to be saved from." But he has this view himself. His standards are those of the nineteenth century, his golden age is his own childhood.

Speaking of the clock Ramona's aunt keeps in her old-fashioned parlor, Herzog reflects:

To own a clock like this you had to have regular habits—a permanent residence. Raising the window shade of this little European parlor with its framed scenes of Venice and friendly Dutch porcelain inanities, you saw the Empire State Building, the Hudson, the green, silver evening, half of New York lighting up. Thoughtful, he pulled the shade down again. This—this asylum was his for the asking, he believed. (p.184)

He is tempted to look for asylum in the European-tinged nineteenth century; he pulls down the shade on the present. His valedictory address in high school was based on Emerson, and while his polemic is now a good deal more sophisticated than it was as a boy (pp.163–65), it remains Emersonian. He praises Martin Luther King for "moral dignity" (p.67). Even his social conscience—paternalistic and utopian—is of the century of Tolstoy: owners of large estates are to give up their land to the peasants.

But more specifically, the basis of his ideas is Jewish. His standard is the Jewish family as he knew it in childhood. Bellow explained to the interviewer for *Show*, speaking of the contemporary apocalyptic romanticism which sees the need for and inevitability of total destruction, "I think the Jewish feeling resists romanticism and insists on an older set of facts."[16] Similarly Herzog resists "the argument that scientific thought has put into disorder all consideration based on value. . . . The peculiar idea entered my (Jewish) mind that we'd see about this!" (p.106). He may bitterly laugh at his own principles, thinking of "young Jews, brought up on moral principles as Victorian ladies were on pianoforte and needlepoint"—but they *are* his principles. In this passage from the interview in *Show*, Bellow clearly reveals his standards and their source:

My mother lived strictly in the nineteenth century and her sole ambition was for me to become a Talmudic scholar like everyone else in her family. She was a figure from the middle ages. In family pictures, her scholarly brothers looked as if they could have lived in the thirteenth century. Those bearded portraits were her idea of what a man should be.[17]

Herzog develops his standards in a similar environment.

Herzog's mother had had a weakness for Jews with handsome beards. In her family, too, all the elders had beards that were thick and rich, full of religion. She wanted Moses to become a rabbi and he seemed to himself gruesomely unlike a rabbi now in the trunks and straw hat, his face charged with heavy sadness, foolish utter longing of which a religious life might have purged him. (p.22)

He is a disgrace to himself, unable to live up to his Jewish, nineteenth century ideal of a man. This ideal comes also from his father, who was "a sacred being, a king" (p.147). It is from this father-king that Herzog derives his belief in the dignity of the individual: "Personalities are good only for comic relief. But I am still a slave to Papa's pain. The way Father Herzog spoke of himself! That could make one laugh. His *I* had such dignity" (p.149). Thus Herzog's standard—and Bellow's—would appear to be the majestic nineteenth century individualist combined with the religious Jew. Here, as in *Augie March*, is a conflict between this standard and the one which derives from the fiction—the simple guru Herzog becomes.

"I do seem to be a broken-down monarch of some kind, he was thinking, like my old man, the princely immigrant and ineffectual bootlegger" (p.39). A broken-down monarch: precisely Herzog's perception of contemporary man, precisely the view of man that Tamkin expresses in his poem in *Seize the Day*. The point is that Bellow's conception of man's greatness is aristocratic. Herzog's valedictory—"The private life of one man shall be a more illustrious monarchy . . . than any kingdom in history—" (p.160) is at once smiled at and believed in by Herzog-Bellow.

Herzog not only derives his standards from childhood, he also longs to return there: it is a golden age for him.

Napoleon Street, rotten, toylike, crazy and filthy, riddled, flogged with harsh weather—the bootlegger's boys reciting ancient prayers. To this Moses' heart was attached with great power. Here was a wider range of human feelings than he had ever again been able to find. The children of the race, by a never-failing miracle, opened their eyes on one strange world after another, age after age, and uttered the same prayer in each, eagerly loving what they found. What was wrong with Napoleon Street? thought Herzog. All he ever wanted was there. (p.140)

Ripped away by growing up, by personal guilt, and by the twentieth century, he feels alienated, he is a Moses-in-exile. Herzog is the bootlegger's boy still; he still recites the ancient prayers, though not in synagogue. We remember the Edenic quest in *Augie March*, the sense of lost childhood in *Dangling Man;* here is the core of Herzog and the source of Herzog's ideas.

We find him setting the truth of apples against scholarship (p.70). Against the "full crisis of dissolution" he argues with Shapiro: "You are too intelligent for this. You inherited rich blood. Your father peddled apples" (p.75). Of his old friend Nachman he thinks, "It was the child with his fresh face, the smiling gap in his front teeth, the buttoned blouse and the short pants that was real, not this gaunt apparition of crazy lecturing Nachman" (p.133). Does he not feel the same about himself—

that his childhood self was the real one, not his present, alienated, scholarly, philandering self?

If all this is true, then Poirier is wrong—the "ideas" in *Herzog* are very much a part of the characterization. They derive from Herzog's childhood. Moreover, we see that Moses Herzog, the defender of Jewish family values, feels himself a renegade to those values; the very intensity with which he defends his ideas indicates his need to justify himself with respect to them.

His guilt at being a renegade, in origin sexual, extends to his romanticism and his despair. That is, those negative forces which he finds in the culture he finds also in himself. For he himself has the sense of a fall from past greatness ("broken-down monarch") which he attacks in Nietzsche (p.54), in Kierkegaard (p.49), and in the culture at large (p.163). If he laughs bitterly at Gersbach's vanity, a symptom of leftover romanticism, he is ashamed of his own, feeling himself "a gesture maker, ambitious, a fool" (p.234) in the eyes of his mother and father. If Mady is ambitious for a reputation, so is he: "His achievements were not only scholarly but sexual. And were those achievements? It was his pride that must be satisfied. His flesh got what was left over" (p.13). If Mady, and society in general, are hungry for fulfillment at any price, every woman demanding "nightly erotic gratification, safety, money, insurance, furs, jewelry, cleaning women, drapes, dresses, hats, night clubs, country clubs, automobiles, theater!" (p.40), he too has followed suit, abandoning his first marriage out of boredom and hunger for fulfillment. If Valentine Gersbach believes that suffering (his loss of a leg and his sense of sin) excuses his actions, Herzog finds himself concurring. In other words, he hides the latter-day romanticism in himself, and conceals its correlate, despair at lack of perfection. For surely underneath the affirmation is intense despair. Poirier is correct in not believing that Herzog "is himself convinced by his snappy contempt for 'the commonplaces of the Wasteland outlook. . . .' "[18] But Poirier makes the mistake of not giving Bellow enough credit. Bellow is aware of Herzog's over-responding, aware that beneath the affirmation is such a statement as this: "people can be free now but the freedom doesn't have any content. It's like a howling emptiness" (p.39).

In many other ways Herzog's character relates to his ideas. The most obvious is that his thinking is compulsive; he has to think and write in order to stay balanced. "Quickly, quickly, more!" he thinks in the middle of a letter (p.68). First, he must vent his feelings somehow; second, his private indignation and despair must be transmuted to public indignation and despair. His letter to the editor concerning radioactivity is a good example of how Moses Herzog handles a personal problem by generalizing it to a cultural one. "Mr. Editor," he writes, "we are bound to be the slaves of those who have power to destroy us" (p.51). Unconsciously he means Mady, but he gains the moral stature and objectivity that come with discussion of a national problem. Third, to understand history and society is to keep a kind of control over them—and at a time when he feels so out of control, this gives him necessary self-assurance. Fourth, as he acknowledges later, he had always done elaborate intellectual work "as if it were the struggle for survival"—as if he would die when thinking stopped (p.265).

But the thinking is more than compulsive. It justifies him, as well. His ideas enable him to feel a victim of sweeping cultural trends—and therefore not responsible: he is a victim of the debased romanticism found in Gersbach and Mady; his self-contempt is the result of cultural self-contempt (p.164). If his problems are universal, they are easier to live with.

"Is this the full crisis of dissolution?" he asks about our culture in a letter to Shapiro, but primarily the dissolution he fears is his own. Hoberly, Ramona's ex-boyfriend who has fallen to pieces when rejected, is a double for Herzog; so when Herzog thinks it possible "that a man like Hoberly by falling apart intends to bear witness to the failure of individual existence," (p.208) we are meant to see Herzog's fear that he, too, bears such witness. Conversely, Herzog's ideological bitterness that "you must sacri-

fice your poor, squawking, niggardly individuality . . . to historical necessity" (p.93), signifies his personal fear that *he* is
crumbling.

Herzog must defend the individual because he feels unworthy.
His attack on "Protestant Freudianism" (p.58) with its "lousy,
cringing, grudging conception of human nature" is a personal
attack against a personal threat: the guilt within himself. Despair
that "Maybe dignity was imported from France. . . . It all belongs in the museum now" (p.193) is really despair for his own
dignity.

Herzog identifies with the culture. Poirier calls *Herzog* "an
insufferably smug book, its smugness nourished by an assumption common to the Jewish fiction of which Bellow is the recognized master. Put simply, the life of the urban Jew, far from
being special, is assumed to be the life of the Modern American
Everyman" (p.264). Bellow is not free of this charge. Herzog, a
marginal figure—a Jew, Canadian-born of Russian immigrant
parents, a neurotic whose problems derive not from a modern
American family situation but from an unstable, rigid, Victorian-
Jewish family situation—is equated by Bellow with the culture:

His life was, as the phrase goes, ruined. But since it had not been
much to begin with, there was not much to grieve about. Thinking, on
the malodorous sofa, of the centuries, the nineteenth, the sixteenth, the
eighteenth, he turned up, from the last, a saying that he liked. (p.3)

In a sense, Herzog is the sum of all Western civilization since the
Renaissance, as if he were reflecting on his personal past. Maybe
Bellow is being satirical, but he is also serious: Herzog is
Representative Man fighting for survival.

However, the equation of Herzog with the culture functions
with respect to his character. He writes the Monsignor who
converted Mady to Catholicism, "the no doubt mad idea entered
my mind that my own actions had historic importance, and this
(fantasy?) made it appear that people who harmed me were
interfering with an important experiment" (p.106). This experi-

ment is to see whether the individual—Moishe Herzog—could live successfully; if so, perhaps there may be hope for Man. It is a courageous experiment; but if Herzog is trying to be an unsung culture hero, he is also acting the paranoiac victim. Here again, the experiment, the paranoia: "The progress of civilization—indeed the survival of civilization—depended on the successes of Moses E. Herzog. And in treating him as she did, Madeline injured a great project" (p.125). The treatment is comic but we feel portents of danger. Hitler and Robespierre had similar ideas; so did the minor Machiavellians in *Augie March*. Soon Moses sees his conflict with Mady and Val as universal—sees himself defending Man against revolutionary mobs "sacking Versailles, wallowing in cream desserts or pouring wine over their dicks. . . ." In other words, dressing up as the defender of the culture may lead to murder for a "good cause."

Finally, Herzog must keep talking to keep the world verbal—to keep it his. Everything becomes an essay. And not only does he use ideas to keep it his own world, but his perceptions are also extremely biased. When Shapiro is speaking with Mady and Gersbach at Ludeyville, Herzog, irritated, watches the garden:

> The lawn was on an elevation with a view of fields and woods. Formed like a large teardrop of green, it had a gray elm at its small point, and the bark of the huge tree, dying of dutch blight, was purplish gray. Scant leaves for such a vast growth. An oriole's nest, in the shape of a gray heart, hung from twigs. . . . I am a prisoner of perception, a compulsory witness. (p.72)

As we have noted, perception is his prisoner. Herzog sees in his garden a duplicate of himself—on an elevation—he feels morally elevated above the others; a teardrop of green—he is sad; a large, isolated gray elm dying of blight, with scant leaves for such a vast growth—he has vast potential but, because of blight, little output (leaves = leaves of a book); a gray heart—his own. Later in the novel he understands that he has not been an objective observer. Herzog says to himself that he has instilled "something of his own into his surroundings. As though he painted them with moisture and color taken from his own mouth, his blood, liver, bowels, genitals. In this mingled way, therefore, he was aware of Chicago, familiar ground to him for more than thirty years. And out of its elements, by this peculiar act of his own organs, he created his version of it" (p.278). Herzog learns this. We remember Augie's comments about Paris—that it was always a version which was seen. We remember Henderson's understanding that he projected himself onto his environment and that "if I stopped making such a noise all the time I might hear something nice." Like Henderson, at the end of the novel Herzog does "hear something nice." But until his transformation he creates the world after his image.

He humanizes the world to keep it safe. Like Augie, who feels sorry for the iguanas, like the narrator in "By the Rock Wall," who wants nature to be a pastorale, Herzog wants a world made for man. Faced with brutality in court, he cannot understand. He rejects the Reality Instructors who "want to teach you—to punish you with—the lessons of the Real" (p.125). Instructors are only too delighted to tell him:

> "They'll kill you."
> "Sandor, quit this."
> "Put you over a barrel. Tear your hide off."
> Herzog held his ears. "I can't stand it."
> "Tie your guts in knots. Sonofabitch. They'll put a meter on your nose, and charge you for breathing. You'll be looked up back and front. Then you'll think about death. You'll pray for it. A coffin will look better to you than a sports car." (p.88)

Although he criticizes the bourgeois attitude that the universe was made for our safe use, he believes this himself. Like all of Bellow's characters, he both recognizes his failings and acts as if he did not. With acute, bitter self-analysis he wonders

> whether he didn't belong to a class of people secretly convinced they had an arrangement with fate; in return for docility or ingenuous good will they were to be shielded from the worst brutalities of life. Herzog's mouth formed a soft but twisted smile as he considered

whether he really had inwardly decided years ago to set up a deal—a psychic offer—meekness in exchange for preferential treatment. (p.154)

Another version of this "psychic offer" is the verse he quotes:

> I love little pussy, her coat is so warm
> And if I don't hurt her, she'll do me no harm.
> I'll sit by the fire and give her some food,
> And pussy will love me because I am good. (p.118)

He has lived his life requiring people to lie to him (p.202). The lie was that he was safe, that his security as a child—protected within a warm family group against a world of hijackers outside —would not crack. He would not be police-bait. He would not die.

Ultimately it is Herzog's fear of death which is at the core of his guilt, his posturings, his ideas. In Bellow, again and again, fear of death is the root motivation; and if Herzog laughs at Tina Zokóly's theories about facing death, he thinks: "True things in grotesque form . . ." (p.269). Bellow rejects the worship of death; but he indicates in book after book that unless you confront your death, you're worshipping it as a secret, malign goddess.

For Herzog, intellectuality has always been a way of humanizing reality through words so as to stifle the reality of death. While his mother is dying, Herzog sits in the kitchen studying *The Decline of the West*, preferring to consider cultural rather than personal decline. As he remembers in court, when he is forced to confront what Asa and Augie call the "darkness," his mother had tried to teach him what death was, rubbing the palm of her hand until the dirt that we come from appeared; he doesn't want to learn. When she enters the kitchen just before her death, her eyes tell him: "My son, this is death." Herzog reflects: "I chose not to read this text" (p.234). He prefers to read cultural history.

It isn't only at the time of his mother's death that he intellectualizes to keep away anxiety over death. He admits, after his transformation has begun, "Did I really believe that I would die

when thinking stopped?" (p.265). Even before this transformation he recognizes his fear: "When we have come to better terms
with death, we'll wear a different expression, we human beings.
. . . *When* we come to terms!" (p.232).

The theme of death is less overt in the early part of the novel
than in *Dangling Man, Augie March, Seize the Day,* or *Henderson.* Herzog's consciousness is all we see, and it has suppressed
the thought of death; he speaks of Mady wanting to "get rid" of
him, wanting to "do him in"; but the theme is muted. Once
released, however, it flows until it dominates the novel. One
important relationship we discover is that for Herzog, desertion
means death. Ramona, he is sure, would not "be despondent in
'desertion' as he would have been—his childhood disorder, that
infantile terror of death that had bent and buckled his life into
these curious shapes" (p.266). Now we can understand Moses'
terror at desertion by Mady and betrayal by Gersbach: they
mean death to him. So when he says that the lovers wish for his
death, the assertion must be understood in this light, not taken as
literal truth. Furthermore, Mady's rejection of him is a symbolical
repetition of his father's rejection; his father had threatened him
with death; he imputes the same threat to Mady.

This, then, is Herzog's character. What about its transformation?

Herzog is burdened, like so many of Bellow's characters, by
the weight of the past. He must get the weight off his back.
Herzog is the bearded Negro he sees pushing women's coats
down Seventh Avenue: the Negro blows a toy trumpet which
cannot be heard, just as Herzog writes unsent letters; the Negro
is burdened with women as is Herzog. How to get rid of his self-
imposed burdens and break out of silence? Or Herzog is like the
ancient building being razed by the wrecking crew. Like the hero
of "The Wrecker" (see Chapter One), he needs to smash down
his false self before he can construct a fresh life. "Is this the full

crisis of dissolution?" Actually, only through dissolution can the human being in Herzog be redeemed.

In the course of the novel Herzog is—and therefore, for Bellow, Man is—partially redeemed, because he accepts himself and he accepts his death.

How is Herzog's redemption achieved? Moses Herzog is at Ramona's, filled with sexual guilt and guilt because he has deserted his traditions. Thoughts of sex lead to thoughts of death; shrimp remoulade leads to shame. He retells his story until Ramona asks him to stop. Finally they make love, and he has some peace that night and the next morning. But then his problems resume. Speaking to Simkin, the lawyer, Moses is told that if he takes Mady to court, he could win custody of his child. Simkin suggests a private detective, but, since detectives are so expensive, drops this idea. He tells Herzog, "They tried to murder you." Herzog takes this as showing Simkin's desire that he admit his wish to kill. He admits this mentally but not to Simkin, although after identifying Gersbach as the depraved revolutionary, he admits sending him a telegram: "Dirt Eaters At The Heart" (p.216)—its initials being, DEATH. Off the phone, he wonders why he expects justice when so few receive it.

Many of these elements are developed in succeeding scenes: sexual guilt and projection of this guilt onto Gersbach, the desire for justice, the use of a detective, the threat of death, the desire to kill.

Immediately Herzog remembers with guilt his first wife Daisy's trials with her mother, who, in her senility, thinks her a prostitute. "Oh Daisy, I am very sorry about this. . . ." (p.222). Then he goes to court—the place he wants to put Mady—to look for Simkin. It is a symbolic quest for justice. On the way, the cabbie asks, " 'You a lawyer? A cop?' 'How could I be a detective in this coat?' 'Hombre, detectives even go in drag now' " (p.223). In a sense, Herzog will be his own detective in the following scenes, snooping on his wife himself. Herzog is not in drag (dressed up as a woman), but he feels that his sports clothes are almost indecent and certainly decadent. And we remember Simkin's laughter at Gersbach for having kissed Herzog. Herzog replies, " 'That's his exuberant Russian personality.' 'Oh, I'm not saying he's queer, exactly,' Simkin said" (p.211). But Herzog himself, a few moments later, connects Gersbach with sexual perversion ("wine over their dicks") and with sexual extremism ("his wife says . . . he was on top of her every night") (p.216). So we have the dangerous combination of a sexual offender and a sexual witchhunter. In the court the second case Herzog sees concerns a homosexual picked up by a detective who had pretended to be homosexual himself (a kind of "going in drag"):

"At seven-thirty-eight P.M. at a urinal in the lower level men's lavatory, Grand Central Station . . . this man (name given) standing in the adjacent space reached over and placed his hand upon my organ of sex at the same time saying. . . ." The detective, a specialist in men's toilets, Herzog thought, loitering there, a bait. (pp.226–27)

It is a scene ambiguous in its relation to Herzog's character. If on the one hand he is seeing Gersbach as a sexual offender and himself as the detective he half-despises, he is, more significantly, seeing himself as on trial.

Let me backtrack a moment. If the trip to court is a symbolic quest for justice, it is both his enemies and himself on trial. As Herzog enters the court he picks up a dropped bouquet of violets. He remembers Mady in Ludeyville, remembers the deodorant Mady sprayed the bathroom with, and then thinks, "These violets smelled to him like female tears." That is, the violets bring up suppressed guilt for the destruction of his marriage(s). They remind him of his sexual perversity on the bathroom floor, and of his responsibility for Mady's unhappiness (female tears). Thus he goes into court a guilty man.

"My client's plea is still the same—not guilty" (p.255). This statement refers not only to the drunk who beat his friend but to Herzog himself. What Herzog sees, Herzog is: perception is his prisoner. This formula applies particularly to the scenes in court.

Herzog, then, pleads not guilty—he has so pleaded throughout the novel even while pretending to accuse himself—but he feels guilty.

To return to the homosexual's trial, we may ask what Herzog sees of himself in his case. First, simply sexual indecency. Second, latent homosexual feelings: the feminine-passive attitude ("Griselda Herzog") with which Herzog hopes to cheat death has homosexual components—specifically, as Reik, following Freud, points out, the desire to be sexually used by the father instead of being castrated or killed by him. But there is no need to turn to external, theoretical formulations; as the courtroom experiences and the trip to Chicago open up parts of his past he had preferred to ignore, Herzog remembers the time in Chicago (the safety of Napoleon Street already gone by) when he was raped by a stranger and offered a nickel. Sexual submission to this man is the price of his life. Even without the offer of the nickel, this scene is crucial in the development of Herzog's guilt: his sense of sex as filthy and of himself as a whore. More than filthy, sex is associated with the devil the evil foot of the rapist, the barking dogs—and so with Gehenna and death. Moses has become tainted. Then when Moses says ironically to Phoebe Gersbach that her husband "had to be led step by step into degeneracy by me" (p.261), part of him believes this. She answers, "He fell for you. Adored you." Later he recognizes that Gersbach "sought me in her flesh" (p.318), just as Allbee sought Asa in the body of the whore. In other words, he is a sexual object for Gersbach, and feeling this, he experiences guilt.

Herzog's sense of being a male whore is projected into the court case of Aleck-Alice, an actual male prostitute. Aleck-Alice carries a toy gun in an attempted holdup—significant because it is an acting-out of Herzog's attempted murder with an antique pistol. Aleck-Alice, like Herzog, sees sex as dirty: he doesn't wash because "filth makes it better, judge" (p.228). Herzog believes that the prostitute's irony is in effect saying, "your authority and my degeneracy are one and the same" (p.229). The judge is himself a "whore." So Herzog sees the respectable world, which includes himself, as guilty.

As the judge sentences the prostitute, he says, " 'Aleck, if you keep this up you'll be in potter's field. . . . I give you four-five years.' " It is like a sentence of death, and it is this sentence, in the context of Herzog's terror of death and expectation of death as punishment for sexual crimes, that leads to Herzog's sudden anxiety. He sees himself as charming and intelligent-looking—he sees himself as "outside police jurisdiction." But he is not sure; he suddenly thinks of calling his lawyer, unconsciously imagining himself as a guilty prisoner, and when he cannot reach the dime, feels sick, burning, blanching. "He saw that the magistrate was staring at him, as though Herzog owed him the courtesy of a nod on leaving his courtroom" (p.230). Clearly this is projection. As he left, "the sweat broke out on his face." Then, outside, he breathes again. But at once he wonders if he might not be having a heart attack.

He has experienced this sickness once before—when he was faced with sexual guilt at Zelda's (p.39). The cause is the same here; but now that we understand Moses' fear of death as punishment for sexual sin, his anxiety, coming upon Aleck's sentence of "death," takes on new meaning, and his worry about a heart attack fits into place.

It is now that Herzog begins to think of death and of his attempt to avoid it. As we have seen, it is more than confrontation of the sordid in humanity which leads to these thoughts; it is his guilt.

In the final court case he sees "a young couple, a woman and the man she had been living with in a slum hotel, uptown . . . being tried for the murder of her son, a child of three. She had had the boy by another man who deserted her" (p.235). In other words, this is the trial he has come for: the trial of Mady and Gersbach, living together with Herzog's child. Of course Gersbach and Mady never murdered the child, but they did keep her locked up in Gersbach's car, alone and weeping, while they had an argument; and Herzog swore, reading the letter from the baby-sitter, "I'll kill him for that" (p.101). So in the trial of a lame, retarded, vicious woman and her boy friend, a porter, Herzog is trying another case. We remember his belief that "sexual practices . . . were a private matter. Except for the children. Never children. There one must be strict" (p.227). If he can (unconsciously) see his own child as a victim of Gersbach and Mady, he has the right—or duty—to kill them.

There are a number of connections between the couple and his wife and Gersbach. Like Gersbach, the girl is lame; like Mady (and like himself), she was sexually abused as a teenager; they had kept the child locked up as Gersbach had locked June up in the car. Of course the differences are enormous, but the similarities help to account for Herzog's trip to Chicago. Dumb with incomprehension, bitter at his own illusory humanism, which expects to find cruelty only in books, he leaves the courtroom sick—and in horror and self-righteousness flies, as judge and executioner, to Chicago.

Then, too, Herzog identifies with the dead boy. Just as he had suffered abuse and the possibility of death at the hands of a pervert, so this boy was actually killed by the couple who wanted to copulate without annoyance. His trip to Chicago is partly an act of revenge for "the buried boy" (p.240)—that is, for his own destroyed innocence. In another way, too, Herzog identifies with the boy. In masochistic fantasy he has written of himself as "writhing under this sharp elegant heel"—Mady's heel. In court, the medical examiner, asking where the bruises were heaviest, replies, "on the belly, and especially in the region of the genitals, where the boy seemed to have been beaten with something capable of breaking the skin, perhaps a metal buckle or the heel of a woman's shoe" (p.237). Here is one more connection between Mady and the killer, one more reason Mady deserves to die.

But the analysis is incomplete. The final, terrible paragraph has more meaning.

The child screamed, clung, but with both arms the girl hurled it against the wall. On her legs was ruddy hair. And her lover, too, with long jaws and zooty sideburns, watching on the bed. Lying down to copulate, and standing up to kill. Some kill, then cry. Others, not even that. (p.240)

Again there are images of revolting sexuality. Generally these are connected with Herzog's guilt—here again. First, Herzog is like the deserter who fathered the child. The case brings up, as "an acrid fluid in his mouth," Herzog's guilt at not being the father he should have been, the Jewish family man. Condemning himself for his treatment of June and Marco, he turns self-condemnation into condemnation of Gersbach and Mady. Second, the filthy lust of the couple reminds him of his own sexual profligacy; even now he sat at court in the very un-rabbinical madras coat and held his hard straw hat. The fact of his guilt is made clear when, hurrying away from the court, he stumbles into a woman with a cane. She is like a figure from another world:

He saw that she wore a cast with metal clogs on the foot and that her toenails were painted. Then getting down the loathsome taste, he said, "I'm sorry." He had a sick repulsive headache, piercing and ugly. He felt as if he had gotten too close to a fire and scalded his lungs. She did not speak at all but was not ready to let him off. Her eyes, prominent, severe, still kept him standing, identifying him thoroughly, fully, deeply, as a fool. Again—silently—*Thou* fool! (pp.239–40)

She is a figure from another world—Napoleon Street. Moments before entering the courtroom he had remembered his mother's messages of death; here is his mother. But more clearly, it is his Aunt Zipporah, the regimenting Reality Teacher so akin to Grandma Lausch in *Augie March*. She is a figure of warning: life, says her cast with metal clogs, is not a madras jacket. More generally, with her weapon she threatens punishment for sin and weakness, like old man Herzog. Herzog goes to Chicago, then, to project his guilt onto Mady and Gersbach, just as Asa projected his onto Allbee. *They* are guilty, *they* will die: not he.

Herzog's actions in Chicago emanate from this projected guilt.

To go there he dresses in an old seersucker suit; that is, he leaves his decadent self (madras jacket) behind and symbolically becomes his father. He returns to his dead father's house, the prodigal son, the lost sheep, to take up his father's values, to judge with his father's criteria.

Everything about the place is ancient and reminiscent of death. His stepmother Taube says she is "the living dead." Indeed, she is a figure of oncoming death. The light in the entry hall reminds Moses of the vigil light in the synagogue: this is a sacred place. In a sense it is a visit to the underworld like those made by Tommy and Augie. No father is here, but the father's presence is strong. As he remembers making love to Ramona, Moses' thoughts shift to death (the punishment for sexual offence)—the blood beats in his head and he remembers that he has come on an errand of death.

"He sat near the very spot where Father Herzog, the year before his death, had threatened to shoot him." Moses now (as then) concurs in his father's judgment of him: a debased convert with a "Christianized smirk." "Croak in a flophouse," his father had said, and had run for his pistol (p.249). Repentant Moses thinks, "he should have pulled the trigger," and he feels guilty at having possibly shortened his father's life (p.250).

It is clear that his father's sentence of death is similar to what the judge tells Aleck: potter's field is similar to the flophouse. The flophouse reminds us also of the cheap hotel where the debauched couple killed the child: his father condemned him for what is to Herzog sexual offence. Moses still feels that the sentence should have been carried out. But he transmutes self-judgment into judgment of Mady and Gersbach; he changes his own sentence of death into theirs. Becoming the father, he takes Father Herzog's antique pistol, wraps it in the Czarist rubles he had played with as a child—thus associating himself with the *ancien régime*, with traditional values, and returning him to the security of childhood—and he goes off to kill his guilt in the persons of Mady and Gersbach. Tamkin says in *Seize the Day* that every murder is a suicide; this murder is to kill the evil that Herzog feels, and cannot handle, inside him.

The very streets he passes through symbolize Herzog's direction: Garfield Street (assassination), Washington Park, where he fears losing his way (the United States?). "He decided to follow Eden's to Congress Street and Congress to the Outer Drive" (p.254). Is it overinterpreting to see this as an allegory of American cultural history: from a pastoral ideal to a bourgeois-democratic reality and past it to nihilistic despair? Half mad, he swears that no one will harm his daughter—and this when he is about to kill her mother! It is he who has the standards of "heart" (p.258); consciously he believes that he is committing a righteous act: "They deserved to die" (p.254).

Of course, no reader expects Herzog to pull the trigger. He sees Mady washing dishes and Gersbach tenderly bathing June. Seeing them as real people, not as versions of the child-murderers in the New York courtroom, he breathes again; he is on the road to transformation. Just as Asa, seeing Allbee as real, lost his contempt for him and thus his self-contempt, so Bellow would have us believe that the incident at the window purges Herzog of his constructions; he sees what is, rather than his version.

This incident is not, however, a believable lever force for such a change: Herzog does not become God's holy fool, nor does he become humble, accepting himself and death, because he has seen the reality of two people who were previously only phantoms of his imagination. If Bellow wanted to show such a change, he would need to write (what seems to the reader an obligatory scene) about Herzog's confrontation of Gersbach and Mady. Instead, we see Mady only for a moment at the police station, there is little confrontation, and we get little indication of a significant change.

But Bellow indicates a second significance of Herzog's inability to shoot Gersbach and Mady through the window. His inability does not mean that he has shaken free of his father and that his father's accusation of him, which he unconsciously has directed onto Mady and Gersbach is now withdrawn. Rather, Herzog is continuing to act out his role as Papa Herzog. Just as Papa Herzog was unable to shoot him, so he is unable to shoot them. Just as "Tante Zipporah told Papa he could never use a gun on anyone. . . ," so Herzog cannot (p.258). Thus even here he is imitating his father and so is still controlled by his father's values. In fact, to some extent Moishe has all his life imitated Papa. For if Moishe was the bad boy not fulfilling Papa's expectation of order, Papa was no genius for order himself. He was an unsuccessful businessman, unsuccessful crook, unsuccessful bootlegger, with appearances of order but, as Aunt Zipporah knew, only appearances. Indeed, Moses thinks of his father not as a monarch but as a "broken-down monarch" like himself.

Now, if we were correct that at the core of Herzog's guilt is oedipal guilt and resultant fear of castration or death, the attempted murder can be seen as a mime of the father's act of vengeance—mimed by the guilty party to relieve himself? He takes the father's power—his gun—and, becoming the father, goes to seek revenge on his wife and the villain who has stolen the wife. That the villain is in a number of ways (especially his vanity) a double for Herzog has already been noted. But Herzog does not kill; it is like saying, "See—father cannot kill, and so, although I am guilty, I am safe."

But whether one sees the scene at the window as representing Herzog's confrontation with the real Mady and Gersbach or whether one sees it as a symbolic enactment of parental revenge and forgiveness, this scene is a watershed in the novel. The couple is safe and so he, too, is safe. Herzog is not, of course, completely changed, any more than Joseph, Asa, Tommy, or Henderson. Herzog, going to visit Phoebe Gersbach, is still anxious to take revenge by gaining custody of June. He still sees Gersbach and Mady as vicious, himself pure. Only now he claims that he's glad to get rid of Mady. "Bless the bitch!" (p.263), he tells Phoebe. And when he leaves Phoebe, there is "a softer kindliness in Herzog's expression, not often seen" (p.264). He kisses Phoebe's head and hand and recognizes "this was an unnecessary visit." It is one of Herzog's first displays of spontaneous affection for another person. He is on Asa's road back from alienation.

In the rented car again, Herzog writes that the human race will soon be free from human dependency; but not he, for he needs other people (p.265). Then—

Blood had burst into his psyche, and for the time being he was either free or crazy. But then he realized that he did not need to perform elaborate abstract intellectual work—work he had always thrown himself into as if it were the struggle for survival. But not thinking is not necessarily fatal. Did I really believe that I would die when thinking stopped? Now to fear such a thing—that's really crazy. (p. 265)

He has partially forgiven Mady and Gersbach—and hence himself—and is therefore less afraid of dying; he is able to admit that underlying his sterile intellectualism was a fear of death. Earlier he remembers the *Beth Olam*—the cemetery, but literally "the dwelling of the multitude." Herzog's fear of joining humanity is a fear of losing his personal identity in death. Now his recognition of his need for others leads him to telegraph Ramona—his first *sent* message of the novel—ending "much love"; and leads him to visit Lucas Asphalter. If once he ran from his friends at the Vineyard, unable to stand kindness, now he welcomes it. And now, for the first time, instead of telling Luke his own troubles, he discusses Luke's problems—he goes out for himself to speak of Luke's unhappiness at the death of his monkey and of Luke's ideas about death. "Don't feel so bad, Luke" (p.271). A simple thing to say—but it is the first time. And for the first time he communicates to another person the ideas which are important to him. Now he is ready to visit his daughter, June, to give her love without becoming outraged about Gersbach.

But then comes the automobile accident. There are two points to be made about this. First, Herzog is still living absorbed in his own world. We get brilliant fragments of police talk, but generally the ride to headquarters is a blank: instead of experiencing it, Moses remembers the time he was sexually abused, and he thinks about Proudhon and Nietzsche. In his "note" to the psychiatrist Edvig he writes, "I am much better now at ambiguities." But is he? We do hear him call Mady and Gersbach "unknowable" and a strange mixture of "pure diamond and Woolworth glass" (p.299). But his view of her is essentially unchanged: she is a vicious bitch who wants him dead. If Bellow wants us to see Herzog as changing, as opening himself up to *what is* instead of to his version, why does he not give us a fresh look at Mady? Possibly Bellow felt that a significantly different view of Mady would overcomplicate the novel and oversimplify Herzog's change; as we have noted, in each novel Bellow is careful to keep change of character ambiguous and tentative. (Possibly Bellow was merely not able to see his fictional material. It has always been difficult for Bellow to write about women; his subject is the solitary man. The fact that Bellow believes he has "created some real women in *Herzog*" shows that to some extent he misunderstands the novel.[19] The women are creations of Herzog's masochistic imagination—not "real" at all.) Second, what a clumsy artistic mistake it would be to show Herzog in an accident just when he is on the path to health—if this were an accident. But the scene is no mistake, the accident no accident. Rather, it is typical of the "accidents" moral masochists arrange for themselves: to touch the brake pedal a bit too hard, knowing that in one's jacket pocket is the accusing loaded pistol. Waking, Herzog knows without having to be told that the pistol wrapped in the *ancien-régime* rubles is in the hands of the police. How strange that this should occur—if we are correct that it was no accident—on a day Moses thinks of as "like the day of Father Herzog's funeral" (p.279). We feel that he is nearly ready to bury the father, to break free of him. But after the accident we find that the father is very much within him; for his carrying of the revolver he calls a "filial deed" (p.289). Or, again, "he took the revolver (his purpose as intense as it was diffuse) because he was his father's son." Indeed, this accident is a symbolic repetition of his father's failure as a bootlegger: Papa Herzog had had the old pistol with him (uselessly) the night his truck was stopped on the road to the border and he was beaten up.

But the accident and booking have a more obvious significance. The whole incident is a closure, a completion, of the action that began the morning Herzog walked into court in New York. From Herzog's entrance into court through his trip to Chicago, his attempt to murder, his accident and booking, one large pattern develops. If on that morning in court he feels symbolically put up for trial—and leaves—now he submits to judgment. It is as if he had to sin in a small way and be taken by the police in order to be released from his guilt. If I am correct that the unsuccessful attempt to kill is an imitation of the father, its purpose being to free Herzog from anxiety, then the accident and booking are primarily a minor punishment to ward off a major one and yet to free Herzog from guilt.

It is significant, of course, that he is taken to court for having the loaded gun. If the imagery of fish in the novel is sexual, then the following observation is important: " 'Do you recognize this gun?' The sergeant held it in his yellow palm, turning it over with delicate fingers like a fish—a perch. The radiance of her look as it rested on the gun was deeper than any sexual expression he had ever seen on her face" (p.300).

It is Herzog, not the author, who compares Mady's look to a "sexual expression." It is for possession of his father's phallic power that Herzog is being booked. Once this possession is acknowledged and agreed to be only "sentimental"—the gun only a paperweight (i.e., something to hold down his multitude of papers, to give him order and control)—he is at least temporarily freed from oedipal guilt. Hence, after leaving the station with his brother, instead of feeling unhappy, Herzog feels cheerful and loving.

It is this temporary—or final—liberation that accounts for Herzog's thought in the squad car:

Proudhon says, "God is *the* evil." But after we search in the entrails of world revolution for *la foi nouvelle,* what happens? The victory of death, not of rationality, not of rational faith. Our own murdering imagination turns out to be the great power, our human imagination which starts by accusing God of murder. At the bottom of the whole disaster lies the human being's sense of a grievance, and with this I want nothing more to do. (p.290)

Here is a typical Herzogian generalization about cultural history —that the destruction of God motivated by revenge leads to the enthronement of death itself. This generalization originates typically out of a personal problem: Herzog renounces his stance as victim and renounces revenge. His guilt is reduced; he has partly forgiven others and forgiven that part of himself which he had projected onto those others. The motive-force for his masochism is lessened. Rejecting the stance of victim on a personal level, he likewise rejects it on a cultural-philosophical level.

Earlier, in Luke Asphalter's apartment, a related transformation begins. Herzog reveals that he had tried to force reality into verbal constructs, and states that the theories of dread and despair proposed by modern philsophers are also constructs. In a kind of sermon of affirmation, Herzog says:

But let's stick to what matters. I really believe that brotherhood is what makes a man human. If I owe God a human life, this is where I fall down. 'Man liveth not by Self alone but in his brother's face. . . . Each shall behold the Eternal Father and love and joy abound. . . . The real and essential question is one of our employment by other human beings and their employment by us. Without this true employment you never dread death, you cultivate it. (p.272)

Unless he lives in brotherhood, a man is not human. We find Herzog trying to move away from selfhood toward brotherhood, to community; trying to cure, in Bummidge's words (*The Last Analysis*) "the Pagliacci gangrene! Caused as all gangrene is by a failure of circulation. Cut off by self-pity. Passivity. Fear. Masochistic rage."[20]

The casting off of selfhood has been the dominant movement

in *Dangling Man, The Victim, Seize the Day,* and *Henderson.* Once again, it is true in *Herzog.* As always, the hero defends his individuality—a defense which is surely Bellow's as well; Herzog thus attacks the Himmelsteins of this world, who believe "You must sacrifice your poor, squawking, niggardly individuality . . . to historical necessity" (p.93). But Bellow also believes that to be redeemed one must lose one's individuality: not lose it to the crowd, not lose it in acquiescence to "historical necessity,"—no, but lose it by becoming one with his fellow man. "Brotherhood is what makes a man human."

Richard Poirier complains, "Nothing but nothing in Herzog's career—are we to think of his surrender of his wife's diaphragm to her messenger Gersbach?—suggests that his selfhood and self-development have been 'this great bone-crushing burden.' "[21] What Poirier means is that Herzog has insufficient grounds for complaint—and Poirier is correct. But selfhood *is* Herzog's burden, for it is Herzog's defense of his Self that leads to his masochistic posturings. Like Joseph, Asa, Augie, Tommy, Henderson, Herzog will not put his burden down. "Should he have been a plain, unambitious Herzog?" (p.43). *Meshugenah,* bohemian Nachman, a quack who like Tamkin and Dahfu knows the truth, tells Herzog,

> We do not love ourselves, but persist in stubbornness. Each man is stubbornly, stubbornly himself. Above all himself, to the end of time. Each of these creatures has some secret quality, and for this quality he is prepared to do anything. He will turn the universe upside down, but he will not deliver his quality to anyone else. Sooner let the world turn to drifting powder. . . . You're blind, old friend. . . . Rooted in yourself. But a good heart. (p.134)

Herzog has been carrying the world on his shoulders. That is, he has been carrying his own world, his special version. After the trip to Chicago he can put it down. He can stop trying to control the world with words and ideas and instead simply live in it. He can stop defending his "special destiny," his individuality, and live unencumbered as another creature in the world that is.

"A man," Herzog thinks in Chicago, "is somehow more than his characteristics, all the emotions, strivings, traits, and constructions which it pleases him to call 'my life'" (p.266). Thus, like D. H. Lawrence, Bellow is trying to get below individuality to something more basic, to get underneath the "old stable *ego* of the character."[22] Like Lawrence, he is concerned with the carbon underlying the diamond and coal—and for Bellow this carbon is a state of transpersonal, mystical unity. "Go through what is comprehensible and you conclude that only the incomprehensible gives any light" (p.266). This incomprehensible, Herzog argues, is not death. Never is it named, because it cannot be named, but the closest word is *love*.

Later, in the woods, this discarding of Selfhood is described (in Whitman's words) as escape "from the life that exhibits itself":

Oh, that's a plague, the life that exhibits itself, a real plague! There comes a time when every ridiculous son of Adam wishes to arise before the rest, with all his quirks and twitches and tics, all the glory of his self-adored ugliness, his grinning teeth, his sharp nose, his madly twisted reason, saying to the rest—in an overflow of narcissism which he interprets as benevolence—"I am here to witness. I am come to be your exemplar." Poor dizzy spook! (p.324)

Herzog discards gesture, this masochistic ham, always acting, especially in suffering; he discards self-contained individuality. "Spook" is accurate, for the man bound to his ego is not living in the flesh but in mental constructions. Now he is living in reality, the reality Henderson enters. Herzog, too, has moved from "the states that I myself make into the states which are of themselves." In the past he had traded on innocence and meekness, he had humanized reality, he had lived in *his* world. Now he buys his daughter a periscope so that she will grow up seeing what *is*, even if it isn't pleasant; and as a guru in the woods he writes this exquisite note to God:

How my mind has struggled to make coherent sense. I have not been too good at it. But have desired to do your unknowable will,

taking it, and you, without symbols. Everything of intensest significance. Especially if divested of me. (pp.326–27)

The passage is built on a paradox: when he stops trying to make
sense, he finds sense. As Augie says, "When striving stops, the
truth comes as a gift." Reality in itself has meaning; Herzog is
content to live in it. Therefore he is content to live in his house,
without being overly concerned with its order. Throughout, he
had identified with his house—bought with his father's money—
sadly in need of repair, as he is himself. Finally he accepts it as
is; he accepts lovemaking in the house; he accepts death (the
birds' bones): he accepts Herzog.

In Ludeyville he lives among the animals and birds that have
taken over his home, not shooting them, as Thea would, not
flitting, like Robey, nor blowing them up, like Henderson. But
he can face death: "I look at myself and see chest, thighs, feet—a
head. This strange organization, I know it will die" (p.340). He
has read Mama's text. He can admit the ugly findings of *African
Genesis*, not imposing human values on nature. Seeing an old
note card on the floor: *"to do justice to Condorcet,"* Herzog
thinks, "Condorcet would have to find another defender." He
does not have to defend the idea of human perfectibility and
social progress; he does not have to defend any theorist's tight
schemas, watertight constructions, even if affirmative. But he
does not emphasize ugliness; he attacks Mermelstein's "doctrine
or theology of suffering" (p.317). This attack is, like Herzog
himself, less bitter, more coherent, and far more humble than
before. Herzog is the holy man in nature, living in peace, free for
the first time of the punishing Mady and of his own burden of
selfhood.

"He was surprised to feel such contentment . . . contentment?
Whom was he kidding, this was joy!" (p.313). Reality, then, is,
finally, not a bitter pill; as Herzog (and Bellow) suspected all
along, its true apprehension is in love and joy: in *amor fati*.
Bellow has spoken of a "spontaneous mysterious proof [of the
justification of life's continuation] that has no need to argue with

despair."²³ He wishes to make us experience this proof in the final pages of *Herzog*.

In doing so, he washes his hands of the two diseases with which society—and Herzog—are infected: the romantic glorification of the self and the devaluation of the self; Faustian striving and the self-contempt of them who, not finding paradise within, see a wasteland both within and without. The cure for both diseases is selflessness. Augie's quest for a special fate, Henderson's "I want, I want," are ended. "But what do you want, Herzog? 'But that's just it—not a solitary thing.'" Accepting life and death, he is "pretty well satisfied to be, to be just as it is willed, and for as long as I may remain in occupancy" (p.340).

Mainly what Herzog accepts is himself as "simply a human being, more or less" (p.317). Like the dead Morgenfrue who played the piano, Herzog must "play the instrument I've got" (p.330). Music is associated with confrontation of death: earlier, Asphalter says he "had to face the music" of death (p.269); now Herzog faces it. In painting an old piano green to send to June, he is symbolically confronting death while he is affirming life.

Herzog's new posture seems like quietism; yet Herzog feels that now, free of Selfhood and of despair, he can truly act in the world. "'I mean to share with other beings as far as possible. . . .' Herzog felt a deep, dizzying eagerness to begin" (p.322).

But can he begin? He is free of guilt and able to enter into community. Into *Community*: but what about *a community*? Like *Henderson* this novel ends with the promise of accommodation to society. But Herzog's loyalty to civilization must be seen in the context of his life in Eden. He is the child, he is the guru in the woods—not the Jewish family man. If Bellow has attempted in *Herzog* to bridge the gap between the isolated self and society, he has not succeeded. Herzog is man communing with God and nature, not with men. He spends time with Willie, writes to Marco, and invites Ramona (reversal of the usual situation) to dinner; but essentially he is still alone.

His final, beautiful affirmation of life is Hasidic.[24] Indeed, there has been a strain of holy joy, of celebration, throughout the novel, like hints of a musical theme which is finally released. "There was no strain in the water, where schools of minnows swam. Herzog sighed and said to himself, 'Praise God—praise God'" (p.91). He speaks of "unexpected intrusions of beauty" (p.218). In the woods Herzog writes "songs, psalms and utterances" (p.327). He blesses the lovers who have used his couch. But this affirmation, while it could be called Jewish and certainly religious, is not at all similar to the affirmation of man and civilization Herzog has been proclaiming throughout the novel. Man as King, whose "*I* had such dignity," is not Man as fool of God. "Marvelous" Herzog is not holy Herzog. Herzog's—and Bellow's—final affirmation is of course not totally different from what has been affirmed throughout: goodness belongs to the old Herzog and the new; if the source of Herzog's values is his childhood, it is to a lost innocence that he returns. Furthermore, in doing so, he is not completely detached from his father's ways, for his father, when he became old, had taken great pleasure from his garden in Chicago. But individuality, which Herzog-Bellow has been defending, is not affirmed in the fictional resolution. If Bellow successfully affirms the possibilities of new life for man against the prophets of doom, what he succeeds in affirming is not the nineteenth century father, not the traditional family life, not civilized society, but the timeless saint and the holiness of reality. Saint more than zaddik, indeed, for the zaddik—the Hasidic rabbi—is the leader of a congregation and is loyal to Jewish law and traditions; Herzog is outside these traditions. Once Isaac Rosenfeld criticized Fiedler for calling Simone Weil "Our kind of saint." No, says Rosenfeld, there is only *their* kind of saint; Weil's sainthood cannot be detached from her neuroses and fanaticism.[25] But Herzog is "our kind" of saint—outside ritual and even stated belief, living in humble awe of what *is* rather than in obeisance to a god: belief or unbelief is irrelevant.

However, Herzog is *not Herzog—duke* in German: he is not

noble in a traditional sense; and Moses is not *Moses*. Certainly, even though the name "Moses" is satirically intended—"Moses wanted to do what he could to improve the human condition, at last taking a sleeping pill, to preserve himself" (p.107)—Bellow does intend his hero to be a new Moses leading his people out of Egypt through the wasteland to a promised land. But the promised land he arrives at is Eden, not the New Jerusalem, and he leads only himself, a blessed Natty Bumppo.

That is—if we can even accept Herzog as blessed.

He believes himself permanently changed; and since there is hope for him, there is hope for man. But is Herzog redeemed? I asked this question concerning Henderson; I ask it here. Does Bellow affirm because he believes in affirming? Perhaps. Bellow has presented us with a careful unfolding of Herzog's psychological transformation. But the transformation, because it is without a believable lever force, seems likely to be temporary and restricted to Herzog while he is alone. His freedom from the accusation of the father within himself may be lost when he is again exposed to human—and therefore sexual—relationships; it seems likely that guilt and the consequent masochistic mechanism will return.

If we as readers are at all convinced that Herzog is a selfless saint, it is because of the rich, lyrical style that ends the novel. Leaving a sterile intellectuality, Herzog speaks simply and without irony. The sentences become shorter, less complex in structure. They are rich in concrete imagery lovingly recorded. He thinks in metaphor, parable, and epigram:

What keeps these red brick houses from collapse on these billows [of plunging, ocean-like land] is their inner staleness. I smell it yawning through the screens. The odor of souls is a brace to the walls. Otherwise the wrinkling of the hills would make them crumble. (p.339)

In this passage I see a new kind of intellectuality, a new kind of humanist philosophy. It is a rich and profound statement of man's significance.

CHAPTER TEN

The Politics of Oedipus:
Mr. Sammler's Planet
To Jerusalem and Back

Mr. Sammler's Planet

Oedipus the immigrant. Who leaves home to rid himself of guilt and make his way in the world. He wins a kingdom—and his mother's heart, but in doing so, he drenches himself in guilt and has to withdraw. When we see him again, he is Old Oedipus, Oedipus not Son but Father, Oedipus at Colonus.

Bruce Mazlich, in his *James and John Stuart Mill*, argues for a *historical* reading of the Oedipus complex.

Somewhere between the late eighteenth and early nineteenth centuries, sons began to adopt a different posture towards their fathers. . . . The Oedipus complex was handled at first in a slightly different, and eventually in a totally new way. A relationship, formerly patterned and secure, became problematic. Filial rebellions became more intense, and their fizzling out into submission less common and complete. The psychic price, in anxiety and guilt, became acute, and its prevalence increasingly epidemic. . . .[1]

Mazlich agrees with Howard Wolf that by the early twentieth century the father figure was fading away and the conflict was no longer so acute.[2] But this situation is very different among immigrant families to the United States in this century. Chicano, Puerto Rican, Jewish—often the entrance to the New World was an entrance into modernity, urbanism, industrialism that created conditions analogous to those facing families in Britain in the nineteenth century. It was a leap in time, forcing new values on the young if they were to prosper in the New World. And so we find in Chicano, Puerto Rican, and Jewish literature a tension between the values of the Old World, often identified with the father, and the values of the new; between "communal insularity" and the pain of dislocation and acculturation;[3] between God and America. The "rise" in *The Rise of David Levinsky* takes place at the cost of his soul. Early in the novel, Levinsky tells us the Talmudic story of Rabbi Matthia, who gouges out his eyes to avoid sexual temptation. Sexuality, it seems, is an important part of the initiation into America. Levinsky, on the other hand, does not gouge out *his* eyes; warned "one becomes a gentile in America," he falls into temptation and enters American sexual and economic modes.

Of course, Saul Bellow is not Abraham Cahan. Born only two years before *The Rise of David Levinsky* was published, Bellow grew up a modern, he did not have to struggle as Cahan did to reconcile his Jewish and American worlds or write with an American voice.[4] And yet his are immigrant roots. Like the character David Levinsky, Bellow grew up with the devotion of a mother who cherished him and longed for him to be devout and study Talmud. Like David Levinsky's, his rise in the world was accompanied by a discarding of his Jewish roots. At the beginning of *To Jerusalem and Back,* Bellow tells of a group of Hasidim flying to Israel in the same plane. "To me," he says, "there is nothing foreign in these hats, sidelocks, and fringes. It is my childhood revisited. At the age of six, I myself wore a tallith katan, or scapular, under my shirt. . . ."[5] The conflict on the plane is comic and charming, but it is a version of the immigrant son caught between the claims of his Judaism and the claims of his modern life in the world.

The immigrant *father* is often already a figure out of place; in Eastern Europe he could be respected as a scholar without the need for economic activity, which was generally the role of the wife. But in America, respect derived from successful economic activity—and economic success did not come easy. And so the tension between generations, between immigrant father and second-generation son, already existed *within* the immigrant father.

Bellow grew up speaking Yiddish as well as English. While we know little of his personal father, we know Bellow grew up in the midst of a tension between contradictory traditions.[6] But more: the American tradition was not simply an alternative but was a tradition *of* the breakdown of old-world values, a tradition of constant change; the conflict was generational—fathers versus sons—at the same time as it was cultural. To survive, psychologically and economically, in the new world was to reject a secure self. "The American experience," Chametzky writes, "was strange, thrilling, exhilarating—the sense of life and its possibilities heightened in its audience as nowhere else—but clashing with a dream-like past that exerts its force and demands to be reconciled with the new reality. In the absence of such a reconciliation, personality remains fractured, incomplete."[7]

Oedipal conflict has existed prominently in Bellow's work since the beginning; in general, the fiction has moved closer and closer to the position of the father in the conflict. Joseph is fully the rebellious son, threatened by his father with Gehenna (Hell). Asa struggles to keep from becoming his paranoid father. Augie is without a father but "tries on" a number of them. Tommy by his very "moniker" denies his identity as his father's son; his father curses him with death, but at the end a sort of symbolic reconciliation takes place over the coffin. Henderson's father rejects him as interloper, but Henderson plays violin to reach him, and at the end he himself becomes surrogate father to the orphan boy. Herzog, as I have shown, finds peace by identifying with his father, taking up the father's gun, and sparing the wayward thief of his wife—sparing, in effect, himself. In *Mr. Sammler's Planet*, almost alone among Bellow's fiction, the protagonist identifies with the father and rejects the children.

I say *almost* alone: in the wonderful short story from the fifties, "A Father-to-Be" (discussed in another context on pp.54-55 above), the protagonist is a young man, Rogin, on his way to dinner at his fiancee's house.[8] Written years before *Herzog*, "A Father-to-Be" shows a fiancee who is amazingly like Mady from *Herzog*, like Denise from *Humboldt's Gift*. She is the boss. She is using Rogin financially—he supports her elegant whims, her psychotherapy, her Christmas gifts. God help him—we know what marriage to Joan will mean. Rogin also knows—but won't acknowledge—won't acknowledge how much she uses him, won't acknowledge his anger. On the subway he notices a dapper man in his early forties. This man looks as if he could be Joan's son by Rogin, and the thought depresses Rogin. That he should be the father of a "fourth-rate man of the world"! That this smug, vain, superficial man should survive while his own traits die out. "The inhumanity of the next generation incensed Rogin. Father and son had no sign to make to each other" (p.409).

We know, of course, that Rogin has displaced his anger at Joan onto this stranger. But, more important for my purposes, he has projected a psychic split: between *father*, with whom he identifies, and *son*, a superficial man of the modern world. It is the situation of Tommy Wilhelm and his father, but here the protagonist represents the father and castigates the son.

Rogin projects his social self onto this stranger, a self he despises; he takes refuge from oedipal guilt by despising the "son." The son represents the new, the father the old. The father, who will die, doesn't deserve to die; the son, who will live, doesn't deserve to live. At the end Joan talks to Rogin in baby talk and shampoos his "pink" scalp. He falls back into the role of dependent infant and forgets his anger.

Rogin is both son and father, and the fiction is interesting because of his comic inner turmoil. Sammler is only *father*. There was a time when he was a dandy, a man of the world, but that young man was buried by the Nazis in a mass grave in Poland; the person who crawled out, barely alive, and survived the war, was another man, "Uncle" Sammler, a character who resolves the oedipal dilemma by burying the "son" within himself, by becoming the father. Unlike Oedipus, he has lost only one eye. But like Oedipus, he is a wanderer, travelling with his daughter, stranger in the land yet one who is felt to have magical powers. A wise man, the voice of wisdom itself, somehow needed by the community, he has come through the whirlwind. Thinking of the fanatical sexuality of the young, he quotes Sophocles himself: "Most gladly have I escaped the thing of which you speak; I feel as if I had escaped from the hands of a mad and furious master."[9] This is a solution to the dilemma of Oedipus that lops off one of the horns. Oediups the Son becomes desexualized into Oedipus the Father.

This accounts, I feel, for the deadness of *Mr. Sammler's Planet*. A number of critics have argued that the concerns of *Mr. Sammler's Planet* are those of Bellow's earlier novels.[10] And this is true. But what has changed is the angle of vision and with it the dramatic focus. What has always involved us in Bellow's fiction is the struggle of his protagonist to redeem himself. *Can Man be saved*—the essential question in Bellow—is more fully expressed as, Can Man *that suffering joker* be saved? Always it is the son, the struggling son who must lose his selfhood and come to grace. Always a hero tries to face the worst and cast it off, tries to throw off the burden of his own past, which prevents him from becoming human. But *not* in *Mr. Sammler's Planet*. Sammler is a static character, the voice of one of the dead, the Fathers, gazing down on the sublunary world with his one fierce eye. Siegel points out the parallel between Sammler and Dr. Adler from *Seize the Day*.[11] But in *Seize the Day* the angle of vision was Tommy's. In *Mr. Sammler's Planet* once again we hear of the unsatisfied *wanters* of the world, who "needed gratification of numerous instincts" (p.74). We remember Henderson's "I want"; Augie's "When striving stops the truth comes as a gift"; Tommy's vision of the Broadway crowd silently expressing their selfhood— "I labor, I spend, I strive . . . I want." But always in Bellow it has been *we* who want and need and must struggle with the foolishness of all that needing; in *Mr. Sammler's Planet* it is *they:* the young. The sexual. The contemporary. Always before we have been able to identify with the fool yearning to be whole; to identify and at the same time laugh at the absurdity of his quest. But in *Mr. Sammler's Planet* we are not permitted to identify. We stand *outside* ("the place of honor"), shaking our heads. Wallace, Elya's son, is very much a Tommy Wilhelm, acting out his disorder to gain his father's attention (see above, pp.69-74). Both are doctors' sons. Both call their father "Dad." Both deny that they want their fathers to die. Both are "dreamy." But we care nothing about Wallace, we can't believe in Wallace. Sammler, sad, aloof, watches this superficial character in his oedipal struggle.

In the paperbound version of the first edition of this book I argued that Sammler had aligned himself with the Fathers and paid the price of withdrawal in the novel's deadness. More recently, Mark Shechner has supported this view. "Sammler," he argues, "is the superego's book."[12] He sees it as a "retreat from a long and difficult line of emotional exploration."[13] He argues that its politics and deadness of style are a manifestation of "Bellow's psychological retrenchment." Exactly. In this essay I am trying to make clear the nature of that retrenchment and its expression in Bellow's political vision.

The characters in *Mr. Sammler's Planet* are, according to Shechner, like Jonson's sharpers and gulls—humors rather than Dickensian comic characters.[14] Sammler as the old Oedipus has an eye that distorts, flattens, caricatures. Even the prose style of the novel is dead. Bellow's wonderful lists, for example—compare this one from *Seize the Day:*

If you wanted to talk about a glass of water, you had to start back with God creating the heavens and earth; the apple; Abraham; Moses and Jesus; Rome; the Middle Ages; gunpowder; the Revolution; back to Newton; up to Einstein; then war and Lenin and Hitler. After reviewing this and getting it all straight again you could proceed to talk about a glass of water. "I'm fainting, please get me a little water."

to this one from *Mr. Sammler's Planet:*

> Because of the high rate of speed, decades, centuries, epochs condensing into months, weeks, days, even sentences. So that to keep up, you had to run, sprint, waft, fly over shimmering waters, you had to be able to see what was dropping out of human life and what was staying in.

As Shechner says, "The language of narrative in *Sammler* abandons sensuousness and detail in favor of generalization and meaning."[15] The style, like Sammler himself, has withdrawn from this planet. Always before, Bellow's moments of transcendence arose from the everyday—Tommy's moment of love in the subway tunnel, Joseph's serenity gazing at the red string. But Sammler has withdrawn his energies from this earth and Bellow his energies from the novel. Compare the dialogue between Sammler and Dr. Lal to similar ones between Henderson and Dahfu or Tommy and Tamkin; the Lal-Sammler discussion is abstract, passionless, dull.

But of course. Bellow is using the angle of vision of a character who has buried his passionate, modern, conflicted self. Bellow is not deceived into pretending that Sammler is a saint. Sammler, as Bellow fully knows, is a repressed man. The contemporary American world *acts out* all that he has discarded from his personality. Just as "Elya . . . had delegated Angela to experience the age for him," so Sammler delegates Shula, Wallace, Angela, and the revolutionary youth culture of the late sixties. Does Bellow understand *how* distorted is Sammler's vision of the age? He has the old man say, "I am of course deformed. And obsessed" (p.230). But are we expected to agree? His Swiftian vision of the young with their sexual odors, of blacks with enormous penises, of revolutionaries who uphold sexual vitality as a standard of truth—these images are not merely embarrassing caricatures of the sixties—they are nearly mad, and I must believe that no matter how cranky Bellow had become by 1969, he was consciously creating a Sammler who was projecting his own repressed life onto his age.

As I shall show, Bellow gives us evidence of that repression throughout the novel. He lets it seep out past Sammler's defenses. As I have shown in earlier chapters, Bellow is a master of the creation of characters whose perceptions reveal more about them than they themselves would be able to express. This novel is clearly within the same mode. True, Bellow's own sympathies are with Sammler; his politics are consonant with Sammler's own. But Sammler is a character distanced ironically from his creator. Bellow, consciously, has created a Sammler who plays the Father, Oedipus at Colonus, in judgment on his age and so keeps at bay anxiety over the buried impulses of his own life.

First, I want to look carefully at this strange character and then define as precisely as I can his relationship to Saul Bellow.

As Bellow knows, Sammler lives out a rebellion of his own—lives it out vicariously. While he believes "he didn't have much use for the romance of the outlaw," he goes *a dozen times* to watch the black thief at work on the bus. "*Illicitly,* he craved a repetition" (p.11, italics mine). Sammler as voyeur: dismayed, still he listens to Angela's tales of her sexual encounters and Bruch's confessions of his fetishism, as he also stares with fascination on the black pickpocket at work—and on his penis, symbol of his illicit majesty. The silent scene, almost hallucinatory, in which the thief forces Sammler to look, is like the thief's expression of the relationship between them, an exaggerated dramatization of Sammler's voyeurism.

His unconscious explodes—and Bellow means it to—in ongoing perception, in memories, and in conceptualization. *Ongoing perception:* there are many ways of seeing New York. Sammler sees phone booth urinals, he sees—and goes back to see again—a powerful black pickpocket seeking whom he might "devour," he sees "the barbarous world of color erupting from beneath" (p.7). The color is often yellow, always the color of the sexual and lurid in Bellow (see above, p.152, *re The Victim*). The sexuality and violence in the city is overwhelming to him. "A barrage of sweetness and intolerable brightness was laid down. Sammler did not really want to experience this. It all rose against him, too dizzy, too turbulent" (p.298). He tells Wallace to censor the mad messages from the unconscious he sends himself; Sammler censors his own messages, but they break through. Girls with sexual odors. Young people like "young dogs with their first red erections, and pimples sprung to the cheeks from foaming beards" (p.37). This image reminds me of the rapist's orgasm in *Herzog:* "And between the boy's thighs the red skinless horrible thing passed back and forth, back and forth, until it burst out foaming." On the street Sammler sees "women with dogs, leashed and unleashed"—always figures of fearful sexuality for Bellow (see above, pp.150-51). Sammler's New York is crammed with the sexuality and violence he is horrified by; it is, in the Jungian sense, his own "shadow."

The black pickpocket is not the object of racist *hatred*. He is compared to an "African prince or great black beast," and this ambivalence is repeated often. He has a "certain princeliness"; he is compared to a "puma." He is Dahfu and the lioness in one image. It is clear that Sammler's revulsion with negritude, with "sexual niggerhood," is, in the psychoanalytic sense, projection and denial. It is Sammler who, as much as Mailer, sees blacks as metaphors for sexuality and violence—for the shadow. But he also sees the pickpocket as royal, as glorious, and is horrified when his son-in-law Eisen (in German, *iron*) smashes the pickpocket with a sack full of his metal sculpture. The black prince is acting out Sammler's buried self.

His unconscious explodes through his *memory:* If Sammler is fascinated by the pickpocket's criminality and sexuality—Sammler, the most gentle of men—underlying this fascination is his memory of his own criminality: the pleasure he felt in murdering the German soldier in the Zamoshet Forest. During the war he touched bottom; he knows how thin a membrane separates him from the "barbarian" who survived the war and knows that his experience has deformed him. Just as Asa needs to separate himself from an Allbee who has touched bottom, Sammler needs to keep at bay the terrible underbelly of his own life. But doing so, he projects it out onto the contemporary world, which becomes a nightmare.

His unconscious boils over in his *conceptualizations:* I refer to how he organizes the nightmare. He sees the world divided into order, tradition, duty, on the one hand, and selfhood—with accompanying violence, sexuality, and rebellion—on the other. He sees the world breaking down, the membrane between civilized and savage, ordered and disordered, tearing. Criminality permeates every level. Twice he compares the pickpocket to a skilled "doctor." The comparison, unconscious for Sammler, is intended by Bellow to remind us of Dr. Gruner's own criminality. And yet he does not condemn upper-class criminality. ". . . It was plain," Sammler thinks, "that the rich men he knew were winners in struggles of criminality, of permissible criminality." But then he reconsiders: "Wait a minute, though: Sammler denied himself the privilege of the high-principled intellectual who must always be applying the purest standards and thumping the rest of his species on the hand" (p.75). When it comes to the "criminality" of the young, however—revolutionaries, sexual profligates, even the unclean—he is disgusted. Ignoring the place his own fantasies play, he imagines revolution as a way of giving the bottom of society the aristocratic privilege of the pleasure of murder (p.144). Bellow must mean for us to understand that Sammler is fearful of his own pleasure in murdering. And Sammler is "testy with white Protestant America for not keeping better order. Cowardly surrender. Eager in a secret humiliating way to come down and mingle with all the minority mobs, and scream against themselves" (p.105).

Minority mobs. Terrified of disorder in himself, Sammler sounds like both an American racist and a British Victorian fearing the "mob." In my chapter on *Herzog*, I discussed Herzog's attack on Valentine Gersbach, vulgar, modern egomaniac. "When I think of Valentine . . . I think of the books I devoured as a boy, on the French and Russian revolutions. And silent movies, like *Mme. Sans Gene*—Gloria Swanson. . . . Anyway, I see the mobs breaking into palaces and churches and sacking Versailles, wallowing in cream desserts or pouring wine over their dicks and dressing in purple velvet, snatching crowns and mitres and crosses. . . . Emancipation resulting in madness." Simkin replies, "I never saw a man pour wine over his dick in any movie—when did you see that?" And adds, "Besides, in your mind, you don't identify yourself with Versailles or the Kremlin or the old regime, or anything like that, do you?" And Herzog backs off: "No, no, of course not." But we don't believe him—and neither does Bellow. This horror of emancipation, of rebellion against the father, Bellow knows to be a projection of Herzog's own guilt. Guilt over his own rebellion. It was Herzog who "devoured" those books as a boy. Now he identifies with the Father—politically, with the old regime. Sammler is in his own way at least as mad as Herzog—but his madness is the obverse of Herzog's frenzy of selfhood. Sammler is half mad with horror at the excesses of individual freedom, of licentiousness and aggression on behalf of the ego. He fears women, blacks, and the young breaking out—breaking out in his own heart.

His essential attack is on the *self*, the megalomaniac ego. Bellow's fiction has *always* seen selfhood, in the Blakean sense, as the obstacle to the discovery of true beauty of the deeper self (see above, pp.113-36).[16] "The self may think it wears a gay ornament, delightfully painted, but from outside we see that it is a millstone. . . . Where is the desirable self that one might be? (*MSP*, p.234). As Stock puts it, "The mere assertion of individuality, the 'non-negotiable' demand for one's own way, the leaps to ecstasy or 'significance' that by-pass duties and commitment to others—such behavior debases the self it seeks to glorify."[17]

There is nobility and nobility. Man is potentially a king, but his very act of separating himself out, becoming "more than human," as Schlossberg says in *The Victim*, keeps him from his true nobility. Because of this paradox, the bundle of metaphors surrounding nobility and aristocracy has been vital in Bellow's work from the beginning (for example, see above, pp.83-88). It is basic to the

defense of the human being. In *Mr. Sammler's Planet* we see a
parody king, "Rumkovsky, king of rags and shit," who ruled the
Lodz ghetto for the Nazis (p.232). And we have the "princely"
black pickpocket with his majestic scepter. I agree with Robert
Boyers that Bellow is sympathetic to this black prince, as he was
sympathetic to King Dahfu. I agree that when the pickpocket is
finally beaten, "Sammler suffers for him not because he is a mere
mortal who has fallen on bad times, but because the idea of noblesse he somehow incarnates has been wantonly soiled by those
who have no real sense what noblesse might mean for all of us."[18]
But Sammler also sees the pickpocket as a "megalomaniac," *self*
glorifying, as one of the pack of self aggrandizing individuals who
are breaking down order in the world. Once again, extravagant
selfhood is the enemy.

These hungry selves walking through the city, patterning themselves on models of rebellion: Sammler's basic attack is not on the
revolutionary or primitive but on the use of *images* of revolutionaries, *images* of primitives to ornament the unsatisfied self.
Sammler is disgusted by the way ". . . human beings . . . mytholo-
gize themselves. They legendize. They expand by imagination
and try to rise above the limitations of the ordinary forms of
common life. . ." (p.147). They try, in other words, to be *more than
human*. Or again, Sammler thinks, "The dreams of nineteenth century poets pollute the psychic atmosphere of the great boroughs
and suburbs of New York" (p.33).

Conceptually opposed to threatening, extravagant selfhood, opposed to the life of personal gesture and egoistic sexuality, is the
corporate sense of life in which the individual is connected to his
fellow creatures, in which the rebellious self is subordinated to
the will of God. This opposition is certainly not new in *Mr.
Sammler's Planet*; we are reminded of Tommy's moments of love
in the subway, of Henderson's "I had a voice that said, I want. *I*
want? I? It should have told me *she* wants, *he* wants, *they* want";
of Herzog's ". . . have desired to do your unknowable will. . . .

Everything of intensest significance. Especially if divested of me."
But in *Mr. Sammler's Planet* the subordination to an order
beyond the self is more severe; indeed, rigid and repressive. It is
not simply a peaceful, ethical, humane life that is being affirmed;
it is a life without sexuality, a life that insists on duty, insists on
following contractual obligations, insists on order. Order is not
necessarily repressive—it can be the condition of freedom; but the
order in *Mr. Sammler's Planet* does not seem a loving harmony in
submission to which the individual can find freedom; rather, it is
like the voice within Herzog, the voice that demands order:
"There is someone inside me. I am in his grip. When I speak of
him I feel him in my head, pounding for order" (see above, p.200).
In my chapter on *Herzog* I argued that this order-giver inside his
head was the oppressive, guilt-producing father. Here again. But
it is much more serious here, for that voice in Herzog's head, the
voice he must reconcile himself with, has *taken over*, has become
the protagonist. And if that voice of order comes to Herzog from
the graveyard, Sammler himself comes from the graveyard. *Literally*. He represents the Fathers, the ancestors, the dead who control us. It seems strange that Sammler, never a practicing Jew,
should play this role; but is not Sammler the one-time cosmopolitan intellectual who does so; it is Sammler the twice-
buried. In *Humboldt's Gift* Bellow's protagonist lives in terror of
burial; in *Henderson the Rain King* and *Seize the Day* we find
images of burial. But in *Mr. Sammler's Planet* Bellow in fact
creates someone who *has* been buried—buried first by the Nazis
in a mass grave, then again, hidden from the Poles in Cieslakie-
wicz's tomb. He speaks with the voice of the dead, voice of
authority, tradition, order, against the modern American world of
extravagant selfhood. Like Bellow himself, he is an immigrant—if
not from the *shtetl*, yet from the "world of our fathers."

I have argued throughout this book that deliverance from "the
body of this death" (*HRK*)—a death the protagonist feels he deserves—is the core motivation in Bellow's fiction. Here again.

This earth was a grave. . . . The planet was our mother and our burial ground. No wonder the human spirit wished to leave. Leave this prolific belly. Leave also this great tomb. Passion for the infinite caused by the terror, by *timor mortis*, needed material appeasement. *Timor mortis conturbat me. Dies irae. Quid sum miser tunc dicturus.* (p.182)

In all of Bellow there is not another passage so clear and specific about the connection between the terror of death and the need for transcendence. But throughout the fiction (see above, pp.97-112, 172-75, 178-83, 196-98, 209-11, 214, and the following chapter on *Humboldt's Gift*) we find the same motivation, the same struggle. This is the basis of the need to defend the self. And note: Henderson, in terror of death, must escape from Lily; specifically he perceives her as unclean, rejects the sexuality she offers, and *runs*. This pattern of sexuality connected to uncleanness and death is found in *Dangling Man, The Victim, Henderson the Rain King, Herzog,* and *Humboldt's Gift*—but it is perhaps clearest in *Mr. Sammler's Planet.* We see a Sammler who perceives woman as unclean and flees from death. The earth—this "grave" Sammler calls it—is also "our mother." Tomb and womb are one. Fleeing death, one must flee the Mother, flee illicit sexuality. To leave "the body of this death" one must, in effect, leave the body, transcend the human condition.

This pattern of withdrawal is the source of the extended metaphor of flight to the moon. Lal speaks of the crush of humanity in India—"crowded in, packed in . . . and human beings must feel that there is a way out." This, he say, perhaps explains his sensitivity to a moon voyage. This same sense of the oppression of the individual by multitudes (often connected to Asia) is found throughout Bellow's work (see especially p.108 above.) To escape death one must escape this "tragic earth." Lal's argument is very rich in suggestion for Sammler. His imagination takes to space travel as it takes to Meister Eckhart. "Philosophers, men of science," Sammler thinks, ". . . are compelled to sue for divorce from all these human states. Then they launch outward, moonward, their flying arthropod hardware" (p.174).

The *tone* of the novel is Sammler's real spaceship. I mean simply that the abstract contemplation, the resigned disdain for this turbulent, rebellious world, lift Sammler off, away from the planet. At age sixteen his mother gave Sammler Schopenhauer's *World as Will and Idea.* (Herzog read the same book at the same age!) He learns that "only ideas are not overpowered by the Will —the cosmic force, the Will, which drives all things" (p.209). "Yes, and come to think of it, according to Schopenhauer, the seat of the Will in human beings is . . ." He stops, Dr. Lal prods him— "Where is it?" And only then, hesitantly, Sammler says, "The organs of sex are the seat of the Will." Ideas as weapons against sexualtiy, weapons offered by his own mother. This connection suggests strongly the way in which ideas function, in which abstraction functions, for Sammler. They remove him from the sexual "body of this death," from the womb and so from the tomb.

But here lies a contradiction, the essential contradiction in Bellow: again and again it is an isolate, an alienatee, who preaches brotherly love and community. Sammler complains of "agitated spirits" who "fled from the oppressiveness of 'the common life,' separating themselves from the rest of their species, from the life of their species, hoping perhaps to get away (in some peculiar sense) from the death of their species" (p.147). These are the egoists, the rebellious, exhibitionistic modern individualists who try to be more than human. But *what else is Sammler himself trying to do?* His flight from this planet is a mirror of the flight of those he condemns. As Bellow knows, Sammler, too, is guilty of a lack of humanity, of a rejection of the human contract.

Sammler tries to defend his own withdrawal. "The best, I have found, is to be disinterested. Not as misanthropes dissociate themselve, by judging, but by not judging. By willing as God wills" (p.236). Lovely! But does Sammler himself come close to meeting this ideal? Throughout the novel he continually judges. He seems, like Gulliver, perhaps like Swift himself, nauseated by humanity. "The place of honor was outside" (p.73). I wonder whether the intensity of the struggle of Bellow himself to defend humanity doesn't derive from a similar revulsion, from anguish at how much needs to be defended. But this seems only one aspect of Bellow himself; it comes close to being the whole of Sammler.

In his transcendence of this plant, Sammler, like Charlie Citrine in *Humboldt's Gift*, is continually *thinking*, continually *explaining*. James Harris argues that in *Herzog* explanation was a goal; in *Mr. Sammler's Planet*, a hindrance.[19] But in fact, although his characters continually try to explain the world, explanation has *never* been a goal for Bellow himself, and it is only when explanation stops that beauty can enter. Herzog seems healed not by coming up with a good five-cent synthesis but by becoming *silent*. In Ludeyville, seeing an old notecard on the floor, "to do justice to Condorcet . . ." Herzog thinks, "Condorcet would have to find another defender." And the novel ends with Herzog at silent peace: "At this time he had no messages for anyone. Nothing. Not a single word." Sammler knows that his mental gymnastics are obsessive. "Sammler had a touch of the same disease" as had the modern Americans he condemns—"the disease of the single self explaining what was what and who was who." It is part of the withdrawal of Sammler, his attempt to turn the world into thought in order to stay aloof and safe.

Sammler's politics are the concomitant of this withdrawal. Sammler retreats into a defense of the old regime. The insane scramble of egos can be seen as a madness derived from capitalism, which alienates the individual, makes him experience impotence, and forces him at the same time to succeed by competing with eveyone else. It is a game in which there are only losers. But while Sammler does not defend capitalism, he accepts it, accepts *its* crimes, and is horrified only by breaches with the status quo. He treats oppressed people as if they were spoiled children, and he does not recognize the ideological function of such moralizing. "Humankind had lost its old patience" (p.162). The universalization of people with specific needs into "humankind" and the use of the moral category is politics posing as morality. *Patience!* It reminds me of the old slave-owning class, teaching the virtues of humility to its captives. Sammler is upset with self-aggrandizing behavior only if it is rebellious.

Sammler is a character who lacks humanity—who *has to* lack humanity in order to survive psychologically. He sighs, "Poor Wells . . . could in the end only blast and curse everyone" (p.28). This is more or less true of Sammler. Projection upon projection. "Like many people who had seen the world collapse once, Mr. Sammler entertained the possibility it might collapse twice" (p.33). The collapse he fears most deeply is his own. The "dangerous staggering violence of fanatics" is his projection of elements he must repress within himself.

And what about Bellow himself? While Bellow means us to see that Sammler's conceptual model is a form of defense, he gives us no way to see beyond that model, no way to humanize the world. In "Distractions of a Fiction Writer," Bellow quotes Simone Weil, "To believe in the existence of human beings as such is love," and goes on to argue that the writer's job is to manifest this love. But where is the belief, the love, in *Mr. Sammler's Planet?* It exists only in Sammler's praise of his nephew Elya Gruner. But this praise exists separately from a dramatic form that would make it mean something. We don't see in the relationship of Sammler and Gruner a model of deep, loving friendship; we don't see in Gruner himself a loving man. The beautiful passage that ends the novel is a rhetorical tag, an ending not derived from the material of the novel. That tag has the resonance of so many lyrical, contemplative passages in Bellow. But the novel as a whole gives us not love but emotional withdrawal.

Is it simply a problem of angle of vision and resulting tone? In a sense, yes, but that angle of vision, that tone, are Bellow's fundamental choices. Besides, it would be possible to write a brilliant and humane fiction in which the angle-of-vision character were bitter, even hateful—but only if that character seethed with the subterranean energy of the writer, as in Dostoyevsky's *Notes from Underground,* or if a standard beyond the character's own standard is implied, as in James Baldwin's "Going to Meet the Man," told from the angle of vision of a racist sheriff.

But, intellectually and emotionally, the reader is given nothing to identify with beyond Sammler. In an interview in 1975, Bellow acknowledged, "I think of *Mr. Sammler's Planet* as a sort of polemical thing."[20] Ben Siegel shows that Bellow's own views during the years he was composing *Mr. Sammler's Planet* were close to those of Sammler; that Bellow, too, in "Culture Now," attacked those groups "bohemianizing" American society.[21] And as I pointed out earlier Bellow was in the late sixties nearly as terrified by disorder as is Sammler; and the color of disorder for both seems to be the same—black. "Angela sent money to defense funds," Sammler thinks, "for murderers and rapists. That was her business of course." We cannot define precisely Bellow's attitude toward this remark, but he did argue in a lecture in 1969 that "Negro slums are not inviting to bohemians, [who] . . . depend upon civilized tolerance."[22] It is Sammler who attacks "the peculiar aim of sexual niggerhood for everyone," but it is Bellow who is so trapped by fantasies of black sexuality as to use as his phallic prince a black man. *Mr. Sammler's Planet* is the obverse of, say, "The White Negro." Not only Sammler but Bellow himself is dealing with the same stereotype as is Mailer—with opposite valuation.[23]

Bellow, like Sammler, is obsessed with the sexuality of the young. Sammler is preoccupied with the revoluntionary who interrupts Sammler's speech to say "his balls are dry"; but it is Bellow who invented such a caricature revolutionary. Not only is such an outburst not *typical*; not only have I never encountered it in the course of hundreds of political meetings; but it is inconceivable that such a fool would not be booed out of the hall or laughed down. The New Left was—Bellow is certainly right—full of foolish acting out; but Bellow's version of that acting out betrays not merely ignorance but obsession, hysteria. Salter suggests, "There are precedents for identifying Bellow's bias and perhaps smugness as something common to Jewish mandarin intellectuals."[24] I agree, and I wonder whether many of Bellow's readers are not delighted to find their reactionary politics rationalized by such a brilliant writer.

Sammler is clearly, in spite of Bellow's awareness of distortions, the normative character. He is a polemical tool that allows Bellow to take a harder line—more repressive and racist—than he could have if he were to argue in his own person. And yet I do not see racism or defense of the status quo as *essential* to Bellow's politics. Essentially, they are the politics of withdrawal, not reaction. Politics and social struggle are *themselves* the enemy for Bellow, here as in *To Jerusalem and Back*. "I think the sixties will be remembered," Bellow said in 1975, "as the decade of frenzy, and violent agitation, having very little to do with literature or art. I think the sixties was the decade of the politicization (a disagreeable word . . .) of writers, painters, and intellectuals in this country."[25] This conception is itself political; in one sense, withdrawal is impossible. Bellow believes that society is "taking [people's] souls away. . . ."[26] In *Mr. Sammler's Planet* Sammler considers Captain Nemo playing Handel on his organ beneath the sea. "To take with one, whether down into the depths or out into space and time, something dear and to preserve it—that seemed to be the impulse" (p.136). That something dear is finally, in Bellow, the *soul* or *true self*. Speaking of the desire to transcend the human condition, Sammler insists that a person "has something in him which he feels it important to continue. Something that deserves to go on" (p.235-36). (*Continue* and *deserves to go on* are the language of Bellow's defense of human life. "If we . . . want [life] to continue . . . in what form shall life be justified?"[27] Again, Bellow's character is struggling, arguing, against the anxiety of deserved death. What is there in me that deserves to live?) Thus, in his withdrawal, Sammler feels he is not standing outside of humanity but is attuned to its core. I understand this as resolving Sammler's personal drama, his oedipal conflict, and yet I also feel the truth of the idea. I feel that this defense of the true self is what Bellow has always been about. He believes now as he has always believed that in the presence of "distraction" we cannot come to ourselves.[28] Withdrawal can be a way of preserving the true self. This desire to preserve the true self underlies his sense of the function of art. Attacking " 'activist' art," he argues that "the power of a true work of art as such is that it induces a temporary suspension of activities. It leads to contemplative states, to wonderful and, to my mind, sacred states of the soul."[29] While the writer may be withdrawn from the social world, he is in contact, Bellow feels, with his own core and thus with everyone else as well: "It so moves his own heart that he feels other people's hearts must be moved in the same way. And this has a value, which has something to do with the solidarity of the species as a whole."[30] In *To Jerusalem and Back*, as I will show, he speaks of art as a third force, which, drawing us away from politics, humanizes us and connects us.

Strangely, this is not far from the *radical* function of art as the revisionist Marxist Herbert Marcuse perceives it—the creation of a space of liberation. "The truth of art lies in its power to break the monopoly of established reality (i.e., of those who established it) to *define* what is real. . . . Art is committed to that perception of the world which alienates individuals from their functional existence and performance in society—it is committed to an emancipation of sensibility, imagination, and reason."[31] "With the affirmation of the inwardness of subjectivity," Marcuse says, "the individual steps out of the network of exchange relationships and exchange values, withdraws from the reality of bourgeois society, and enters another sphere of existence . . . the domain . . . of the inner resources of the human being: passion, imagination, conscience."[32] But for Marcuse the space must be indeed a *liberating* one; it must be committed to "the Life Instincts in their fight against instinctual and social oppression."[33] It is foolish for me to hold up Marcuse as a yardstick against which to measure Bellow; my point is that Bellow's desire for an art that is attuned to a core self and that connects us all is in contradiction to the *kind* of withdrawal undergone in *Mr. Sammler's Planet*—not into human brotherhood but into misanthropic isolation and an acceptance of the status quo. Most of Bellow's fiction, however, *does* make me feel the potentiality of brotherhood, of a connection among us all on a very deep level. As Tommy Wilhelm thinks,

When you are like this, dreaming that everybody is outcast, you realize that this must be one of the small matters. There is a larger body, and from this you cannot be separated. The glass of water fades out. You do not go from simple *a* and simple *b* to the great *x* and *y*, nor does it matter whether you agree about the glass but, far beneath such details, what Tamkin would call the real soul says plain and understandable things to everyone. There sons and fathers are themselves, and a glass of water is only an ornament; it makes a hoop of brightness on the cloth; it is an angel's mouth. There truth for everybody may be found, and confusion is only—only temporary, thought Wilhelm.

I sense a longing in this passage that cannot be fulfilled within "the old regime"—a longing for a loving brotherhood. "Not to submit to what societies and governments consider to be important."[34] This, according to Bellow, is the deep political function of poetry. In *Mr. Sammler's Planet* I do not find this refusal to submit. I hear a voice that denies eros, denies love. It is a voice from the dead.

To Jerusalem and Back

In *To Jerusalem and Back* Saul Bellow is speaking in *his own person*—a persona but not a separate character—about Israel; if we are interested in Bellow's political vision, it is a good place to look.

The first thing I notice is how *different* the persona is from the character of Sammler. The narrator is humane, gentle, funny, terribly open, not at all a crank. His descriptions are those of a man with *two* good eyes in his head: "The Archbishop is, to use an old word, a portly man. His cassock, dark red, swells with the body. On his breast two ball-point pens are clipped between the buttons. He has a full youthful clever face; a black beard, small and tidy. The eyes are green" (p.6). His characterizations are enormously enjoyable; for example, this sketch of Teddy Kollek, Mayor of Jerusalem:

Kollek is ponderous but moves quickly—a furiously active man. His is a hurtling, not a philosophical soul. His face does not rest passively on its jowls; its creases are those of a shrewd man. His nose is straight, short, thick, and commanding; his color is ruddy; his reddish hair falls forward when he goes into action. Balzac would have taken to the Mayor. Kollek is to Jerusalem what Old Goriot was to daughters, what Cousin Pons was to art objects. But no category will hold a phenomenon of such force. On duty (he is never really off), he bangs about the city in his car. He takes you on a tour of the new suburbs he has built in East Jerusalem. Computerlike, he retrieves the names of philanthropists and his secretary writes them down. "We can fit a little playground into that space. Let's send So-and-So a letter about that." (p.113)

Such memories are acts of love! Unlike *Mr. Sammler's Planet*, *To Jerusalem and Back* is full of love; love for his friend John Auerbach, who has lost his son, for Kollek, for all the Israelis who are "actively involved in universal history" (p.62).

Sammler, like Bellow himself, went to Israel during the 1967 war. Both see a terrible abundance of corpses. But then Sammler retreats again to his apartment in New York; Bellow certainly does not. Bellow's book itself records his involvement in the world, even while it also records his distaste with that involvement. Sammler reads Meister Eckhart, while Bellow reads and discusses political theory.

Of course, Bellow wrote *To Jerusalem and Back* in 1976, seven years after *Mr. Sammler's Planet*. Between them comes *Humboldt's Gift*, which is a return to Bellow's earlier mode, the more expansive mode of the rebellious son. The dead father is temporarily buried again. But the main change is from *character* to *persona*. And when we look underneath this surface change, we find that the politics are not very different. Surely Bellow's persona is no cranky conservative. But *To Jerusalem and Back*, as much as *Mr. Sammler's Planet*, records Bellow's perception of a choice between capitalism and violent rebellion out to destroy civilization, between essentially good Jews and barbarians and their chic defenders; it records his deeper politics—a revulsion, a withdrawal from the noise and the distraction of politics to art and to the sacred place at the core of the self, the place that connects us as human beings.

The stance of Bellow's narrator is of an "interested amateur." He is so evenhanded, objective, that he irritates an Israeli friend. Can there be two sides to the question of survival (p.51)? He balances theorist against theorist and only a few times declares a position. When he satirizes Professor Fisch for his fanatical nationalism he does so very gently. He acknowledges that Israel has not given enough attention to the payment of indemnities to Arabs whose land was taken. When he quotes Soviet dissidents about the dangers of communism, he does so with little comment —merely says that they seem "wakeful" and the West "asleep."

Beneath the narrative persona of impartiality, however, we know very well where Bellow stands politically. Bellow's tone of moderation is itself his strongest weapon for putting to sleep *our* critical questioning. Bellow makes us trust him as a man of broad sympathy and with no axe to grind. He builds up far more sympathy by his portrait of decent people cultivating their land and trying to live moral lives than any rational argument could possibly win. He quotes a taxi driver whose friend was killed by a terrorist bomb: "And this is how we live, mister! Okay? We live this way" (p.57). I am not criticizing Bellow for his strategy. The essential argument of the book is one I share: the human heart and human experience against any theory that would try to subsume that experience under its rational categories; and a very important part of this argument is conveyed through the narrator's modelling of a sympathetic, fully responsive human being to the living experience underlying "politics."

His compassion, however, is dispensed to selected groups; it is intensely felt for the Israelis, for victims of terrorist attacks anywhere in the world, and for the victims of Soviet totalitarianism. He quotes the old Tolstoy speaking of the growing horror he saw around him: "I can't make out how mankind can go on living like this . . ." (p.61). And thinking of the Israelis Bellow says, "These people are actively, individually involved in universal history. I don't see how they can bear it" (p.62). But he shows little sympathy for the victims of Israeli retaliatory raids. The corpses from the '67 war horrify him, but he places full responsibility on Nasser, not on Israel. It is understandable that Bellow would feel more instinctive sympathy for the suffering Jews than for the suffering Palestinians; it is unfortunate that he does not take his emotional bias into account. Bellow's sympathy is essentially one-sided and is used as an ideological weapon. The Jews are victims and potential victims. The Jews are civilized, cultivated, hard-working, intelligent. The Palestinians are barbarians and/or terrorists.

Arabs are hardly human in this book. They are seen as treacherous and vicious, even with one another. They live better in Israel than anywhere else—a defense of Israel similar to the South African government's defense of its treatment of black Africans. The book builds toward the horror of the speech before the Syrian National Assembly by a Syrian general. It is truly a barbaric speech, praising a hero who decapitated Israelis and devoured the flesh of one. I am sure that Bellow does not believe that most Arabs are cannibals, but the impression left by the book is that they are fearful barbarians.

The barbarians at the gates. Violence and cruelty occur only on the revoluntionary *left* and in the communist world in *To Jerusalem and Back*. Bellow is concerned with the plight of Soviet prisoners; but he is not concerned with the plight of political prisoners in Brazil, in Chile, in Israel itself, which has also been accused (by Amnesty International, for example) of crimes against prisoners. He is not concerned with the lives of the Arabs in Israel. He excuses Israeli injustice just as Sammler excused the crimes of the wealthy and powerful in *Mr. Sammler's Planet*: has there ever been a just society? Why are Jews called upon to be more moral than others?

We should, Bellow feels, awaken from sleep and take warning

against communism. He does not concern himself with the crimes of the status quo, the injustices of the class system, the oppression of the human spirit under capitalism. Consistently he attacks *ideology*. But nearly all the ideology he attacks is of the left. In doing so he himself becomes an ideologue of the status quo—and a particularly dangerous ideologue, identifying compassion with a conservative politics, allowing his reader to feel that somehow Israel, liberal democracy, and capitalism represent a politics of compassion.

Underlying Bellow's politics is a defense of Israel and the capitalist West precisely analogous to the defense of man found in all his fiction. The question, Can man survive?—becomes here, Can Israel survive? Can liberal capitalist democracy survive?

Throughout this examination of Bellow I have emphasized his defense of human life—against the metaphysicians of the wasteland, against all who see man as *done for*. This defense is once again at the core of *To Jerusalem and Back*. But now it fuels a specific ideological position so that to support the position seems equivalent to supporting man himself.

Here is Bellow's essential cry:

Even the Chinese, who know little of Jews, are Israel's enemies. Jews, yes, have a multitude of faults, but they have not given up on the old virtues. (Are there new ones? If so, what are they?) But at this uneasy hour the civilized world seems tired of its civilization, and tired also of the Jews. It wants to hear no more about survival. But there are the Jews, again at the edge of annihilation and as insistent as ever, demanding to know what the conscience of the world intends to do. . . . The Holocaust may even be seen as a deliberate lesson or project in philosophical redefinition: "You religious and enlightened people, you Christians, Jews, and Humanists, you believers in freedom, dignity, and enlightenment—you think you know what a human being is. We will show you what he is and what you are. Look at our camps and crematoria and see if you can bring your hearts to care about these millions." (p.78)

The tone is that of Bellow defending human life itself: *survival, annihilation, what a human being is.* I think of Schlossberg's great speech in *The Victim:* Schlossberg attacks those who argue, "a man is nothing, his life is nothing." He declares, "If a human life is a great thing to me, it *is* a great thing." Schlossberg rejects the philosophical redefinition Bellow himself arraigns. In "The Writer as Moralist" Bellow argues, "Either we want life to continue or we do not. . . ." A people at the edge of annihilation: in the passage on Israel's survival we are dealing with the survival of human life.

The life that must survive is a traditional life—a life of the "old virtues," a life that, even for Israeli nonbelievers, is at least "quasi-religious" (p.72). The whole humanist and Judeo-Christian traditions are absorbed into the image of the Jew. The book—like all Bellow's books—becomes a drama of survival against death. And the rhetoric of survival—which moves me as much as any reader— allows Bellow to blur political questions and ignore political problems.

This same rhetoric of annihilation/survival Bellow uses to dignify—without the need for argument—capitalism and liberal democracy: "Much of Western Europe believes that capitalism is *done for* and that liberal democracy is *perishing*" (italics mine). Again, Bellow has covered his politics with the drama of human survival. "Is this the full crisis of dissolution?" Herzog writes Shapiro. "We are talking about the whole life of mankind." And so he is again. But wait a minute: "capitalism" and "liberal democracy" are *not* sacred institutions. How can you identify them with "man" and "civilization"?

There is a personal drama underlying Bellow's discussion, the same personal drama that his protagonists act out in the novels: a defense of human life in context of a terror of death. I believe that Bellow *sees* in these terms and that he has formed his political vision around them. I would argue further that survival of mankind, for Bellow, depends on survival of the Fathers, of what he considers traditional life, of the *old regime.* He defends the Jews and defends capitalism against the Jean-Paul Sartres of the world on the same grounds Herzog used to defend mankind against the

Shapiros: "You are too intelligent for this. You inherited rich blood. Your father peddled apples." Traditional Jewish life of the Fathers is the standard in this book too. It is one solution to the peculiar oedipal drama of the immigrant, cultural drama in which the father represented tradition against modernity, Jew against gentile. I don't believe that capitalism itself is a significant part of the drama. Bellow understood in *Seize the Day* how destructive of human dignity capitalism has been; it is the manifestation in society of the egocentricity of a Dr. Adler or a Mr. Rappaport and the other clients of the stock market office, keeping information for themselves, grabbing what they can, ignoring deeper feelings. How can Bellow defend it here? I believe that capitalism simply gets dragged along as part of the old regime, becomes a figure in the drama in which rebellion becomes equated to a cheapening of life, in which revolutionaries become either barbarians or superficial modern intellectuals, enemies of mankind.

And yet in the midst of this drama, Bellow does not close his pages to theoreticians who support Eurocommunism or ask Israel to compromise with the Arabs. He paraphrases or quotes from intellectual after intellectual. This is a large part of what gives the book such a sense of openness and evenhandedness—and a large part of why readers felt *To Jerusalem and Back* to be unfocused, amorphous. But read carefully, all this theorizing is an important part of Bellow's political strategy: finally, what matters, Bellow insists, is not theory but human fact; not Professor Averni's mistaken view of communism but the fact that he is "an engaging fellow, far from heartless"; not the foolish rationalizations of revolutionary socialism by an ex-account executive but the human faces that Bellow sees in Israel, faces that are so familiar to him. It is the child playing Mendelssohn on the violin, reminding Bellow of his own childhood, or the shell-shocked dog or John Auerbach, whose son died in a helicopter crash. Returning from a discussion of American policy, Bellow feels "no longer in a Sabbath mood." He brings roses to his wife. "They are dark red, almost a black-crimson color. She is very pleased with them" (p.138). This passage closes a chapter—closes it beautifully. It establishes a conflict between the Sabbath and politics and ends by reasserting that Sabbath in the gift of flowers.

Politics versus the Sabbath: this conflict is at the heart of the book. The enemy in *To Jerusalem and Back* is not the Arabs but the intellectuals. Bellow warns of the "dangers that 'thinkers' can constitute for the rest of humanity." He sees their ideas coming "down over us like butterfly nets" (p.153). This is typical Bellow, reminding us of Joseph's attack on ideal constructions or Augie's laughter at the great individuals, each building his own Tower of Babel, his "version" of reality. Or Sammler's disgust with the "explainers."[35]

The *conservative* thinkers, however—Russian dissidents especially—*warn* us of dangers. *They* are trying to wake us up. No, the danger lies in left-wing intellectuals, in particular the French intelligentsia. "France is a country whose thinkers, sitting in Paris, feel they know all they need to know about the world outside. That outside world is what they declare it to be. . . . Paris, for centuries the center of European civilization, grew rich in collective representations, in the indispensable images or views by which the civilized world conceived of itself" (p.67). But the French, Bellow says, with their Marxist categories and romantic view of revolution as "cleansing," are cut off from the real world, the world of human fact. He attacks Michel Tatu, foreign-news editor of *Le Monde*; the portrait is delightfully vicious: Tatu "is one of those short men who have learned to hold their ground against big ones." Again, ". . . Tatu does not have the look of a man whose life is easy and I don't see why I should spoil his Jerusalem dinner for him—in his diary it would probably be entered as 'An enchanted evening in Le Proche Orient with an Armenian archbishop.' I decide to let him enjoy his dinner" (p.7). And so our narrator persuades us that he himself is more powerful than the superficial Frenchman with his easily injured ego. When Tatu agrees with the Archbishop that the Russians have retreated, Bellow writes, "So that, as they say in Chicago, is where the smart money is" (p.9). Tatu is not to be taken seriously—nor is his newspaper, which has taken an anti-Israeli position (*and* declined to publish Bellow's letter).

But the role of Satan is reserved for Jean-Paul Sartre. Sartre is the anti-poet in the book, one of the "masterminds." Bellow's strategy is to attack Sartre's tendency to turn the world into great theater and to see Sartre's attack as inspired by aristocratic contempt for the United States. Bellow asks, "Did this influential thinker and prominent revolutionist" (*prominent* is particularly nasty!) "know what he was saying?" (p.156). "A definition is a definition. Sartre is not conspicuously flexible. He has what I call the Larousse syndrome." He sees Sartre as caught up not only in theory but in out-of-date theory, still operating out of Lenin's theory of imperialism. "In taking positions or advocating actions that may cost people their lives one should be as clear as possible about historical facts. Here the danger that 'thinkers' can consti-tute for the rest of humanity begins to be very plain" (p.158). Sartre is a fool locked into his theories and ignoring—in 1949—the Russian concentration camps, as he ignores *now* the murderous violence of the Arabs against Israel. "A great deal of intelligence," Bellow sighs, "can be invested in ignorance when the need for illusion is deep" (p.162). Bellow's tone is ironic and bitter. He parodies Sartre's theory of "glorious, ineffable revolution": "An explosion of a hundred million Arabs can tear a huge hole in the rotting bourgeois structure. After an ecstatic time of murder will come peace and justice. The fellahin, their manhood recovered, will learn to read and be citizens, etc." (p.164). Again we see, in the parody, Bellow's distorted perception of the Arabs as barbar-ians. But his attack is on the theoretician who will encourage these barbarians to destroy whatever is decent in civilization.

In opposition to theory, what does Bellow assert? Essentially, the human heart and poetry. I mean not only that he is *more interested in* the human heart than in the theoretical but also that he *asserts the supremacy of* art and primary experience over any theory that would deny them.

And so he satirizes Professor Fisch for speaking of "fate" and "reclaiming our land according to God's promise," satirizes largely by placing him into conjunction with Tzvi Lamm, who speaks of the loss of realism in Israel itself, the change from saving the Jews to "redeeming the land." But while Bellow seems to agree, he does not argue the position, because to do so would be paradoxically to *defeat* his position.

To participate actively in political debate, political questioning, is agony to Bellow. Again and again the narrator retreats from politics, retreats, for instance, to a flagstone court in the Greek quarter, where he is "tempted to sit down and stay put for an aeon in the consummate mildness" (p.122). It is a moment of serenity, like Joseph's in contemplation of the piece of red string, like Herzog's at Ludeyville, Like Tommy's in Roxbury. Bellow goes on to say, "The origin of this desire [to stay put for an aeon] is obvious—it comes from the contrast between politics and peace." As in *Mr. Sammler's Planet*, as in *Humboldt's Gift*, Bellow is concerned with "screening out the great noise of modern life" (p.123). What a strange basis for a book about politics!—but it is precisely what gives this book its special quality. The politics of *To Jerusalem and Back* are, essentially, *poetry*: "Not to submit to what societies and governments consider to be important" (p.28). This is the political value and human value, Bellow says, of poetry. He remembers the modern writers who died in Soviet prisons: "Perhaps to remain a poet in such circumstances is also to reach the heart of politics. Then human feelings, human experience, the human form and face, recover their proper place—the foreground."

And so a scene in *To Jerusalem and Back* more central than the conversations with Peres or Rabin or Eban is the day of relief—sightseeing, drinking, talking with two poets in (significantly) the Old City; not central in its ideological content but in its emphasis on ordinary life, on *letting go* of politics, on human connection: "Drink and poetry and feeling for a dead friend [John Berryman]. . . . I couldn't help grieving over Berryman's suicide, when I recited some of his *Dream Songs*, but it wasn't senseless grief. Something else mingled with the heaviness. The transforming additive: the gift of poetry." And he contrasts people with this gift to "some of the politicians" he has met: "admirable, intelligent men. . . . But in them the marvelous additive is lacking" (p.106). Poetry is a way into the human core of politics, the human core politics *should* refer to. Instead, it is a buzz of noise, of self-referential language. Bellow withdraws.

A withdrawal—not, as in the case of Sammler, to a misanthropic single eye and a small apartment but to an art that celebrates human life and sensuous experience. A withdrawal from the *presentation* self to the *true* self. He cites a passage from Alexandr Blok in which Blok speaks of art as a "third force," a world belonging neither to him nor to others yet connecting them. Blok seems to indicate awed, silent, rapturous contemplation as the experiential feature of this world, and so it is close to what Bellow quotes David Pratt as calling "aesthetic surfaces": "lingering, loving contemplation of flavors, colors, shapes, fragrances" (p.123). The human heart; a state of contemplation and a mystical state in which "the barriers of rationality" are let down and mystery is communicated. Without mentioning God, Bellow is speaking of an opening to sacral reality. As I said in connection with *Mr. Sammler's Planet*, there is a contradiction between existing society and this space—a space that Bellow does not simply define but lets us—in novel after novel—enter. It is a deeply liberating space; whatever Bellow's surface politics may be, I am grateful for it.

To Jerusalem and Back exemplifies Bellow's longing for that space. The book itself is a venture into the noisy political world punctuated by withdrawals to the true "Jerusalem," the Jerusalem of "Next year in Jerusalem," as Jews of the diaspora have always sighed. And *back*. Bellow reluctantly, out of a sense of concern, pain, duty, opens himself to the struggles of a suffering people to survive and to make sense out of their position. Then he retreats again. Exemplifying the role of poet, he is caught between the demands of the political and the human; his synthesis is that the human and poetic is the core of any real politics.

He is rejecting the world of—as Blake calls them—*spectres* in favor of the world of what Bellow, quoting Blake, calls the *human form and face*. Bellow's revulsion from political ideology and practice is understandable—on the one hand it is terribly unreal and on the other it can have powerful effects in the real world; it can kill. Yet I find that Bellow is untrue to his own position. If Bellow wishes to defend inner space against the noise of ideologues, against the distraction of politics; if he is going to defend the experience of the true self against "what societies and governments consider important," then he ought not to *defend* those societies and governments. Bellow *does* take a political stand—a stand in favor of the old regime. Yet it isn't clear that capitalist societies make accessible much spiritual space to the majority of people. Bellow refuses to confront *his own* ideology, which, in the name of spiritual truth and human dignity, defends a status quo Bellow knows to be anything but sacred. It is easy for the class in power to appear neutral, to make the class *out* of power look like ideologues. Easy and misleading. Bellow himself is a "dangerous thinker" when he puts sensibility at the service of those in power and permits us to retreat in spiritual comfort from the pain of other people.

CHAPTER ELEVEN

Humboldt's Gift:
Transcendence and the Flight from Death

Once again in *Humboldt's Gift*, as in every novel except *Mr. Sammler's Planet*, Bellow is dealing with the struggling soul—with the fool wanting a new life. In the world of distraction, the world in which the ego, the social self, moves, man cannot be saved. But there is always *another* world in a Bellow novel: it is a world of love, of search for the light of God and the will of God, a world in which the person is no fool, or is a holy fool, in which the soul (not the ego or personality but something deeper, truer) *is* worthy of salvation.

These two opposed worlds are expressed in two opposed voices: the external world of distraction is given to us with comic energy; it is idiosyncratic, demonic, oppressive. Bellow pours out lists, creates a wonderful jazzy, idiomatic language. The inner world, the world of love, is given to us lyrically. It is full of quiet mystery.

It is as if Bellow's protagonists were in exile from a Platonic world of the real, enmeshed in a shadow world of distractions. The comedy of the novels is to watch them trying to extricate themselves from distraction, and, as if it were flypaper, getting more and more stuck. But the beauty *behind* the comedy is in the intimation of that other world, of a "home-world" (as Humboldt calls it). "Banished souls . . . longing for their home-world. Everyone alive mourned the loss of his home-world," says Charlie, thinking of Humboldt. Without this sense of a home-world Bellow would be simply a skillful, realistic, and comic writer. But infused through his narratives, encountering manic or oppressive distractions, is the "inner miracle," the "core of the eternal in every human being," intimation of a truer, higher, deeper life than this crazy mess we're surrounded by, this crazy mess that is, finally, our absurd, hungry selves. "We never seem to lose our connection with the depths from which these glimpses come," Bellow says in his Nobel Prize address.[1]

So that yes, Man *is* saveable, but which Man? Not the bourgeois ego, the self who, in *Humboldt's Gift,* buys Gucci slacks and sleeps with sexy young women and worries about fancy cars and plans literary magazines and builds his body and is the innocent victim of poets, hoods, and castrating ex-wives. Not the wheeling-dealing self figuring out how to survive his lawyers and the IRS, a big shot flying a helicopter over suffering New York, away from suffering lost Humboldt—not that self but the "listening soul that can hear the essence of things and comes to understand the marvelous." In his Nobel Prize address, Bellow said that "a novel moves back and forth between the world of objects, of actions, of appearances, and that other world from which 'true impressions' come. . . ."[2] Not the social self, but the inner self, the poet. The poet has the "Power to cancel the world's distraction, activity, noise, and become fit to hear the essence of things."

Oh, but it's not easy! "Society," Charlie says, "claims more and more of your inner self and infects you with its restlessness. It trains you in distraction." Go on—retain a poet's vision while you engage in legal battles and sexual encounters, while you try to be part of America with its machines and money and miracles of power. *Your* power sleeps. If you're lucky enough to survive in this world, you betray your soul, you become a kind of cannibal, a person with no inner being. Less lucky, you destroy yourself, performing the drama of the tragic, sensitive self-destructive poet, the drama America is pleased to buy.

Yet *Humboldt's Gift* would be a tedious, dull novel without Rinaldo Cantabile throwing $50 bills, made into origami birds, off the steel ribs of an unfinished skyscraper, without Renata, in the middle of the Palm Court of the Plaza, giving herself an orgasm with Charlie's foot, without Thaxter or the Señora stealing him blind, and, especially, without Humboldt leading him through intrigues and subjecting him to mad discourses on, as Charlie tells us, "Freud, Heine, Wagner, Goethe in Italy, Lenin's dead brother, Wild Bill Hickock's costumes, the New York Giants, Ring Lardner on grand opera, Swinburne on flagellations and John D. Rockefeller on religion." This is the pleasure of the novel— Bellow's pleasure, too—and yet it is also the world of distractions. In this world, everyone teaches Charlie (as they taught Tommy, Augie, and Herzog) how to survive, how to make it. Reality teachers, they try to make their materialistic reality his, to save him from solitude, from his innocence, make sure he's got a bagman, a Swiss bank account, a beautiful woman, a piece of the action.

Humboldt's Gift sets us between the two worlds. On the one hand is modern, slick, crowded, money-hungry Chicago; on the other is the "obsolete" past, Jewish ghetto life, the Russian baths, the dead. While others forget, Charlie can't help remembering, and remembering is a form of love, an assertion of value. He wouldn't remember, he tells his rich brother, if "the whole thing was nothing but a gyp." "No one would put so much heart into things doomed to be forgotten and wasted." This world of the past, world of the dead, is a correlative for the inner life, a temple of the inner life.

On the one hand is the toughness of the reality instructors, the world of business and power; on the other is the innocent heart, which is never totally destroyed.

On the other hand is the modern individual, man as God, a kitsch existential hero demanding satisfaction; on the other is a view of the universe in which the human being is part of an ordered cosmos, a "great chain of being," in which God is God and man bows to his will.

On the one hand is the experience of distraction; on the other is Charlie's experience of an inner light; in the one world the poet is fool; in the other he is at moments in touch with sacred reality.

On the one hand is a view of man as part of a natural world, his end absolute death; on the other is a view of man as part of a supernatural world, his end immortal life.

The form of the narrative in *Humboldt's Gift* is built on the same dichotomy. Early in the novel Charlie lovingly describes Humboldt's conversation—rambling brilliantly and wildly. Then he says, "in the midst of these variations the theme was always ingeniously and excitingly retrieved." Charlie's narrative form repeats Humboldt's conversational form. Compared to the two earlier first person novels, *Augie March* and *Henderson the Rain King*, Charlie's way of telling a story is incredibly complicated, flitting from digression to digression, memory to meditation to current event: a whirl of distraction, but in the midst of the distraction, Charlie returns to the theme, returns to his attempt to maintain his soul and find the power to defeat distraction. This accounts for the movement between brilliantly realized comic action and abstract, often long-winded, meditations. Charlie gets on a plane and *thinks*. He is arrested and *thinks*. He is about to make love and *thinks*. Often this makes for dull fiction; but in a sense it is a modelling of the activity of the inner being trying to defeat distraction. Of course Bellow and the reader see the incessant thinking as comic. And yet at the end of the novel, what is the hero prepared to do rather than write a screenplay?—"a very different activity": to think his way into an answer to the question of death and the disease of modern egoism. What I am arguing is that while all this thinking is fictionally a weakness, it is a representation of the very thing that needs to be saved *and* of the mode of that salvation.

The struggle between the inner world and the world of distraction accounts also for the insistence on parody, burlesque, and farce. *Humboldt's Gift* is tossed between a serious statement of the tragedy of the artist in America (the tragic story of Humboldt)

—and a parodic statement of that story in the exhibitionistic, self-presenting Cantabile, with Charlie the artist as clown; between a serious statement of flawed love between Humboldt and Charlie and a parodic version of love in the relationship, quasi-homosexual, between Charlie and Cantabile. In a sense the Humboldt story (which in itself is a mixture of tragedy and comedy) contains a parable of the struggle of the poet with the powers of distraction; the Cantabile story contains a parody of the problem. The Charlie-Cantabile story is the Humboldt-Charlie story in baggy pants. It both underscores the absurd elements of the Humboldt story and at the same time serves to keep it tragic.

The form of parody expresses what happens to the noble truth seeker in the veils of maya and on the streets of Chicago. Remember the actual legacy of Humboldt—the scenario of the writer who lives out a beautiful month of love with his mistress, then, to deceive his wife about the lyrical book he's written, repeats it with her: so the lyrical story is subjected to parody and the soulful writer becomes fool who loses wife and mistress both.

The job of parody in *Humboldt's Gift* is to pull the lofty hero back to earth, to give weight to the comedy of distraction. The job of the transcendent elements is to keep alive the yearning for and possibility of redemption of the suffering, humble fool.

II

And so in *Humboldt's Gift* the question, Can Man be Saved? comes down to: Can the soul be saved from the power of distraction? But underlying that abstract question is a simpler, more concrete one: *Can I be saved from death?* Overshadowing each of Bellow's protagonists is this terror of death—in some, disguised, in some, more direct, in all fused and confused with the question of human survival and the survival of humane values.

Charlie tries to connect the two questions: the question of death to that of the power of the poet to defeat distraction. This power, Charlie believes, is tied up by terror of death. So the poet sleeps—as Charlie himself has been sleeping for years. Sleep is a response to boredom, and the first principle of modern boredom, according to Charlie, is acceptance of the "metaphysical assumptions about death everyone in the world had apparently reached ... either you burn or you rot." But the poet's power can be released: "To assume, however queerly, the immortality of the soul, to be free from the weight of death that everybody carries upon the heart presents, like the relief from any obsession ... a terrific opportunity. ... Terror of death ties this energy up but when it is released one can attempt the good without feeling the embarrassment of being unhistorical, illogical, masochistically passive, feebleminded." Then the poet does not, like Humboldt, have to destroy himself to testify to the glory of his good. His energies can be used.

But this connection between the power of the soul, of the poet, and the question of death and immortality, is not experienced, not a living part of the fiction. We *hear* that Charlie is less afraid of death after reading Rudolf Steiner. We *hear* about his belief in the immortality of the soul. We *hear* that Charlie has experienced an inner light. But none of this does Bellow make real for us. He simply lets Charlie report it. And Bellow is too competent a writer not to know how weak is Charlie's newfound faith, how impossible as fictional development. I believe we are meant to take it as longing and as *denial*, defense against anxiety. In "The Heavy Bear," Delmore Schwartz, the prototype of Humboldt, wrote:

> The strutting show-off is terrified,
> Dressed in his dress-suit, bulging his pants,
> Trembles to think that his quivering meat
> Must finally wince to nothing at all.

These lines could be an epigraph to *Humboldt's Gift*. For if the faith in immortality is not realized fictionally, the terror of death is powerfully rendered. Again and again we are made to suffer the terror of being buried. Charlie could "conclude how bourgeois it was that I should be so neurotic about stifling in the grave," but it wasn't comforting, and he was not able to attend funerals. "I couldn't bear to see the coffin shut and the thought of being screwed into a box made me frantic." At the time he is telling us his story, he is much less afraid of death, but death anxiety nevertheless permeates the book.

One of the core scenes in *Humboldt's Gift*—brought back again and again—is of Charlie the successful man of letters, who flies above New York with Senators Javits and Kennedy, attends a fancy luncheon looking "in great shape," and suddenly sees Humboldt in the West Forties, a seedy section of New York: Humboldt eating a pretzel; Humboldt looking like death. His friend—whom he loves—but Charlie runs. Leaves the senators and flies home for consolation.

"Between the radically unlike there is no love," Bellow has said,[3] and this attempt to reject kinship with Humboldt is a refusal to love based on fear of death. As Schlossberg says in *The Victim,* "We only know what it is to die because some people die, and, if we make ourselves different from them, maybe we don't have to?" Charlie stands on his head, plays paddle ball, runs from a mugger as he runs from death. He deserts the near-dead; he *survives*—and feels intense guilt.

Again and again Charlie remembers how he refused connection with Humboldt. Charlie, the *macher,* survives. He feels guilt not merely over his denial of dying Humboldt but over his own survival. Like Joseph in *Dangling Man,* who would rather be a "victim than a beneficiary," like Henderson, who feels intense guilt over inheriting the legacy that should have gone to his dead brother, Charlie is obsessed with his role as a survivor. He feels anguish at being the beneficiary of the dead. "I stayed where I was on the sofa sinking into the down for which geese had been ravished." As a biographer, of course, Charlie knows, "the deceased were my bread and butter." We are reminded of Dr. Pep, in the wonderful monologue Bellow wrote early in his career, advising us to accept the fact that we live off death; to stop disguising the dead animals we eat by grinding them into hamburgers and croquettes. But Charlie can't accept this. Running from the dying Humboldt, he flies to Chicago, where his sensitive nose can still smell the stink from the now-defunct stockyards: the smell of death. And so when he sees Humboldt as the Poet-in-America, as exemplar to the survivors, he imagines Americans thinking, " 'If I were not such a corrupt, unfeeling bastard, creep, thief, and vulture, I couldn't get through this either.' So this, I was meditating, is how successful, bitter hard faced and cannibalistic people exult." Clearly, it is Charlie who feels like that guilty survivor. A cannibal, one who directly lives off the dead, his fellow men. Remember the scenario of Caldofreddo that Charlie and Humboldt wrote, the scenario which becomes a hit movie: Caldofreddo, on a polar expedition with Umberto Nobile, is set adrift on an ice floe. He survives by eating his companions. Years later, discovered in a Sicilian village, a sweet old man who peddles ice cream, at first he tries to kill the journalist who can expose him, but finally confesses to the townspeople. The film ends in a "choric scene of forgiveness and reconciliation—just as Humboldt, with *Oedipus at Colonus* in mind, would have wanted it."

As I showed earlier, the other wacky scenario, of the writer who enjoys his month of love only to have to repeat it in farce, is a parable of the conflict between the poetic soul and the powers of distraction. The seeker of high qualities who slips on a banana peel. In the same way the scenario of Caldofreddo is a parable of the ennobling of Man the Cannibal. It focuses on the guilt of the survivor and on his liberation from guilt.

Charlie is no cannibal. "Strictly speaking," he says, "I was no killer. But I did incorporate other people into myself and consume them." Consume them: Freud connects the identification with a lost love object in mourning or melancholia to a "cannibalistic oral phase;"[4] Whether Charlie is or is not aware of this connection, Bellow certainly is. And so, although he is no cannibal, Charlie, like Joseph, like Asa, like Tommy, like Henderson, like Herzog, feels guilt for surviving. Humboldt is his Allbee—the loser he might have been. Herzog and Tommy groan that they are being murdered, bled to death, devoured. Secretly—but clearly—they feel intense guilt for surviving, for being the devourers—and fear a death they deserve.

I have spoken of the *conflict between the soul and the power of distraction;* I have talked about the *guilty fear of death.* In order to connect these meaningfully, I must continue to use psychoanalytic formulations; in particular, formulations of oedipal conflict. I do not consider myself primarily a Freudian critic. As I explained in some detail in "The Politics of Oedipus," above, I see intense versions of the Oedipus complex as historically limited—limited to family structures in which the father dominated, the mother nurtured, and within a social context of severe conflict between generations.[5] The late nineteenth and early twentieth-century immigrant family fits this pattern very closely.

Bellow grew up in the midst of a conflict between contradictory traditions. This conflict was generational—father versus sons—at the same time as it was cultural. The modern world, the American world, assumes a life without God, a life in which death is final. Essentially, the world of distraction is this modern American world of the *sons* while the inner, *true* world is the "world of our *fathers.*" The struggle between these worlds, which energizes the novel, is oedipal at the same time as cultural—is oedipal *because* it is cultural.

The oedipal conflict is left vague, shadowy, in Bellow's fiction, dealt with directly only in *Seize the Day* and *Herzog.* But it is there. When Bellow attempts to create a larky, uncomplicated character, he finds it necessary to make him fatherless. Ironically, *Augie March* is the novel Bellow dedicated to his own father. And still the falsity of Augie's larkiness begins to put pressure on the picaresque structure of that novel. But Tommy is told by *his* father, "I'm not going to pick up a cross. I'll see you dead, Wilky, by Christ, before I let you do that to me." Herzog's father threatens to shoot him and Herzog feels deserving of being shot.

Charlie's father is dead, and we learn little about him; however, Humboldt is there to play surrogate father.

"For me he had charm, he had the old magic." Charlie is talking about Humboldt, but this sentence could as well have been spoken of Herzog. Herzog sees his father as a "broken-down monarch." Both have dignity, both are failures. Charlie's real father is, like Herzog's, a poor man who tries to maintain his position as a gentleman. Perhaps Bellow felt he had written in *Herzog* all he needed about that figure. Besides, here we have Humboldt, his spiritual father. Like Herzog's papa, Humboldt, too, attacks and accuses his "son" of betrayal—of entering the world of distraction. And Humboldt claims that Charlie has betrayed him with regard to his wife Kathleen: Charlie, he says, knows where Kathleen has gone. He tells New York of Charlie's betrayal and pickets the theater where Charlie is making a success. Like Herzog's father, Humboldt has a gun and with it threatens a "young critic," sure that Kathleen has run off with him. The surrogate father, jealous of his wife: a transformed drama of Oedipus. And Charlie feels the pressure of the dead Humboldt just as Herzog feels the pressure of his father. Finally, both leave legacies to the protagonist, and these legacies are in each case connected with the protagonist's salvation.

In a sense, Humboldt's legacy is Humboldt himself. Charlie, once Humboldt is dead, feels he has to act out that part of himself which formerly was acted out by Humboldt. He must play the role of self-destructive artist, and we see even the jealousy and fantasies of persecution (in a less extreme form) of his spiritual father. Freud (in "Mourning and Melancholia") pointed out how in mourning, and in its fantasy image melancholia, the lost love object is introjected by the mourner. The mourner identifies with the lost person. The introject is taken into the ego and is attacked by what Freud later termed the superego. Karl Abraham argued that sometimes this figure is taken into not the ego but the superego and becomes itself a powerful attacker.[6] Both dynamics are at work in Charlie's case. He acts like Humboldt, begins to fall apart, and attacks himself for his disaster. In this, Charlie is Joseph, Leventhal, Wilhelm, Henderson, Herzog: their stories begin when their defenses are crumbling, they are beginning to fail; they condemn themselves. But Humboldt is also the accuser, representation of the "world of our fathers" threatening Charlie with the curse of an empty life, worthy of death.

The real mourning is for the Father—not the literal father but the fantasy figure from childhood, figure of love and terror, worshipped and rebelled against. The real "work" in the novel is the detachment of the ego from the introjected father. Here, as in all Bellow's work, the Father is an ambiguous figure—a judge and failure both. The struggle of the protagonist is to survive both the judgment and the failure of the internalized Father. But the fictions can never permanently end the struggle. They resolve it temporarily in a symbolic form; temporarily the accuser/failure is put to sleep in the psyche. Then again it erupts. This may account for the dissatisfaction critics feel with the endings of Bellow's novels. The protagonist may be successful, but we're not sure how he came by his success, and it occurs in a realm in which it can't be tested.

The condemning father, the guilty modern son: this is again and again the situation in Bellow's novels. *Dangling Man, The Victim, Seize the Day, Henderson the Rain King, Herzog, Mr. Sammler's Planet* (where the point of view is that of the father), and *Humboldt's Gift* (where the father is not literal but spiritual). The imago of the condemning father is also projected onto other characters in the fiction, so that it becomes one aspect of the protagonist's whole world: surrounding the figure of the son are more or less angry, judgmental reality instructors. "Very well, Moshe Herzog," thinks Herzog to himself while Sandor Himmelstein wildly attacks, "If you must be pitiable, sue for aid and succor, you will put yourself always, inevitably, in the hands of these angry spirits. Blasting you with their Truth." Tommy Wilhelm might as easily be saying this about his father.

The ultimate reality teacher is the black pickpocket in *Mr.*

Sammler's Planet, who demonstrates his power in the size of his
penis, silently warning Sammler not to cross him and indicating
what Sammler takes to be the modern scepter of authority. This
scene brings into the realm of adulthood an image that recurs in
Bellow's fiction—the child molested or raped by the pervert.
Sammler, helpless as a child, is not touched, but the scene connects emotionally with the earlier passages (see above,
pp.104-105). The protagonist acquiesces before this male power. I
am *not* arguing that such an experience may have happened to
Bellow himself; I am arguing that the image haunts him, tugs
deeply at his fantasy life; it is an ambiguous scene: the rapist is a
horrible figure of illicit sexuality, the black pickpocket a figure of
rebellion and aggressive pride: they are, in Jung's sense, *shadow*
figures. But the scene is connected as well to a child's fantasy of
punishment at the hands of an angry, powerful father. The scenes
of rape represent acquiescence to the father, a passive homosexual acquiescence that fends off castration or death.[7]

The reality teachers are not, however, necessarily enemies;
often they love the protagonist, want, in the manner of a father,
the best for him. But it is in the manner of a father, a judgmental
father, and the protagonist *opens himself up* to their judgment.

Bellow's women, if they are not passive, generous, loving versions of Mama, are tough bitches: Joan in "A Father-to-Be," Thea
in *Augie March,* Mady in *Herzog,* Denise in *Humboldt's Gift.*
They are castrating women. They are dangerous, a challenge;
they cause the hero premature ejaculation, they weaken him sexually, they may betray him. They are rule givers, they demand.
Whereas the male reality instructors love as well as judge, the
female ones give almost nothing but judgment. The protagonist is
certain that they desire his death and feels they are in fact des-
troying him.

Essentially, like the male reality instructors, these women are
versions not of the mother but of the father imago. Herzog plays
"Grizelda" to Mady. He is "female," she, "male." These women

have financial as well as sexual power over the protagonist. Tommy, Herzog, Humboldt, acquiesce.

By acquiescing to the father imago, the protagonist stays safe. He plays the role of gentle, good fool, caretaker of the innocent heart. If, as Fenichel puts it, "aggression . . . plays a considerable part in the case of anxiety centered around a morbid fear of death,"[8] the first strategy of the protagonist is to avoid imputation of, or conscious experience of, aggression. "The persistent feeling of being wronged by everybody," Fenichel says, "is a projective defense against the opposite feeling of being guilty. . . . The conflicts around the guilt feeling may represent old conflicts with the father. . . ."[9] Karen Horney, in "The Self-Effacing Solution," describes perfectly the response to conflict of characters like those in Bellow's fiction:

His idealized image of himself primarily is a composite of 'loveable' qualities such as unselfishness, goodness, generosity, humility, saintliness, nobility, sympathy. Helplessness, suffering, and martyrdom are also secondarily glorified. . . . A premium is also placed on feelings— feelings of joy or suffering, feelings not only for individual people but for humanity, art, nature, values of all sorts. To have deep feelings is part of his image.[10]

Horney connects this emotional strategy with growing up under the shadow of someone, often "a benevolently despotic father." She sees the strategy as an externalization of guilty self-hate and as a search for affection through means by which it was available as a child—self-subordinating devotion.[11] Fenichel, and Freud, see the same pattern essentially as projection: it is not I who am the killer, it's the others. A search for affection, projection of aggression—both dynamics seem to be operating in Bellow's characters.

Denying their aggression, such characters project it out onto the world. If Humboldt experiences the world as his enemy, forming plots against him, Charlie, too, is the world's victim. Horney's description of one who effaces himself to solve psychic conflict is precisely to the point: "His terror of wrongdoing simply compels him to feel himself the victim. . . . He may provoke others to treat him badly, and thus transfer the inner scene to the outside. In this way, too, he becomes the noble victim suffering under an ignoble and cruel world"(p.223).

Charlie foresees what will happen to him in court: "I'll represent human dignity and they'll give me hell." Carrying an "old accusing smell" like a righteous judge into the courtroom where he is to *be* judged, he represents the innocence he knows is laughable in the modern world. He himself laughs, as Herzog does, at his own "obsolete" feelings. What neither understands, but Bellow certainly understands, is that his "innocent" heart and his higher feelings protect him from the death he secretly feels he deserves.

Charlie, like Herzog, is guilty not only of repressed aggression but also of illicit sexuality. Both sleep with too many women, and if they are proud of this, it is their modern, superficial selves that are proud; more deeply, both are obsessed with the uncleanness and criminality of their sexuality. Renata, says Charlie, was wonderful to him because "she was in the Biblical sense unclean, had made my life richer with the thrills of deviation and broken laws." The fascination of the criminal—what Herzog feels but denies, what Sammler is forced to admit to himself—all Bellow's heroes despise, yet manifest. Even making love with his fiancee felt criminal to Charlie—"There was always a trace of crime in the way Demmie did the thing, and there had always been a trace of the accessory in me."

In *Humboldt's Gift* as in *Herzog* this illicit sexuality is strongly connected with death. In both books, at a moment just prior to lovemaking, the protagonist thinks about "the cemetery bit." Herzog remembers a sexual joke about burial; Charlie thinks about Chicago as onetime slaughter capital of the world. Then he listens to fire trucks, ambulances, imagines incendiarism in black slums, thinks of the night as a rape and murder night. All this while Denise sits naked on the bed, brushing her hair, waiting for him to make love. Lawlessness, licentiousness—we are almost in the nightmare world of Sammler, projecting onto the young his own guilty desires. Charlie laughs at his own "obsolete sensibility," laughs at himself mourning for Humboldt instead of making love with Denise. But I would argue that his "obsolete sensibility" is something he holds onto to defend himself against his sexuality and his guilt—he is a good man, a loving man, who remembers the dead. It is the woman who is naked while he mourns. But the defense doesn't work, and death sits on his shoulder.

Sexuality and aggression are only two aspects of a total betrayal of the father. His whole immersion into the world of distraction has removed Charlie from his Jewish roots—from traditional roles, traditional virtues. Just as Herzog feels shame and guilt for wearing his fancy sportsjacket, feels trivial, foolish, deserving of his father's wish to kill him, Charlie feels uneasy at playing the role of the celebrity who flies from continent to continent with beautiful women, eats at expensive restaurants, hobnobs with mafioso chiefs. The Cantabile plot, which sucks him further into the world of distraction, begins at George Seibel's card game. Who are the other players?—a detective from *homicide*, an *undertaker*, a man in tuxedo (I think of the corpse in *Seize the Day*) who tells the story of his *dead girlfriend*. And of course, Rinaldo Cantabile, who threatens Charlie with death and later has him play the part of a contract killer. What does all this say about the world Charlie is entering? It is a world of death. Driving up Madison to Bronson's office with Cantabile and Thaxter, Charlie thinks about Waldheim Cemetery, where his parents lay buried. "But of course," he says, "we were not bound for the cemetery." The irony is twofold: (1) They should be bound for the cemetery, should concern themselves with the dead. What are they doing instead? (2) In fact they are, in spite of their manic denial, heading for the cemetery. And they deserve it. A strange paradox that runs through Bellow's work is that the survivor, who makes it in the corrupt, modern world, is a cold-hearted bastard and is worthy of death; the hero has to avoid seeming like this figure. He has denied the world of our fathers. *But* the loving, worthy man is obsolete, the victim of the corrupt world, which will do him in. *Humboldt's Gift* struggles with this double bind, trying to come up with another alternative.

Innocence is finally Charlie's, Tommy's, Herzog's con—a defense against guilt before the father. But the protagonist has to do more. Like a member of a tribe—of a traditional society—he feels the need to communicate with and placate his significant dead. Henderson plays the violin to his father, Herzog keeps his parents living in his heart and writes letters to the dead, Charlie reads to the dead and by hysterical memorialization and belief in immortality insists that the dead are not dead.

By *hysterical memorialization* I refer to the intense, vivid acts of remembering in *Humboldt's Gift.* Charlie says, "For my part there was nothing that I could forget." And so it seems. He remembers everything about his parents' old boarder, Menasha, down to the name of his music teacher. " 'Your teacher,' I said, 'was Vsevelod Kolodny, room eight sixteen in the Fine Arts Building. Basso profundo with the Imperial Opera, Petersburg, bald, four-feet-ten, wore a corset and Cuban heels.' " He remembers how his father "came home and hung his white overalls behind the bathroom door so that the can always smelled like a bakeshop and the stiff flour fell off in scales. And he slept handsome and angry, on his side all day, with one hand under his face and the other between his drawn-up knees." The memories are beautiful, they are acts of love; in the same way, Herzog's memories of Napoleon Street are the richest part of that novel. But my point is that they serve to keep the dead alive. They also portray the protagonist as One Who Has Not Forgotten.

"I wish I knew why I feel such loyalty to the deceased. Hearing of their deaths, I often said to myself I must carry on for them and do their job, finish their work." He is furious that Humboldt's poems are no longer reprinted by anthologists, those "literary funeral directors." He must remember Humboldt as he remembers his own childhood, must keep Humboldt alive. Charlie's narrative, rich with wonderful memories of Humboldt, does just that.

The inner life, the spirit that confronts the world of distraction, is in opposition to modernity. His daughter, Charlie tells us, knows that "Papa is quite willing to manifest the old time feelings. In fact, I must transmit these feelings." If, on the one hand, he is a disgrace as family man, as traditional Jew, on the other hand, he is all the more a defender of the dead, defender of tradition. He mourns for a lost Chicago, being pulverized by wrecking ball and bulldozer, a lost ghetto. "The ruins of time," he says of an old Jewish section of Chicago, "had been bulldozed, scraped, loaded in trucks and dumped as fill." The past, discarded. The buildings are like the dead of his past—cast away, allowed to rot, forgotten.

Only the Russian baths seem to have survived this Chicago Holocaust. Their dignity (and comedy) are set off against the Downtown Club and against the modern world. "Upstairs at the Russian Baths," Charlie tells us, "in the television screen in the locker room, little dudes and grinning broads make smart talk or leap up and down. They are unheeded." Of course, Charlie fears that he is nothing but a dude making smart talk, and so he defends the ways of the past all the more strongly. He has been given a legacy; he must nurture it against the Holocaust.

Politically, the defense of the past is a defense of the old regime, projection of lawless rebellion onto the young, blacks, and revolutionaries—"mobs breaking into palaces and churches and sacking Versailles. . . . emancipation resulting in madness." In *Humboldt's Gift*, unlike *Mr. Sammler's Planet*, there is very little of an explicit politics. But the dudes and grinning broads, the vulgar and forgetful modern world, are set off against the declining decency of traditional virtue. The connection between death anxiety and politics is expressed at one point in an interesting metaphor: ". . . Unless you conceive Death to be a violent guerrilla and kidnapper who snatches those you love, and if you are not cowardly and cannot submit to such terrorism as civilized people now do in every department of life, you must pursue and inquire and explore every possibility. . . ." Death as guerrilla is the enemy; civilized people are threatened but should not acquiesce; to do so is cowardly. Later Charlie pursues and inquires and explores every possibility when his aristocratic friend Thaxter is kidnapped by actual guerrillas. To defend the dead, to defend the values of the dead, the traditional values of bourgeois civilization, is joined in Bellow's thought to a kind of political conservativism, a defense *not* of American capitalism, represented by Brother Ulick, but of traditional virtues, which are endangered even more by revolution than by capitalism. But one reason *Herzog* and *Humboldt's Gift* are more interesting books than *Mr. Sammler's Planet* is that if their protagonists represent the old regime, they are also the rebellious sons, dandies, modern dudes. Charlie is fighting, first of all, himself. Still, he sees himself as a defender. His magazine, meant to help in that defense, is called *The Ark*. He is a modern-day Noah in the flood, trying to preserve himself and his species both. The flood reminds me of Elya, in *Mr. Sammler's Planet,* whose brain is flooded at his death and of his son Wallace, who floods the attic of his house, looking for a cache of money. The enemy, then—the "flood"—is both death itself and anarchic, rebellious modern individualism.

Charlie does not, however, simply defend traditional values. He believes that the great ideas of the last few centuries are exhausted. "The radiance [Humboldt] dealt in was the old radiance, it was in short supply—what we needed was a new radiance altogether." A new radiance—and yet his metaphors are certainly meant to remind us of Wordsworth's Nineteenth-century radiance. The beautiful "Ode on the Intimations of Immortality" must have been very much in Bellow's mind as he wrote *Humboldt's Gift*.

> There was a time when meadow, grove, and stream
> The earth, and every common sight,
> To me did seem
> Apparelled in celestial light. . . .

"Humboldt," says Charlie, using the same metaphor of spiritual light as clothing, "wanted to drape the world in radiance." Of course, Bellow puts a delicious comic twist on the metaphor: "[He] didn't have enough material. His attempt ended at the belly. Below hung the shaggy nudity we know so well." Again the nobility is undercut by the comedy. But Wordsworth is certainly the source of that radiance.

> What though the radiance which was once so bright
> Be now for ever taken from my sight. . . .

The radiance, for both Wordsworth and Charlie Citrine, comes from within, renders the world glorious, and gradually is lost to the "growing boy." A light from within: "I want to be clear," Charlie says, "that I speak as a person who had lately received or experienced light. . . . I mean a kind of light in the being. I knew long ago what this light was. Only I seemed to have forgotten that in the first decade I knew the light and even knew how to breathe it in." This is different from Wordsworth: shades of the prison house that had closed around Charlie were lifting. For both, the light is clearly connected to childhood, a world he shared with the now dead. Both move toward a "faith that looks through death" and connect that immortality with the vision of childhood. This light and faith are what deny the power of death.[12]

If one recurrent scene in *Humboldt's Gift* is the flight from the dying Humboldt, a second is the memory of Charlie's stay in a TB sanatorium when he was eight years old. The memory is of a little boy who weeps for the loss of his parents, weeps because he might "never make it home and see them." That same terrible sense of separation, that same threat of death, are still upon him. Ultimately, the "home world" Humboldt and Charlie talk about is the childhood home, the painful, loving home nothing has ever replaced. To keep the dead with him, to stay loyal to their values, is to preserve in his heart the core of his childhood world. It is an antidote to his own anxiety over death.

Nearly all Bellow's fiction turns on the protagonist's confrontation with the fact of his own death. But mostly what he "learns" is to accept "the terms of his existence," to accept death as Henderson did through the death of King Dahfu. In *Humboldt's Gift,* on the other hand, the narrative moves toward *denial* of death. The fact of death makes the protagonist turn—here as elsewhere— to an assertion of significant life. But here death itself is finally negated. It is negated universally, and so negated for Charlie, too. He flees the world of distraction for solitude because the world of distraction is a dying world.

This is, of course, a traditional view held by Christian culture. It is hardly a Jewish view, for in Jewish tradition heaven is in this world, redeemed. While there is great tension between the world as it is and the redeemed world, they are also one and the same. Throughout Bellow's work there is a concern for redemption in the here and now. Joseph's moment of serenity is in the contemplation of a piece of string. Herzog accepts his life as it is—"I must play the instrument I've got," he says. Tommy experiences a moment of love and compassion in a filthy subway. Always the world of love and goodness lifts up from, transcends the everyday world, and yet it *is* that world, transformed. Even in *Mr. Sammler's Planet,* with its yearning for other-wordly transcendence, the weight of the book falls on the dying Elya, who "fulfills his contract" in *this* world—the virtuous (though flawed) husband, father, friend. In *Humboldt's Gift,* however, the yearning for transcendence is much more complete—a Platonic transcendence, stretching towards an unrealized, abstract world of light, rejecting this "tragic earth." Like Bunyan's Christian, Charlie flees a world of death, a world in which he himself will die. And he asserts, or at least receives intimations of, immortal life in the spirit. If Sammler read Meister Eckhart, Charlie reads that modern mystic Rudolf Steiner.

Under the recent influence of Steiner, I seldom thought of death in the horrendous old way. I wasn't experiencing the suffocating grave or dreading an eternity of boredom, nowadays. Instead I often felt unusually light and swift paced, as if I were on a weightless bicycle and sprinting through the star world. Occasionally I saw myself with exhilarating objectivity, literally as an object among objects in the physical universe. One day that object would cease to move and when the body collapsed the soul would simply remove itself.

This is where all the connections with the dead lead us. Charlie has made the dead live in the narrative in order to break down our "metaphysical denial" of them. They live and therefore so will Charlie live. Converting—as he had once done—the terror of death into "intellectual subject matter" could "not take the death curse off." His exploration had to be of a different kind—"Real questions to the dead have to be imbued with true feeling. . . . They must pass through the heart to be transmitted." The death curse is lifted by his love of and communication with the dead. That is the real legacy of the dead, the legacy of Humboldt.

Humboldt, in his tender, loving, beautiful, sad letter to Charlie, tells him, "we are not natural beings but supernatural beings." Exactly the position toward which Charlie himself moves. This letter from the dead is like the dream Charlie repeatedly has of Humboldt understanding everything. But now it is a reality. The dead and the living are in communion. The two screen treatments are also significant parts of the spiritual legacy from Humboldt, intensifying the identification between the dead and the living.

Most important, the letter and legacy are an act of reconciliation. That's really what takes the death curse off Charlie. Herzog identifies with his dead father, takes his father's gun, his role of accuser—but forgives the guilty betrayer; then he is at peace, his own self accusation quieted, his guilt symbolically relieved. In the same way Charlie's oedipal drama is (temporarily) concluded by this act of forgiveness, blessing, from his spiritual father. Humboldt even seems to offer Charlie his wife, Kathleen—arranges that Charlie and Kathleen come together. At the end of the novel, he is about to see her, just as Herzog is about to see Ramona.

Finally, Humboldt blesses Charlie's new life, his life in the spirit, for it is Humboldt's gift that gives Charlie the money he needs to pursue his philosophical investigations and spiritual exercises. Thus, he will not be forced to reenter the world of distraction. As in most of Bellow's fiction we end up with a solitary hero who shows promise of "redemption." But whereas Henderson and Herzog are eager to act in the social world, whereas Joseph joins the army and Leventhal becomes a better family man and worker, whereas even the isolate Sammler praises Elya, the active member of society, Charlie looks forward to solitary spiritual development, which only later will he share with the rest of us.

With his legacy, Charlie is able finally to bury the dead. Humboldt's Uncle Waldemar and Menasha, his parents' old boarder, rebury Humboldt and his mother at Valhalla Cemetery (clearly a place for culture heroes). Menasha is a representative of Charlie's significant dead, Waldemar of Humboldt. It is his seeking them out and remembering that has won Charlie the legacy—his memory and devotion let him pass a kind of spiritual test, so that the guardian of the legacy yields it up. Now Charlie and the two old men act as pallbearers. The coffin is fearfully light, emphasizing both how much is gone and how much of a human being cannot be enclosed. "Of course," he says, "I no longer believed that any human fate could be associated with such remains and superfluities." He is still aching with the thought, ". . . how did one get out? One didn't, didn't! You stayed, you stayed!" But the moment ends with the motif of rebirth, from the tradition of pastoral elegy: "What's this, Charlie, a spring flower?" Bellow closes the book with a gorgeous comic undercutting of the elegiac tradition, which in no way denies it: "Search me. I'm a city boy myself. They must be crocuses."

Humboldt's Gift is built on the conflict between the world of distraction, a world in which people live meaninglessly and die with finality, and a spirit that transcends that world. Clearly this is not an abstract question in the novel but is motivated by the flight from guilt and death, a flight from oedipal conflict that is both personal and cultural. Finally, Bellow, through Charlie, is able to say *yes*, the human being can be saved, saved from death of the soul.

Humboldt's *gift:* the title has two meanings: his "gift" in the sense of poetic powers to struggle with the world of distraction, and his "gift" in the sense of a legacy that strengthens Charlie to continue that struggle, a gift from the dead to the living. Finally, that gift is the intimation of immortality.

But how seriously should we take this gift? Does Bellow mean us to read Charlie's transcendence of the world of distraction as credible or as, in the psychoanalytic sense, denial? Both, I suppose. If Bellow spins out his own longings into his character, he does not, unlike Charlie, permit himself any easy spiritual solutions. He maintains ironic distance from Charlie as he did from Herzog—and yet uses Charlie to express his vision of the struggle of the human soul to survive. One part of Saul Bellow is of course the nutty Charlie, as one part of Goethe is Faust. But Bellow sets that part of himself dancing, as he sets Henderson dancing bear-like around the plane, while Bellow the artist enjoys the dance.

- 4 -

Saul Bellow as a Novelist

CHAPTER TWELVE

The Unity and Development of Bellow's Fiction

Most novelists tell one fable again and again—some more obviously than others. This fable is not at all the story of the novelist's life; indeed, it may not even be the record of his personality.
His acquaintances may not recognize it as in any way connected
to the man. It is the story of an important, possibly unresolved,
portion of the writer's psychic life projected into fiction. If the
writer is in touch with himself, this fable will be extremely close
to the psychic lives of most of us.

The fable underlying Bellow's fiction begins in a ghetto-Eden.
The specifically Jewish character of the setting is important but
not essential. What is essential is the combination of suffering and
family love, the combination of a brutal exterior world with a
close family world—though one of conflict (DM, V, AM, H). The
boy worships and fears his loving and punishing father, while he
is given comfort and shelter by his gentle mother (SD, H). In the
background, besides brothers and sisters, is a Reality Teacher—an
older aunt or grandmother—who threatens the whole family with
the ruin that they are bringing upon themselves. She is hard on
the boy, and is able, he feels, to see through him to his core of
worthlessness (DM, AM, H).

The boy does, indeed, feel worthless. Filled with oedipal guilt
and having the secret sense that his being protected, loved, even
spoiled, will in the end wreak greater destruction, he anticipates
in fantasy castration (HRK, H) and death. He clings to his family,

particularly to his mother, to help him fend off anxiety and storms —economic pressures, the wrath of his father. At any time his Eden might fragment and collapse, but he prefers it, filled though it is with misery and guilt, to the blank uncertainty outside. The danger of disintegration is made real by the family's move out of the ghetto (H) or by sickness, death, or desertion of its members (V, AM, SD, HRK, H, MSP, HG). Partly, the progress in the fable is toward a reintegration of the hero into the loving family group on a larger scale, toward a return to Eden. The orphan (V, AM, SD, HRK, H, HG) goes to a new home. But before his partial transformation, the hero moves in submerged terror toward deserved doom. His problem is to avoid this doom.

There are, essentially, four ways in which the hero hides from death: (1) he plays the suffering shlemiel (DM, V, SD, HRK, H, HG); (2) he garbs himself in a sense of importance, of special destiny; he isolates himself from others to avoid their condemnation. which he secretly feels he deserves, and to avoid association with those who die (DM, V, AM, HRK, MSP, HG); (3) he turns reality into a construct in which he can live safely (passim); (4) he acquiesces to the Father and/or identifies with the Father (H, HG, MSP).

(1) To accept a role as victim, as shlemiel, as sufferer, seems a strange way of avoiding doom. But it works. It allows the hero to reduce his guilt by accepting minor in lieu of major punishment and renouncing rewards he "doesn't deserve" as a penance. Not only does this reduce guilt; it justifies the hero as morally superior. In another version of the same pattern, the hero splits into two—the Good-for-Nothing and the Father who judges him; thus he can control his punishment.

(2) The hero constructs a self to which ordinary laws and limitations do not apply: hence death does not apply. The sad, guilty boy becomes the unique individual with a "special destiny." He wears cothurni, like the walking abstractions in Genet's *Balcony;* he is in the rickshaw, not one of the coolies. The hero becomes "more than human."

(3) In the same way he turns reality into a construct in which he can live safely. In terror of the world-that-is, he constructs his own version of the world. Similarly, he creates a cloak of abstraction to keep off the Darkness. Instead of living in the here-and-now, he transmutes living reality into philosophical problems that he can handle in verbal form. In particular, *Am I worthy?* becomes *Is Man worthy?*

(4) Increasingly in the development of Bellow's fiction, the hero avoids doom by taking the position of the one who dooms, the Father: not merely the personal father but the Father as social authority, tradition, and order. In *Herzog* and *Humboldt's Gift* this solution takes the form of wayward rebel identifying with the position of the Father; in *Mr. Sammler's Planet* the hero begins as Father; the modern son has already been destroyed as a threat, though his echo is heard in a number of minor characters.

But these solutions aren't perfect—they are recognized by the psyche as false—and so the hero is not well protected against guilt and the terror of death. Besides, the solutions are damaging to the hero, especially in his relations with other people. Finally, the hero is faced with some new condition in which the old defenses are no longer viable; he is forced to confront reality directly.

In solving the old problem in the light of the new condition, the hero is surrounded by teachers. These are of two kinds (although sometimes the two are to be found in one character): The Reality Teacher, who shows the hero that reality is brutal, telling him to be tough, self-seeking, shrewd, to impose his power on the world or to accept the reality situation; and the Savior, an eccentric who teaches the hero that there are possibilities for Man, that the hero should cast off the burdens of past and future, should live in the here-and-now, for by seeing himself as merely human, he can be redeemed. Man can be redeemed. In *Dangling Man* Joseph's brother Amos is the most important Reality Teacher; there are no significant Saviors. In *The Victim* Harkavy is a gentle Reality Teacher, Allbee a harsh one; Schlossberg and, at times, Allbee, are Saviors. In *Augie March* brother Simon is the leader of a great number of Reality Teachers—Bateshaw and Thea are others; Mintouchian is the primary Savior, though not so important as Dahfu in *Henderson*. In *Seize the Day* we find the primal, split situation: Dr. Adler, Tommy's father, is the Reality Teacher, while Tommy's foster father, Dr. Tamkin, is the eccentric Savior. In *Henderson the Rain King*, Willatale and Dahfu are Saviors, but they are also Reality Teachers, because, finally, the world of the Darkness is also the world of redemption. *Herzog* has a succession of Reality Teachers, Mady in particular; there are no Saviors. In *Mr. Sammler's Planet* the minor characters are all in a sense Reality Teachers, expressing the cheapness of modern life; the Nazis are in the same way Reality Teachers; and the black pickpocket is the strongest Reality Teacher, denying with his powerful penis the ethical idealism Sammler tries to maintain. At the end of the novel Elya Gruner becomes the image of the Savior, the model of a human being who fulfills his "contract." In *Humboldt's Gift* Rinaldo Cantabile takes on the role of Reality Teacher; so do Charlie's lawyers and friends. Humboldt is cast in the role of eccentric, Tamkin-like Savior; Rudolf Steiner, the philosopher, is a more serious version of Savior. Of course, none of the heroes absolutely needs either kind of teacher—both are within him as fears and hopes, as contrary states of his soul: thou shalt die; thou shalt live.

Unable to employ the old avoidances, the hero must change. His present self is worthy of death. How can he leave "the body of this death"? Only by discarding his self. Yet it is precisely this self that he fights not to give up, for its loss is an image of final death. In other words, fearful of death, he holds onto his self; yet only by discarding this self can he conquer death.

What does it mean to discard the self? It means getting rid of the sense of being set apart from other people. When the hero sees himself as not special but only another creature, he can breathe without death-deserving guilt—he is no worse (if no better) than everyone else. In addition it means casting off the burden of the past and future. The true "I" is, like Sartre's *pour-soi*, nothing more than the total, spontaneous, developing system of contacts in an organism/environment field—the self is a construction formulated out of past action and future predictabilities. To live in the present is to cast off the death-deserving guilt of the past and the anxiety about the future.

The self can be discarded in ways related to each of these meanings. The isolated individual is brought to brotherhood (DM, V, SD, H), and therefore loses the sense of being set apart, by seeing the other person as real, sympathizing with him, feeling one with him. Or the hero learns to live in the here-and-now by yielding to reality as it is. His defenses crack; his vision crumbles; he lives before the awesome and lovely face of what *is* instead of imposing himself upon it—instead of substituting self-derived constructions for reality (DM, AM, HRK, H). To yield to reality, to live in the world as it is, is in part to confront the Darkness that lies outside human values, a darkness found both in nature and in man himself, a darkness grounded in death; thus, to conquer death the hero must confront it (DM, V, AM, HRK, H, MSP, HG).

Casting off selfhood is not like casting off the skin of a snake: it is a partial, not a complete process; it is learned and forgotten. For moments the hero stops striving—stops trying to make himself into someone who transcends the human creature, stops trying to live in an ideal construction and yields instead to reality; then, as Augie says, "the truth comes as a gift." It comes to Joseph, to Asa, to Augie, to Tommy, to Henderson, to Herzog, to Charlie. Each, touched by the truth, is imperfectly reborn as an Adam confronting the world with original eyes, is imperfectly changed into a loving member of the human community. Discarding the self, the hero has solved his problem of avoiding the doom he fears is deserved; at the same time, his joining other men in brotherhood is a return to the Eden he lost as a child: the loving, if suffering, family is simply larger.

Bellow's version of (partial) salvation proposes that a new kind of greatness is possible for men. Since the hero's personal life is justified, so is the life of each man and of society. Man's life is a thing of dignity, of value, of greatness—not the greatness of a Napoleon but that of a simple, loving man (DM, V, SD, H, MSP) or of a holy fool (HRK, H, HG).

The fable can be simplified still more. Once upon a time there was a boy who lived in a safe house on the edge of Disaster. His papa loved him but was stern; his grandmother warned him of the curse of Disaster awaiting him; his mama loved and protected him.

The boy felt that Disaster would come to him; he even deserved it. And when his father rejected him—or was it that he felt he deserved rejection?—he left the house, like an orphan.

Somewhere, Disaster was still waiting. To fool it, the boy—the man—wore a mask, and to fool himself he pretended that there was no Disaster and that he deserved nothing but the best.

But he knew. And so to placate Disaster he submitted to minor troubles, never fully believing that he would win.

One day the man's ordinary life stops being possible. And so he has to face what life is like outside his formulation; wisdom comes through suffering.

And what wisdom? It is that a man can't hide from Disaster but that he is no more susceptible to it than any other man. By seeing himself as part of the human brotherhood, by seeing all men as one, he can be freed from his curse—the curse that is, finally, his selfhood.

We have seen a very consistent pattern in Bellow's novels. Each arises out of the same need, each portrays a similar hero with similar obstacles to pass before he can become truly human. Each sees the same path to redemption. Then how has Bellow developed as a novelist?

All critics have noted the great change that comes over Bellow's style in *Augie March*. Actually, two short pieces published while *Augie March* was brewing give advance notice of the new style: "A Sermon by Doctor Pep" and "Address by Gooley MacDowell to the Hasbeens Club of Chicago." Both are in Bellow's metaphor-saturated later style—what Irving Howe refers to as a "neo-baroque" style,[1] mixing grandiose philosophy and slang, peculiar facts and eccentric theories. But certainly the style first appears full-blown in *Augie March*.

In *Dangling Man* and *The Victim* Bellow's style is reportorial, flat, perceptual. Whether in first person or in third, the style is all eye and very little I. In *The Victim* Bellow remains detached, in Flaubert-James style, from Asa Leventhal, following him around the city, seeing the city through his perceptions; in *Dangling Man* the hero himself seems detached from his own life. He philosophizes about an event afterwards, but interprets little while it is taking place. We interpret his life not so much with the philosophical tools he provides as with psychological tools. There are flashes of metaphorical statement, but generally the prose works through the acuteness and intensity of its *seeing*. Both *Dangling Man* and *The Victim* are brief, narrow in scope, limited in characters. At the beginning of *Dangling Man* Joseph promises to ignore the code of Hemingway and to open his heart, to introspect, to talk freely about his feelings. But he never does:

> At eleven I had a haircut. I went as far as Sixty-third Street for lunch and ate at a white counter amid smells of frying fish, looking out on the iron piers in the street and the huge paving bricks like the plates of the boiler-room floor in a huge liner. Above the restaurant, on the other corner, a hamburger with arms and legs balanced on a fiery wire, leaned toward a jar of mustard. I wiped up the sweet sediment in my cup with a piece of bread and went out to walk through large, melting flakes. I wandered through a ten-cent store, examining the comic valentines, thought of buying envelopes, and bought instead a bag of chocolate creams. I ate them hungrily. Next I was drawn into a shooting gallery. I paid for twenty shots and fired less than half, hitting none of the targets. (pp.106-107)

He is a brilliant camera, utterly detached from his feelings. He does not live the experience but records it; he is miles from himself. He implies an emptiness. We may associate the bricks like boiler-room plates with the terrible engine room in Asa Leventhal's imagination (V)—a vision that hints to Asa of the Darkness—but Joseph tells us nothing. He implies a futility worse than anything Roquentin experienced, but nowhere in the passage does he break from the terse style of a man examining an insect. He simply records absurd, disconnected images and then tells of two choices: he rejects valentines and envelopes for chocolate creams; that is, he rejects the possibility of love and communication and instead acts self-indulgently; he acts out his aggressive feelings in the shooting gallery but—typically for Joseph—won't let them materialize (misses the target and doesn't finish). A terse, teeth-clenched self-hatred is revealed in Joseph's style.

There are many foreshadowings of a later Bellow. The psychological concerns, the hero who longs to return to community, the metaphysical references: "The clouds were sheared back from a mass of stars chattering in the hemispheric blackness—the universe, this windy midnight, out on its eternal business" (DM, p.106). The philosophical passages anticipate *Herzog*. Most of all, the introspection of a crippled hero sets the model for all Bellow's fiction. But this is a tight, bitter beginning.

The Victim is more feeling, more human. Asa is alienated from others but not nearly so detached as Joseph. Asa cannot escape into himself; he must talk to Allbee, not to a Spirit of Alternatives. The acute perceptiveness continues, but there is more the sense of a struggling human being weighed down by the burden that is, finally, himself.

The Victim's style is generally naturalistic. Human life is limited and severely limiting; there is a naturalistic sense of inevitable consequences of actions and the constriction of an individual by the environment. Here is an example:

Just then, the blink of a yellow light in the middle of the street started him into a trot. An eddy of exhaust gas caught him in the face. He was behind a bus. A tearing of gears carried it forward, and he came up on the curb, breathless. He rested a moment and then went on, gradually slowing to his ordinary pace. His head ached. There was a spot between his eyes that was particularly painful; the skin itself was tender. He pressed it. It seemed to have been the dead center of all his

staring and concentration. He felt that his nerves were worse than ever
and that his rage had done him harm, affected his very blood. He had
an impression of bad blood as something black, thick, briny, caused by
sickness or lust or excessive anger. His heart quickened again. He cast a
glance behind. Several people were going in the other direction. "Let
him better not come near me," he muttered. (p.148)

Flat, declarative sentences, painstaking details, an intense relationship of individual and environment: Asa's physical depression
is precisely delineated and specifically connected to the smells
and pace of a hot city. This is a man struggling, a man caught.

A sense of freedom comes through in scenes with Allbee. The
very irrationality of a confrontation with a man who years ago lost
his job because of Asa; the arbitrariness of choosing Asa in the
first place and the absurdity of his refusal to let Asa alone, as if
Allbee were some strange angel sent to guide Asa back to humanity—these add a dimension of openness to *The Victim* that is
not found in *Dangling Man*. There, the Spirit of Alternatives
provides liberation only within the confines of Joseph's mind. *The
Victim* is also closer to *Augie March* in the pattern of the hero's
transformation. If there is hope at the end of *Dangling Man* that
intimations of death and spring may point to the birth of a new
Joseph, that hope is partly realized here. Asa is partially liberated
from the burden of himself.

Augie March seems to need no liberation; he is riding the
waves. Unlike the first two novels, this is a book of adventures, a
series of exciting events in which the central character takes part.
Augie, the picaro, steals, goes to jail, gambles, has a succession of
women, and escapes with ease from situation after situation. As
Hassan says about this novel, "Bellow's teeming images of our cultural life specify; they do not, like the images of Dreiser, say, or
like those of Farrell, attempt to *determine*."[2] The environment is
not an oppressive or constricting element; it is enthusiastically
loved. Augie is excited by and forgiving of the world around him,
so that when he is insulted by Anna Coblin, he says, "how could
you keep a grudge against anyone so terrific?" (p.19). Unlike Asa,

anti-Semitism does not affect him: "And sometimes we were chased, stoned, bitten, and beat up for Christ-killers, all of us, even Georgie. . . . But I never had any special grief from it, or brooded, being by and large too larky and boisterous to take it to heart" (p.12). There are no consequences of early poverty, no consequences of mistakes. The Reality Teachers, like Grandma Lausch, are always pointing fingers threatening, "Gedenk, Augie, wenn ich bin todt" (p.34); they are always warning, "Don't push your luck. Don't take a risk with the clap. Don't tell your secrets to anybody to satisfy their curiosity. Don't get married without a six-month engagement. If you get in dutch I can always spare you a few bucks" (p.468). But the Reality Teachers are wrong. *Augie March* is not so much a naturalistic novel as a romance. The plot, like those of romances and picaresque novels, is open-ended. Like Candide and Tom Jones, Augie can go anywhere. Unlike James's *The Ambassadors,* the novel does not turn in upon itself; it has no necessary direction, no necessary conclusion. Augie's adventures might go on indefinitely. Augie throws himself on life, and no matter what is chosen for him, he cannot lose. It is like Don Quixote loosing the reins of Rosinante at the crossroads: any road is the right one. Similarly, when Einhorn brings Augie to the whorehouse to lose his virginity, it is the whore who chooses *him*—as do Thea and Stella later on—and, of course the encounter is lucky: "I knew later I had been lucky with her, that she had tried not to be dry with me, or satirical, and done it mercifully" (p.124). Even when a bitter incident occurs, we are in a less constricting world than Asa's:

Factory smoke was standing away with the wind, and we were in an industrial sub-town-battlefield, cemetery, garbage crater, violet welding scald, mountains of tires sagging, and ashes spuming like crests in front of a steamer. Hooverville crate camps, plaque and war fires like the boiling pinnacle of all sackings and Napoleonic Moscow burnings. The freight stopped with a banging and concussion, and we jumped out and were getting over the tracks when someone got us by the shoulders from behind and gave us each a boot in the ass. It was a road dick. He

wore a Stetson and a pistol hung on the front of his vest; his whisky
face was red as a winter apple and a crazy saliva patch shone on his
chin. He yelled, "Next time I'll shoot the shit out of you!" So we ran,
and he threw rocks past us. I wished that I could lay for him till he
came off duty and tear his windpipe out. (p.170)

The sordid, even evil environment is here, but it does not define
Augie's life. We are reminded of what Padilla (involved in a
stolen textbooks racket) tells Augie: "I might get into a little
trouble, but I never would let them make it my trouble, get it?"
(p.190). The fumes of the bus exhaust enter Asa's mood, his very
body; the rocks the cop throws just make Augie angry for awhile.
His essential lack of involvement with the environment can be
seen in the style: the description of the cop is unrelated to how
Augie feels, it relates to the cop himself, in his "crazy saliva
patch." We could be made to feel how Augie is hunted by this
animal-like person; instead we focus on the exuberance of description. The rendering of the landscape also is seen without relation
to Augie; it is a wildly shifting, metaphorical description, which
generalizes beyond the scene to the world of war and international politics.

The generalizing quality is part of the overspilling that occurs
throughout the novel. "I am an American," Augie begins. Bellow
is trying to affirm the possibilities of life, freedom, and greatness
in America. Like Whitman, Bellow hurls exuberant lists at the
reader. Augie rides in the City Hall elevator, for example, with

bigshots and operators, commissioners, grabbers, heelers, tipsters,
hoodlums, wolves, fixers, plaintiffs, flatfeet, men in Western hats and
women in lizard shoes and fur coats, hothouse and arctic drafts mixed
up, brute things and airs of sex, evidence of heavy feeding and system-
atic shaving, of calculations, grief, not caring, and hopes of tremendous
millions in concrete to be poured or whole Mississippis of bootleg
whisky and beer. (p.39)

There is a grand, generous quality to the book; it is crammed with
enough characters for a half dozen novels; it is as spendthrift of
incidents as Simon is of money. The "cult of experience" that

Rahv finds in American writing is well illustrated here. And not
only experiences but ideas: the book is loose-bellied; it contains
passage upon passage of philosophical dialogue disconnected
from plot. Like Whitman's *Song of Myself,* like Melville's *Moby
Dick,* many episodes, many conversations could be eliminated
without injuring the book: because the essence of the book is not
in its detail but in its accumulation. As Howe says about the style
of *Augie March,* it functions "to communicate, above all, the sense
that men are still alive."[3] The style says that life is open, is possibilities, is freedom. The earth is "terra incognita"—a place that no
Reality Teacher can systematize. Keith Opdahl, noting the less
dense texture of this novel, says that the listing and the avoidance
of concrete particulars show Augie's distaste for reality (in spite of
what Augie may pretend);[4] but I think that while Bellow's use of
style is mainly intended to defend himself against the bitterness of
life, it is, nonetheless, an honest expression of love, embracing,
just as Whitman wanted to, all America. It expresses possibilities:
life is not definable but open and mysterious. A naturalistic style
would not have been able to express this open world. Here, for instance, is a list describing the students at the city college Augie
attends:

In the mixture there was beauty—a good proportion—and pimple-
insolence, and parricide faces, gum-chew innocence, labor-fodder and
secretarial forces, Danish stability, Dago inspiration, catarrh-hampered
mathematical genius; there were waxed-eared shovelers' children, sex-
promising businessmen's daughters—an immense sampling of a tremendous host, the multitudes of holy writ, begotten by West-moving,
factor-shoved parents. Or me, the by-blow of a traveling man. (p.125)

Energy emanates, even grandeur. Long philosophical statements
rich in metaphor and conjoining slang and metaphysics introduce
many of the chapters. Metaphor, as in the following example (and
the example just quoted), magnifies description:

We went through Gary and Hammond that day, on a trailer from Flint,
by docks and dumps of sulphur and coal, and flames seen by their heat,

not light, in the space of noon air among the black, huge Pasiphae cows and other columnar animals, headless, rolling a rust of smoke and connected in an enormous statuary of hearths and mills—here and there an old boiler or a hill of cinders in the bulrush spawning-holes of frogs. If you've seen a winter London open thundering mouth in its awful last minutes of river light or have come with cold clanks from the Alps into Torino in December white steam then you've known like greatness of place. (p.90)

Here the outskirts of Chicago are given mythological significance and the permanence of statuary; they are ennobled by comparison with a godlike London and a majestic Torino. They are made strange by the long, broken sentence and the peculiar syntax— "space of noon air," "December white steam." As Norman Podhoretz has said, Bellow's style in *Augie March* "expresses not an attempt to wall off the Philistines, but precisely a sense of joyous connections with the common grain of American life."[5]

It seems strange that this book should have been written between 1949 and 1952, a period for which *Joe McCarthy* and *Korea* are symptomatic words; strange to find an affirmative book in a period that sees the breakdown of the last remains of the wartime entente between the United States and the USSR and the election of Eisenhower as president and of conservative majorities in Congress.

Yet the affirmative quality of *Augie March* is in keeping with the views of the editors and many of the contributors to *Partisan Review*, to which Bellow contributed (see chapter one), which was managed by his friends, and to which other friends contributed—Isaac Rosenfeld, Delmore Schwartz, Wallace Markfield, Alfred Kazin. In 1952 *Partisan Review* conducted a book-length symposium called "Our Country and Our Culture," which asked whether the relation between American intellectual and America had not changed; whether the intellectual was not now ready to accept life in America, whether he had not in fact already come out of exile. The implication of the opening editorial statement was that he had, and that this was for the better:

We have obviously come a long way from the earlier rejection of America as spiritually barren, from the attacks of Mencken on the "booboisie," and the Marxist picture of America in the thirties as a land of capitalist reaction. . . . Obviously this overwhelming change involves a new image of America. Politically, there is a recognition that the kind of democracy which exists in America has an intrinsic and positive value. . . . More and more writers have ceased to think of themselves as rebels and exiles. They now believe that their values, if they are to be realized at all, must be realized in America and in relation to the actuality of American life.[6]

With this affirmative view Bellow concurs—or wants to. In 1964 he told an interviewer something that throws strong light on his shift of style and affirmative attitude: "Well, I am a melancholic—a depressive temperament. But I long ago stopped enjoying melancholy—I got heartily sick of my own character about fifteen years ago [around 1949-50]. Sometimes I think these comic outbursts are directed against my own depressive tendencies."[7] This is a surprising statement—the admission of a decision to be affirmative in opposition to his own character—surprising especially in the light of the following quotation from "Distractions of a Fiction Writer":

Today it is hard for . . . [the writer] to declare with Joseph Conrad that the world is a temple. He would have to assert, 'It *is* a temple.' And that would already be a mistake. The feeling of sacredness is beyond price, but the assertion has very little value. *Therefore the novelist will make no assertion for the sake of strengthening himself.* (p.2, italics mine)

But this is exactly what Bellow admits to having done, and so we question the assertion. In the same way, we may question Augie's *amor fati*, or "mysterious adoration of what occurs" (AM, p.523). For in an article on Dreiser written in 1951, while in the middle of *Augie March*, Bellow wrote that "Dreiser bitterly, grudgingly admits his *amor fati*. This is what is so moving in him, his balkiness and sullenness, and then his admission of allegiance to life."[8] To feel this allegiance in spite of the low facts of existence may be "beyond price"; but perhaps what Bellow has done is to wish he could feel it. At least, he has exaggerated his allegiance to life, has been forced in his affirmation. He exemplifies the intellectuals Irving Howe criticizes in the 1952 symposium in *Partisan Review*. Howe, rejecting the affirmative views of the editors, suggests that "it is the readiness of certain intellectuals to make their peace or strike a truce with the status quo that impels them to willed affirmations about America which many of them, in their hearts and bones, do not feel."[9]

In *Augie March* Bellow seems self-consciously to choose hope, but to be uncertain in the choice. Perhaps this is why he feels the novel is unsuccessful, too "effusive and uncritical," and the hero "too ingenuous."[10] Perhaps, too, this is why Maxwell Geismar feels the novel to be "a declaration of insight and intention rather than a record of achievement."[11]

In "Distractions of a Fiction Writer," Bellow insists that the writer remain removed from the marketplace and bowling alley. There, as in "camp and barracks, you drew sneers and hatred if you read books or spoke in your own style . . . Don't drag after the mob protesting that you're not a writer at all but a fisherman or farmer. It would be fear only that made you say such things: the shame of being divorced by differences from other men, and also the fear of the savage strength of the many." Regretfully, Bellow, unlike the *Partisan Review* editors, assumes the necessity of the alienated artist. The writer must remain alone and out of the stream of his society's energy. Bellow continues:

Once in a while he is visited by the thought that he is sitting still in the midst of the most widespread destruction. . . . Under it all, perhaps, he reflects, is a hatred of individual being. 'Let it be obliterated' is the secret message that we hear. . . . If that is the case, the writer, like the minister of a religion, feels that perhaps he is anachronistic. (pp.11-12)

Bellow's image of the artist is of the late nineteenth century: a kind of priest bringing value to the world, a mad world that rejects the individual. Bellow defends him, and in so doing cites

Whitman: " 'The priest departs, the divine literatus comes' "
(p.12). But the effect is of a priest in the presence of a hostile mob
and a ticking bomb. As an answer Bellow tells the writer to care
about his characters: such a manifestation of love is an antidote
for our culture (p.18).

That this is despairing hope is clear, as is the fact that Bellow's
yea is more meaningfully a nay. Clear also is his intent: to combat
"widespread destruction" as well as his own "depressive tendencies" through his craft—therefore the *Adventures,* therefore
the overflowing style and the possibility of love and freedom for
an individual.

Seize the Day is Bellow's finest novel. I think the reason is that
Bellow is able to fuse the psychological naturalism of *Dangling
Man* and *The Victim* with the lyrical, cosmic quality of *Augie
March.* This is a lyrical novel of high intensity in which the concrete, everyday world is intensely present. The world is to be suffered and to be loved. The New York of *Seize the Day* is there—
every agonized breath of it. How acutely we feel the weight of
Tommy's gross body, the pressure of the crowded broker's office;
but acute too is the spring of Tommy's unsatisfied love, his
yearning for a true life in the false city. More than with Joseph or
Asa, we suffer with Tommy and we long for his deliverance
largely because he seems so rich in potentiality of love and imagination. In the materialistic brutality of the city Tommy's story
hints at a world of beauty and mystery.

The richness of Augie's style is not lost in *Seize the Day.* The
third person narrative cannot be as exuberant and lyrical as
Augie's first person narrative, but the language of Tommy's
thoughts and perceptions is metaphorical and slangy. It is filled
with questions, abrupt transitions, and unexpected insights:

> On that very same afternoon he didn't hold so high an opinion of this
> same onrush of loving kindness. What did it come to? . . . It was only
> another one of those subway things. Like having a hard-on at random. . . .
> Wilhelm had a queer feeling about the chicken industry, that it was
> sinister. On the road, he frequently passed chicken farms. Those big,

rambling, wooden buildings out in the neglected fields; they were like prisons. The lights burned all night in them to cheat the poor hens into laying. Then the slaughter. Pile all the coops of the slaughtered on end, and in one week they'd go higher than Mount Everest or Mount Serenity. The blood filling the Gulf of Mexico. The chicken shit, acid, burning the earth.

How old—old this Mr. Rappaport was! Purple stains were buried in the flesh of his nose, and the cartilage of his ear was twisted like a cabbage heart. Beyond remedy by glasses, his eyes were smoky and faded. (pp.85—86)

The perceptions are fantastic; they have an intensity and clarity that makes them seem to grope out toward a realm of psychological or metaphysical reality. "A long perfect ash formed on the end of the cigar, the white ghost of the leaf with all its veins and its fainter pungency. It was ignored, in its beauty, by the old man. For it was beautiful. Wilhelm he ignored as well" (p.87). This is Bellow's mature style: rich in perception, rich in value. It stretches concrete images until they point to a place beyond words. Such style is illustrated in a passage describing a passing mood of Tommy's. Tommy Wilhelm has just denied wishing the death of his father: when his father dies, he will, he feels, be robbed. Tamkin, half-fake, half-guru, asks, "You love your old man?"

Wilhelm grasped at this. "Of course, of course I love him. My father. My mother—" As he said this there was a great pull at the very center of his soul. When a fish strikes the line you feel the live force in your hand. A mysterious being beneath the water, driven by hunger, has taken the hook and rushes away and fights, writhing. Wilhelm never identified what struck within him. It did not reveal itself. It got away. (pp.92—93)

It "got away," as did the truth in Asa's dream and in his moment of near discovery at Harkavy's, as did the moments of understanding of Joseph and Augie. Intangible truth avoids Tommy Wilhelm just as final understanding of the novel avoids the reader. Perhaps it is largely for this indication of a significant pattern in human life—indication without definition—that we read

the Arnewi or Wariri represent, or the lioness, or the tomb-house, does not matter so much as that they *do* represent. Like Ahab's doubloon or the whale itself, they demand a search for equivalents, for a near allegorical reading. The texture, then, is symbolical-allegorical even if we cannot read the novel as consistent allegory. Indeed, Bellow's image of life in *Henderson the Rain King* is of a highly patterned reality with symbolic meanings. So much so that Henderson's affirmation does not seem an affirmation of our world, only of his; not of America but of a mental, metropolitan Africa.

Just as, after *Augie March,* Bellow retrenched with *Seize the Day,* returning to a real city environment, a naturalistic base for metaphysical operations, so after *Henderson* Bellow returns to the city in *Herzog.* But the novel is as hermetically sealed off from society as *Henderson.* What is real is the mind of Herzog, a kind of *mental* traveller. The novel is full of ideas, as if Bellow were trying consciously to create an American philosophical-social novel, the lack of which Philip Rahv had decried in "The Cult of Experience in American Writing." But the ideas are really correlatives of Herzog's alienation and masochism and of his desire to become human. So we don't get a reliable picture of contemporary America—only of Herzog's mind. It is exciting to see this mind concern itself with ideas, to see an intellectual bringing ideas into his emotional life. But largely we feel about the idea-filled Herzog (just as Bellow means us to) the same way Herzog feels about Nachman, his visionary friend: "Herzog could still see him as he had been at six. In fact he could not dismiss his vision of the two Nachmans, side by side. And it was the child with his fresh face, the smiling gap in his front teeth, the buttoned blouse and the short pants that was real, not this gaunt apparition of crazy, lecturing Nachman" (133).

It is not the "crazy, lecturing" Herzog who is real; it is Herzog as a child; it is the world of his Montreal-Jewish childhood that is most real in the novel. That world and a few vivid scenes: Mady putting on her make-up, the trials in the courtroom, the death of

Herzog's mother. They have the power and the intensity not of myth but of ordinary life experienced in a state of heightened consciousness; they have the perception of Bellow's naturalistic fiction, pulsating with reality beyond the here-and-now.

Herzog represents a conscious effort by Bellow to write of an intellectual cut off from friends and country who struggles, largely with success, to return to community. But just as Henderson can make contact only by letter with Lily and by dance with a symbolic Child, so Herzog can experience only joyful communion in the woods of Massachusetts. Once again, Bellow has been able to forget the hardboildom of the Hemingway school, which Joseph attacks in *Dangling Man*. Once again, he has created a character most beautiful in his longing to be beautiful. But once again, he has been unable to bring this character back convincingly into full community. Bellow has to persuade us of Herzog's potential loving kindness and sociality by *style*—particularly by the weaving of Moses Herzog's lyrical suffering and loving into informational letters and cityscape descriptions, the weaving of wisdom passages and metaphysics into prosaic narrative. We feel in the complex tone a mysterious human solution in whom coexist poetry and prose, absurdity and bitterness and irony and intellectuality and passion and sorrow and guilt and dignity: a style well fitted to a fiction attempting to affirm the value of human life.

In the earlier edition of this study, I hoped that "in Bellow's next novel the hero will begin with a sense of community and struggle to live in and create *a* community—to make in our society a community in which a man can find fulfillment." That next novel was *Mr. Sammler's Planet*. Belief in the human community, in one's responsibility to be an active, ethical member of that community, is made explicit in the novel; but there is little evidence of living by that belief. Mr. Sammler's *planet* is inhabited by one man, a man at least as solitary as Joseph. Joseph's voice in *Dangling Man* is terse, cold, ironic, but tense with energy, even if much of that energy is the product of self-hatred. The narrative voice in *Mr. Sammler's Planet* is without tension or energy. It is as I have tried to show, a voice from the grave, one not of self-hatred, as in the case of Joseph the rebellious son, but of the self-righteous authority of Sammler the authoritarian father. The metaphysical speculations do not derive from the realities of life in the novel—as they do, for example, in *Seize the Day*—but are imposed as a substitute for and refuge from such life. *Mr. Sammler's Planet* has fascinating moments—especially those with the black pickpocket and in memories of the Nazi Holocaust and of the Six Day War, but as a novel, it fails—a victim, I believe, to a distorted form of the very "politicization" Bellow himself decries,[12] and to a desire on Bellow's part for an easy solution to his pyschic war.

Humboldt's Gift is a return to the voice and consciousness of the longing fool. Told in Bellow's lyrical comic style, it is full of wonderful moments. The whole of the story of Von Humboldt Fleisher, most of which was written before the contemporary episodes, is beautiful; it is rich in the contradiction between the "child's soul" of the narrator and the noisy comedy that violates that soul. Humboldt himself manifests the same contradiction: between the bizarre, pill-popping wheeler-dealer of the arts and the true poet longing for his "home world." "Below, shuffling comedy; above, princeliness and dignity." The contemporary episodes, almost purely comic, have many wonderful passages: the courthouse scene, the first rendezvous at the hotel with Renata, the reunion with Brother Ulick, are scenes I am grateful for. But generally, the scenes multiply without being fruitful. They seem like arbitrary inventions and carry no emotional weight. Instead, whatever ballast there is for this inventiveness comes from speculations, metaphysical spiels. As Updike argues, "the events of the novel pull away from the issues, and effusion replaces conversation (with everybody . . . sounding like Charlie). . . ."[13]

There is a connection between these two criticisms. Bellow loses his grasp on the connection between speculation and fictional reality. The thinking seems to come out of nowhere. In the

same way, the characters become mouthpieces for the authorial
imagination, cut off from their dramatic identities. Renata speaks
like Charlie; even Naomi, the woman he almost married years
before, speaks like Charlie. In my discussion of *Humboldt's Gift* I
showed one reason why Bellow felt it necessary to turn to long
passages of thinking cut off from dramatic conflict: it exemplifies
the acitivity of the inner being trying to defeat distraction. Still, it
is *very boring*. By the time Charlie and Renata board the plane at
O'Hare, I am quite ready for some new *direction* to the fiction.
But while the *plot* certainly advances, requiring the trip to New
York, where Charlie receives the legacy and the spinning out of
the result of the legacy, emotionally the novel becomes paper thin
once outside Chicago—all clever invention. The plot cannot
handle the significant materials of the novel: the relationship of
Charlie to the dead Humboldt, to the dead in general, and to the
noisy distraction of modern life. The plot is itself distraction; of
course, this is its point—but then, the only refuge is the ending of
"plot," the ending of life! What is not there, as it is in *Seize the
Day*, is the weight and significance of life in spite of and beneath
the distraction. It is as if life itself—metaphysically—has *lost* its
significance, is nothing more than this noisy funhouse. The Real
world is elsewhere. "Real life," Charlie says, "is a relation
between here and there." In an early review Richard Gilman asks,
"Is it too much to say that real art is the depiction of this relation?"[14] If this is true, Bellow has broken that relation in the contemporary episodes in *Humboldt's Gift*, especially in the latter
half of the novel. In "Starting Out in Chicago," published the
same year as *Humboldt's Gift*, Bellow writes, "I had to learn that
by cutting myself off from American life in order to perform an
alien task, I risked cutting myself off from everything that could
nourish me."[15] Twenty-five years before, in "Dreiser and the
Triumph of Art," Bellow asked that writers pay—as Dreiser paid—
"an admission of allegiance to life."[16] This novel fails to the extent
that it cuts itself off from life, to the extent that its allegiance is

merely speculative. But, to the extent that it is at points in deep contact with life, it succeeds.

I feel a strong conflict within Bellow's later work between these two positions. Will he in future work root his yearning for transcendence in the common life, or will he float beyond our planet into a sphere not accessible to fiction? In all his novels it is his sympathy with struggling, foolish humanity as it exists in the noisy world, his apprehension of the mystery inherent in living human beings, that make his fiction so nourishing. I am grateful for that fiction; I would be sorry not to see it continue.

Notes
Selected Bibliography
Index

NOTES

1. In Desperate Affirmation

1. AM, p. 38. See list of abbreviations at front of book.
2. Saul Bellow, "The Writer as Moralist," *Atlantic Monthly*, CCXI (March 1963), 62.
3. Saul Bellow, "Personal Record," *New Republic*, CXXX (Feb. 22, 1954), 21.
4. Alfred Kazin, "My Friend Saul Bellow," *Atlantic Monthly*, CCXV (Jan. 1965), 21.
5. Leslie Fiedler, Remarks during a symposium "On the Novel Today," YMHA in New York City, March 28, 1965; also see John W. Aldridge, "The Complacency of *Herzog*," *Saul Bellow and the Critics*, ed. Irving Malin (New York, 1967), pp. 207–210.
6. Marcus Klein, *After Alienation* (Cleveland, 1964), pp. 47–51, speaks of Bellow's heroes casting off their burdens; also see Irving Malin, "Seven Images," *Saul Bellow and the Critics* (New York, 1967), pp. 142–46.
7. In SD, pp. 193–211. The volume includes four short pieces and the novel.
8. From "A Profile of Saul Bellow," television conversation with Eric Goldman, on *The Open Mind*, NBC, June 6, 1965.
9. Saul Bellow, *The Last Analysis* (New York: Viking, 1965), p. 97.
10. Saul Bellow, "Distractions of a Fiction Writer," *The Living Novel*, ed. Granville Hicks (New York, 1957), p. 14.
11. Probably by Bellow, although unsigned, in "Arias," *The Noble Savage*, IV (Chicago: Meridian, 1960), p. 5. Keith.Botsford, second editor.
12. Saul Bellow, "Dreiser and the Triumph of Art," *Commentary*, XI (May 1951), 503.
13. "Distractions," p. 20.

14. Saul Bellow, "Dora," *Harpers Bazaar*, LXXXIII (Nov. 1949), 199.
15. Lionel Trilling, "The Two Environments," *Encounter*, XXV (July, 1965), 11.
16. Susan Sontag, "Notes on Camp," *Partisan Review*, XXXI (1964), 515–30.
17. William Phillips, "The New Immoralists," *Commentary*, XXXIX (Apr. 1965), 67.
18. Saul Bellow, *Recent American Fiction* (Washington: Library of Congress, 1963), p. 7.
19. Raymond Williams, *Culture and Society: 1780–1950* (New York, 1960), passim.
20. Edward Dorn, "1st Avenue," *The Moderns* (New York, 1963), ed. LeRoi Jones, p. 57.
21. Saul Bellow, "Sealed Treasure," *Times Literary Supplement*, July 1, 1960, p. 414.
22. *Recent American Fiction*, p. 2.
23. Ibid., pp. 8–9.
24. Ibid., pp. 5–6.
25. "Profile."
26. "Profile."
27. "Distractions," p. 11.
28. "Writer as Moralist," p. 61.
29. "The Thinking Man's Wasteland," *Saturday Review*, April 3, 1965, p. 20. Adaptation of Bellow's National Book Award acceptance speech.
30. In interview with Nina A. Steers, "Successor to Faulkner?" *Show*, IV (Sept. 1964), 37.
31. I am indebted to Professor Sypher's unusual book, *Loss of the Self in Modern Literature and Art* (New York, 1962). See especially pp. 58–86.
32. Charles Glicksberg, *The Self in Modern Literature* (University Park, Pa., 1963), p. 107.
33. (New York, 1964), p. 26.
34. *Recent American Fiction*, p. 11.
35. Nathalie Sarraute, *The Age of Suspicion* (New York, 1963), pp. 36, 40, 55, 62.
36. "Writer as Moralist," p. 61.
37. Leslie Fiedler, *Waiting For the End* (New York, 1964), p. 168.
38. Nathalie Sarraute, *Portrait of a Man Unknown* (New York, 1958), pp. 67–69.

39. John Barth, *End of the Road* (New York, 1960), pp. 31, 55.
40. William Burroughs, "The Cut-Up Method," *The Moderns,* p. 345.
41. "The Thinking Man's Wasteland," p. 20.
42. *Recent American Fiction,* p. 11.
43. Ibid., p. 2.
44. "Saul Bellow on the Modern Novel," radio lecture, July, 1961.
45. Eugene Ionesco, in *Four Plays* (New York, 1958), p. 109.
46. "Sealed Treasure," p. 414.
47. "A Profile of Saul Bellow," television conversation with Eric Goldman, on *The Open Mind,* NBC, June 6, 1965.
48. *Recent American Fiction,* p. 12.

2. Bellow's Cultural Context

1. Interview with Nina A. Steers, "Successor to Faulkner?" *Show,* IV (Sept. 1964), 38.
2. Maurice Samuel, *The World of Sholem Aleichem* (New York, 1956), p. 43.
3. Quoted by Irving Howe, "Introduction," *A Treasury of Yiddish Stories* (New York, 1954), p. 51. This 74 page introduction contains the best discussion of Yiddish literature I have seen, a discussion to which I am indebted.
4. Harold Rosenberg, "Pledged to the Marvelous," *Commentary,* III (March 1947), 150. Note: in this discussion of Jewish culture I am referring only to the non-assimilated Eastern European and American ghetto life from which Bellow comes.
5. Isaac Rosenfeld, *An Age of Enormity* (Cleveland, 1962), p. 77.
6. Steers, p. 38.
7. Martin Buber, Tales of the Hasidim: Early Masters (New York, 1961), p. 127.
8. "A Profile of Saul Bellow."
9. Samuel, p. 11.
10. Rosenberg, p. 149.
11. Abraham Heschel, quoted by Irving Malin, *Jews and Americans* (Southern Illinois University, 1965), p. 104.
12. Granville Hicks, "His Hope's on the Human Heart," *Saturday Review,* October 12, 1963, p. 32.
13. Howe, "Introduction," pp. 37–38.
14. Maxwell Geismar, "Saul Bellow: Novelist of the Intellectuals," *American Moderns* (New York, 1958), pp. 216–17; p. 221.
15. Rosenberg, p. 150.

16. See David Daiches, "Breakthrough?" *Commentary*, XXXVIII (Aug. 1964), 61–64.

17. Steers, p. 38.

18. See Howe, "Introduction," p. 30; p. 8.

19. Buber, p. 131.

20. Isaac Bashevis Singer, "The Spinoza of Market Street," in *The Spinoza of Market Street*, trans. Martha Glicklich and Cecil Hemley (New York, 1962), p. 24.

21. Howe, "Introduction," pp. 41–42.

22. Malin, p. 132.

23. Bruce Jay Friedman, *Stern* (New York, 1962), p. 13.

24. Anon., "Saul Bellow," *Current Biography*, XXVI (Feb. 1965), 3.

25. Leslie Fiedler, *Love and Death in the American Novel* (New York, 1960).

26. Leslie Fiedler, *Waiting for the End* (New York, 1964), p. 84.

27. Ralph Ellison, *Invisible Man* (New York, 1955), pp. 19–20.

28. Of course this innocence, which Hassan also insists on in *Radical Innocence* (Princeton, 1961), is found in the whole novel tradition. But the innocence of a hero who says *No!* is more accentuated in American than in any other national fiction, even Russian.

29. Marcus Klein, *After Alienation: American Novels in Mid-Century* (Cleveland, 1964).

30. Hassan, *Radical Innocence*, p. 329.

31. Saul Bellow, "Dreiser and the Triumph of Art," *Commentary*, XI (May 1951), p. 503.

32. Malcolm Bradbury, "Saul Bellow's *The Victim*." *Critical Quarterly*, V (Summer, 1963), pp. 127–28.

33. Saul Bellow, "Distractions of a Fiction Writer," *The Living Novel*, ed. Granville Hicks (New York, 1957), p. 19.

34. Saul Bellow, "The Writer as Moralist," *Atlantic Monthly*, CCXI (March 1963), p. 58.

35. Fiedler, *An End to Innocence*, (Boston, 1956), p. 204.

36. Susan Sontag, "Notes on Camp," *Partisan Review*, XXXI (Fall 1964), p. 529.

37. Lionel Trilling, "The Two Environments," *Encounter*, XXV (July 1965), p. 13; p. 8.

38. Philip Rahv, "Bellow The Brain King," *Book Week, The Sunday Herald Tribune*, Sept. 20, 1964, p. 1.

39. Trilling, p. 4.

3. *Alienation and Masochism*

1. Maurice Samuel, *The World of Sholem Aleichem* (New York, 1956), p. 115.
2. Harold Rosenberg, "Pledged to the Marvelous," *Commentary*, III (March 1947) p. 150.
3. Irving Howe, "Introduction," *A Treasury of Yiddish Stories* (New York, 1954), p. 51.
4. *A Treasury of Yiddish Stories*, p. 316, p. 350.
5. Benjamin DeMott, "Jewish Writers in America," *Commentary*, XXXI (Feb. 1961), 123.
6. Leslie Fiedler, *Waiting for the End* (New York, 1964), p. 84.
7. Isaac Rosenfeld, *An Age of Enormity* (Cleveland, 1962), p. 68.
8. Harvey Swados, *A Radical's America* (Boston, 1962), p. 167; p. 156.
9. Wallace Markfield, *To An Early Grave* (New York, 1964), pp. 137–38.
10. Fiedler, *Waiting*, p. 90.
11. Bruce Jay Friedman, *Stern* (New York, 1962), p. 55.
12. Maxwell Geismar, *American Moderns* (New York, 1958), p. 216.
13. Norman Podhoretz, "The Adventures of Saul Bellow," *Doings and Undoings* (New York, 1964), p. 214.
14. Nina Steers, "Successor to Faulkner?" *Show*, IV (Nov. 1964), p. 37.
15. Saul Bellow, "On Gide," *The New Leader*, June 4, 1951, p. 24.
16. See Tony Tanner's excellent article, "Saul Bellow: The Flight from Monologue," *Encounter*, XXIV (Feb. 1966), 58–70. Also see Tanner's short book on Bellow, *Saul Bellow* (London, 1966).
17. Ihab Hassan, *Radical Innocence: Studies in the Contemporary American Novel* (Princeton, 1961), p. 299.
18. Jean Paul Sartre, *Nausea* (New York, 1964).
19. Saul Bellow, "A Trip to Galena," *Partisan Review*, XVII (1950), 791.
20. "The Author," Portrait in *Saturday Review*, Sept. 19, 1953, p. 13.
21. Tanner, p. 60.
22. Fyodor Dostoyevsky, *Notes from Underground*, in *The Short Novels of Dostoyevsky*, trans. Constance Garnet (New York, 1951), p. 131.

23. Keith Michael Opdahl, "'The Crab and the Butterfly': The Themes of Saul Bellow," unpublished dissertation (Univ. of Ill., 1961). See Chapter II, "The Generalized Man," pp. 32–62.
24. Opdahl, pp. 52–54.
25. For a study of Tommy's masochism see Daniel Weiss, "Caliban on Prospero: A Psychoanalytic Study on the Novel *Seize the Day*, by Saul Bellow," *American Imago*, XIX (Fall, 1962), 277–306.
26. Bernard Berliner, "Role of Object Relations in Moral Masochism," *Psychoanalytic Quarterly*, XXVII (1958), 38–56.
27. Weiss, p. 286.
28. Wilhelm Reich, *Character Analysis* (New York, 1963), p. 226.
29. Weiss, p. 288. I quote Weiss in order to delineate precisely what elements of this chapter derive from his article.
30. Weiss spends a large part of his article discussing Tommy's infantile state; he shows, for example, that Tommy's sucking of his coke bottle is symptomatic of regression to the nursing infant (pp. 286–87).
31. Robert Alter, "The Stature of Saul Bellow," *Midstream*, X (Dec. 1964), p. 8.
32. See Opdahl, pp. 112 ff.
33. Steers, p. 37.

4. Construction of Self and World

1. Leon Trotsky, "Life in the Socialist Future," *Literature and Revolution*, excerpted in *The Marxists*, ed. C. Wright Mills (New York, 1962), p. 286.
2. Leslie Fiedler, "Saul Bellow," *Prairie Schooner*, XXXI (1957), 107.
3. "Saul Bellow on the Modern Novel," radio lecture, July, 1961.

6. Transformation

1. Saul Bellow, *Recent American Fiction* (Washington: Library of Congress, 1963), p. 12.
2. Marcus Klein, *After Alienation* (Cleveland, 1964), p. 34.
3. Richard Lehan, "Existentialism in American Fiction: the Demonic Quest," *Critique*, III (Summer, 1960), p. 69.
4. Charles Glicksberg, *The Self in Modern Literature* (Univ. Park, Pa., 1963), p. 138.
5. Bellow, *Recent American Fiction*, p. 12.

6. *A Treasury of Yiddish Stories*, ed. Irving Howe (New York, 1954), p. 414.
7. Wilhelm Reich, *Character Analysis* (New York, 1963), pp. 377–79.
8. Klein, p. 41.
9. Wylie Sypher, *Loss of the Self in Modern Literature and Art* (New York, 1962), p. 129.

7. The Victim

1. For instance, Marcus Klein, *After Alienation* (Cleveland, 1964), p. 37; Harvey Swados, *A Radical's America* (Boston, 1962), p. 170. I am grateful for the assistance of Mr. James Hoffman, whose unpublished study contains a discussion of many of the parallels between *The Victim* and *The Eternal Husband*.
2. "Saul Bellow," Interview with Jay Nash and Ron Offen in *Literary Times* (Chicago), Dec., 1964, p. 10.
3. Leslie Fiedler, *Waiting for the End* (New York, 1964), p. 99.
4. Fyodor Dostoyevsky, *The Eternal Husband*, in *The Short Novels of Dostoyevsky*, trans. Constance Garnett (New York, 1951), p. 443.
5. Keith Michael Opdahl, " 'The Crab and the Butterfly': The Themes of Saul Bellow," unpublished dissertation (Univ. of Illinois, 1961), p. 75.
6. Fernando Molina, *Existentialism as Philosophy* (Englewood Cliffs, N.J., 1962), p. 109.
7. Dimitri Chizhevsky, "The Theme of the Double in Dostoyevsky," *Dostoyevsky*, ed. René Wellek (Englewood Cliffs, N.J., 1962), p. 127.
8. Leslie Fiedler also quotes this passage in *Waiting for the End*, p. 99. Fiedler emphasizes the "passionate" nature of the relationship between Jew and mythical gentile, not the moral significance of the scene.
9. Fiedler, *Waiting for the End*, p. 99.
10. Norman Podhoretz, "The Adventures of Saul Bellow," *Doings and Undoings* (New York, 1964), p. 214.
11. Opdahl, p. 76.
12. Maxwell Geismar, *American Moderns* (New York, 1958), p. 222.

8. Henderson the Rain King

1. Nina Steers, "Successor to Faulkner?" *Show*, IV (Nov. 1964), 38.
2. Robert Alter, "The Stature of Saul Bellow," *Midstream*, X (Dec.

1964), p. 10; also Keith Michael Opdahl, " 'The Crab and the Butterfly': the Themes of Saul Bellow," unpublished dissertation (Univ. of Illinois, 1961), p. 10. Robert Detweiler, who calls *HRK* a "comic treatment of the idealist," in "Patterns of Rebirth" in *Henderson the Rain King, Modern Fiction Studies*, XII (Winter, 1966–67), p. 413, sees a pervasive irony beneath the symbolism.

3. "Arias," *The Noble Savage*, I (1960), pp. 249–51.
4. Leslie Fiedler, *Waiting for the End* (New York, 1964), p. 98.
5. Marcus Klein, *After Alienation* (Cleveland, 1964), pp. 65–69. Bellow denies the parallel to Nietzsche: "Saul Bellow," Interview with Jay Nash and Ron Offen in *Literary Times* (Chicago), Dec. 1964, p. 10.
6. *New York Times Book Review*, Feb. 15, 1959, p. 1, p. 34.
7. Saul Bellow, *Recent American Fiction* (Washington: Library of Congress, 1963), p. 11.
8. Marcus Klein, p. 54.
9. Steers, p. 38. As a number of critics have noted, *Henderson* is quite obviously a symbolic novel in spite of Bellow's injunction, "Deep Readers of the World, Beware" (see Note 6 above) published one week before the publication of *Henderson*.
10. Norman Podhoretz, "The Adventures of Saul Bellow," *Doings and Undoings* (New York, 1964), p. 225, believes that Henderson *learns* from Dahfu that "reality is you"—that this is Bellow's wisdom. Hardly! It is Bellow's *fear*: until Henderson goes beyond this wisdom he cannot be saved.
11. Philip Toynbee, *"Henderson the Rain King,"* *Encounter*, XIII (Sept. 1959), p. 70.
12. Steers, p. 38.

9. *Herzog*

1. Philip Rahv, "Bellow the Brain King," *Book Week, Herald Tribune*, Sept. 20, 1964, p. 1, p. 14, p. 16.
2. Richard Poirier, "Bellows to Herzog," *Partisan Review*, XXXII (1965), pp. 267–68.
3. Leslie Fiedler, remarks during a symposium "On the Novel Today," YMHA in New York City, March 28, 1965.
4. Anonymous article in *New York Post*, March 14, 1965, p. 47.
5. Maxwell Geismar, "The Great *Herzog* Schande," *The Minority of One*, VI (Dec. 1964), p. 30. Geismar's attack is not representative; Geismar viciously misreads the novel, calling Bellow a

"sellout," declaring him "commercial and corrupt." He speaks of the "deterioration of Bellow's craft into sheer nihilism, into nastiness, and even a kind of spiritual obscenity." Geismar reports Herzog as looking "back upon the ruins of his own life without any sense of understanding, or recognition, or, God forbid, any possible sense of his own personal or moral responsibility, and he then declares that therefore contemporary life, society, culture, and history are also without any meaning, and are simply a comic farce." Such a gross misreading indicates a preconceived hatred of Bellow's fiction and probably of Bellow himself. While Geismar has always attacked Bellow's morbidity and guilt as un-Jewish (*American Moderns*), he has never gone so far in his attack.

6. Jack Ludwig, "The Wayward Reader," *Holiday*, XXXVII (Feb. 1965), pp. 17–18.
7. Poirier, p. 265.
8. Saul Bellow, "The Writer as Moralist," *Atlantic Monthly*, CCXI (March 1963), p. 61.
9. Saul Bellow, *Recent American Fiction* (Washington: Library of Congress, 1963), p. 7.
10. Thomas Meehan, "Claus," *New Yorker*, Jan. 9, 1965, p. 27.
11. Geismar, p. 30.
12. Meehan, p. 27.
13. "The Author," *Saturday Review*, Sept. 19, 1964, p. 38.
14. Leslie Fiedler, symposium.
15. Nina Steers, "Successor to Faulkner?" *Show*, IV (Nov., 1964), p. 37.
16. Ibid, p. 38.
17. Ibid, p. 38.
18. Poirier, p. 268.
19. Steers, p. 38.
20. Saul Bellow, *The Last Analysis* (New York: Viking, 1965), p. 78.
21. Poirier, p. 269.
22. *Novelists on the Novel*, ed. Miriam Allott (New York, 1959), pp. 289–90.
23. "Writer as Moralist," p. 62.
24. Also noted by Edgar Stanley Hyman, "Saul Bellow's Glittering Eye," *The New Leader*, Sept. 28, 1964, p. 17.
25. Isaac Rosenfeld, *An Age of Enormity* (Cleveland, 1962), p. 296.

10. *The Politics of Oedipus:*
Mr. Sammler's Planet, To Jerusalem and Back

1. Bruce Mazlich, *James and John Stuart Mill* (New York, 1975), p. 18.
2. Mazlich, p. 17.
3. Earl Rovit, "Jewish Humor and American Life," in *Herzog: Text and Criticism*, ed. Irving Howe (New York, 1976), p. 514. Also see Jules Chametzky, *From the Ghetto: The Fiction of Abraham Cahan* (Amherst, 1977), p. 63.
4. Chametzky, "Our Decentralized Literature: A Consideration of Regional, Ethnic, Racial, and Sexual Factors," *Jahrbuch für Amerikastudien*, XVII (1972), pp. 61-66.
5. *To Jerusalem and Back: A Personal Account* (New York, 1977), p. 1; also *Mr. Sammler's Planet* (New York, 1970). After this all references will be to these editions and will be found in parentheses in the text.
6. Nina Steers, "Successor to Faulkner?" *Show*, IV (Nov. 1964), p. 38.
7. Chametzky, *From the Ghetto*, p. 65.
8. Originally published in *The New Yorker*, XXX (Feb. 5, 1955), pp. 26-30; collected in *Seize the Day*, 1st ed., in 1956.
9. Cited in *The Republic*, Book One.
10. For example, see Irvin Stock, "Man in Culture," *Commentary*, L (May 1970), pp. 89-90, 92-94; and Ben Siegel, "Saul Bellow and Mr. Sammler: The Absurd Seekers of High Quality," in *Saul Bellow: A Collection of Critical Essays*, ed. Earl Rovit (Englewood Cliffs, N.J., 1975), pp. 122-34.
11. Siegel, p. 126.
12. Mark Shechner, "Down in the Mouth with Saul Bellow," *American Review*, XXIII (1975), p. 67. Shechner's attack is consonant with Richard Poirier's interesting essay "Herzog: Bellow in Trouble," in Rovit, *Saul Bellow*.
13. Shechner, p. 64.
14. Ibid., p. 63.
15. Ibid., p. 66.
16. Stock, p. 89.
17. Ibid., p. 92.
18. Robert Boyers, "Nature and Social Reality in Bellow's *Sammler*," *Salmagundi*, XXX (Summer 1975), p. 37.

19. James Neil Harris, "One Cultural Approach to *Mr. Sammler's Planet*," *Twentieth Century Literature*, XVIII (Oct. 1972), p. 238.

20. Robert Boyers, "Literature and Culture: An Interview with Saul Bellow," *Salmagundi*, XXX (Summer 1975), p. 22.

21. See Siegel, op. cit.

22. From tape recording of lecture given at California State College at Hayward, Spring 1968.

23. See the surprising and useful essay by Earl Rovit, "Saul Bellow and Norman Mailer: The Secret Sharers," in Rovit, *Saul Bellow*, pp. 161-70.

24. D. P. M. Salter, "Optimism and Reaction in Saul Bellow's Recent Work," *Critical Quarterly*, XIV (Spring 1972), p. 64.

25. Boyers, "Interview," p. 13.

26. Ibid., p. 11.

27. Bellow, "The Writer as Moralist," p. 62.

28. Bellow, "An Interview with Myself," *The New Review*, II (1975), p. 54.

29. Ibid., p. 55.

30. Boyers, "Interview," p. 7.

31. Herbert Marcuse, "Excerpt from *The Aesthetic Dimension*," *American Poetry Review*, VII (March-April 1978), p. 14.

32. Ibid., p. 13.

33. Ibid., p. 14.

34. *To Jerusalem and Back*, p. 28.

35. In Boyers, "Interview," p. 7, Bellow speaks of the dangers of systems based on great metaphors—systems of Freud, Marx, Kant, etc. "Once you've given yourself over to one of these systems, you've lost your freedom in a very significant degree."

11. *Humboldt's Gift: Transcendence and the Flight from Death*

1. Reprinted in *The American Scholar*, XLVI (Summer 1977), p. 325.

2. Ibid.

3. "Distractions of a Fiction Writer" p. 12.

4. "Mourning and Melancholia," in Standard Edition of *The Complete Psychological Works of Sigmund Freud*, ed. James Strachey (London, 1958), XIV, pp. 249-50.

5. In this view I have been influenced by Richard Noland, my colleague at the University of Massachusetts. See his "Psychohistory, Theory and Practice," *Massachusetts Review*, XVIII (Summer 1977), pp. 295-322.

6. Selected Papers (London, 1927). Cited by Otto Fenichel, *The Psychoanalytic Theory of Neurosis* (New York, 1945), p. 398.
7. See Freud, "Psychoanalytic Notes on an Autobiographical Account of a Case of Paranoia," *CP*, XII, pp. 3-82; also "A Case of Paranoia," *CP*, XIV, pp. 261-72. Also see Reich, *Character Analysis* (New York, 1949), pp. 218-29.
8. Fenichel, op. cit., p. 208.
9. Fenichel, p. 433.
10. From *Neurosis and Human Growth* (New York, 1950), p. 222.
11. Horney, pp. 222-23.
12. From another perspective, Charlie's solution is to identify with his own prepubescent innocence, innocence of a self that doesn't deserve to die.

12. *The Unity and Development of Bellow's Fiction*

1. Irving Howe, "Odysseus, Flat on his Back," *The New Republic*, Sept. 19, 1964, p. 23.
2. Ihab Hassan, *Radical Innocence* (Princeton, 1961), p. 305.
3. Howe, p. 23.
4. Keith Michael Opdahl, "'The Crab and the Butterfly': The Themes of Saul Bellow," Ph.D. diss., University of Illinois, 1961, p. 23.
5. Norman Podhoretz, "The Adventures of Saul Bellow," *Doings and Undoings* (New York, 1964), p. 216.
6. "Editorial Statement," *Partisan Review*, XIX (1952), pp. 283-84.
7. Steers, p. 38.
8. Bellow, "Dreiser and the Triumph of Art," pp. 502-503.
9. Irving Howe, statement in symposium, "Our Country and our Culture," *Partisan Review*, XIX (1952), pp. 577-78.
10. Steers, p. 38.
11. Geismar, *American Moderns*, pp. 216-17.
12. Boyers, "Interview," p. 13.
13. John Updike, "Draping Radiance with a Worn Veil," *The New Yorker*, LI (Sept. 15, 1975). p. 125.
14. Richard Gilman, "Saul Bellow's New, Open, Spacious Novel about Art, Society and a Bizarre Poet: *Humboldt's Gift*," *New York Times Book Review* (August 17, 1975), p. 1.
15. *American Scholar*, XLIV (Winter 1974-75), p. 75.
16. *Commentary*, XI (1951), p. 503.

SELECTED BIBLIOGRAPHY

A. Major Work by Bellow

Fiction

Novels (in editions cited in text, but given in order of initial publication)

1. *Dangling Man*. New York: Meridian, 1960.
2. *The Victim*. New York: Compass, 1956.
3. *The Adventures of Augie March*. New York: Compass, 1960.
4. *Seize the Day*. New York: Compass, 1965.
5. *Henderson the Rain King*. New York: Compass, 1965.
6. *Herzog*. New York: Viking, 1964.
7. *Mr. Sammler's Planet*. New York: Viking, 1970.
8. *Humboldt's Gift*. New York: Viking, 1975.

Chief Short Fiction

Uncollected

9. "Two Morning Monologues." *Partisan Review*, VIII (1941), 230-36.
10. "A Sermon by Doctor Pep." *Partisan Review*, XIV (1949), 455-62.

Collected

11. *Mosby's Memoirs, and Other Stories*, New York: Viking, 1968. Includes title story and items 12-16.
12. "A Father-to-Be."
13. "Looking for Mr. Green."
14. "The Gonzaga Manuscripts."
15. "Leaving the Yellow House."
16. "The Old System."

Chief Plays

17. "The Wrecker." In *Seize the Day*.
18. *The Last Analysis*. New York: Viking, 1965.

Chief Nonfiction

General Discussions of Literature and Culture (in chronological order)
19. "Distractions of a Fiction Writer." In *The Living Novel*, ed. Granville Hicks. New York, 1957.
20. "The Writer as Moralist." *Atlantic Monthly*, CCXI (March 1963), 58-62.
21. *Recent American Fiction*. Washington: Library of Congress, 1963.
22. "The Nobel Lecture." Reprinted in *The American Scholar*, XLVI (Summer 1977), 16-25.
23. *To Jerusalem and Back: A Personal Account*. New York, 1977.

Studies of Individual Writers
24. "Dreiser and the Triumph of Art." *Commentary*, XI (1951), 502-503.
25. "Isaac Rosenfeld." *Partisan Review*, XXIII (1956), 565-67.

B. Chief Interviews and Biographical Studies

26. Steers, Nina. "A Successor to Faulkner?" *Show*, IV (Sept. 1964), 36-38.
27. Anon. "Saul Bellow." *Current Biography*, XXVI (Feb. 1965), 3-5.
28. Bellow, Saul. "An Interview with Myself." *New Review*, II (1975), 53-56.
29. Bellow, Saul. "Starting out in Chicago." *The American Scholar*, XLIV (Winter 1974-75), 71-77.

C. Significant Related Studies of Jewish Fiction

30. Howe, Irving. "Introduction." *A Treasury of Yiddish Stories*. New York, 1954, pp. 1-71.
31. Malin, Irving. *Jews and Americans*. Carbondale, 1965.
32. Chametzky, Jules. "Notes on the Assimilation of the American-Jewish Writer: Abraham Cahan to Saul Bellow." *Jahrbuch für Amerikastudien*, IX (1964), 172-80.

D. Studies on Bellow
Bibliography

33. Nevius, Blake. *The American Novel: Sinclair Lewis to the Present*. New York, 1970.
34. Lercangee, Francine. *Saul Bellow: A Bibliography of Secondary Sources.* Brussels, 1977. (Also see items 35, 36, 37, 38, 42.)

Book-Length Studies

35. Cohen, Sara B. *Saul Bellow's Enigmatic Laughter*. Urbana, Ill., 1974.
36. Malin, Irving. *Saul Bellow's Fiction*. Carbondale, 1969.
37. Opdahl, Keith. *The Novels of Saul Bellow: An Introduction*. University Park, Pa., 1967.
38. Scheer-Schazler, Brigitte. *Saul Bellow*. New York, 1972.

Collections of Criticism

39. *Saul Bellow and the Critics*, ed. Irving Malin. New York, 1967: Leslie Fiedler, "Saul Bellow"; Maxwell Geismar, "Saul Bellow: Novelist of the Intellectuals"; Richard Chase, "The Adventures of Saul Bellow: The Progress of a Novelist"; J. C. Levenson, "Bellow's Dangling Men"; Ralph Freedman, "Saul Bellow: The Illusion of Environment"; Daniel Hughes, "Reality and the Hero: *Lolita and Henderson*"; Marcus Klein, "A Discipline of Nobility: Saul Bellow's Fiction"; Daniel Weiss, "Caliban on Prospero: A Psychoanalytic Study on the Novel *Seize the Day*, by Saul Bellow"; Irving Malin, "Seven Images"; Earl Rovit, "Bellow in Occupancy"; Forest Read, "*Herzog*: A Review"; John Aldridge, "The Complacency of Herzog"; Saul Bellow, "Where Do We Go From Here: The Future of Fiction."

40. Saul Bellow issue, *Critique: Studies in Modern Fiction*, VII (Spring-Summer 1965): James D. Young, "Bellow's View of the Heart"; Robert Crozier, "Theme in *Augie March*"; Allen Guttman, "Bellow's *Henderson*"; James Mathis, "The Themes of *Seize the Day*." (*Critique* also ran a Bellow issue in Summer 1960.)

41. Saul Bellow issue: *Salmagundi*, XXX (Summer 1975): John Bayley, "By Way of Mr. Sammler"; Ben Belitt, "Saul Bellow: The Depth Factor"; Robert Boyers, "Literature and Culture: An Interview with Saul Bellow"; Robert Boyers, "Nature and Social Reality in Bellow's Sammler"; Harold Kaplan, "The Second Fall of Man."

42. *Saul Bellow: A Collection of Critical Essays*, ed. Earl Rovit. Englewood Cliffs, N.J., 1975: John Clayton, "The Victim"; Denis Donoghue, "*Dangling Man*"; Gordon L. Harper, "Saul Bellow: An Interview"; Irving Malin, "Bummy's Analysis"; Richard Pearce, "The Ambiguous Assault of Henderson and Herzog"; Richard Poirier, "*Herzog*: Bellow in Trouble"; M. Gilbert Porter, "The Scene as Image"; Earl Rovit, "Introduction"; Earl Rovit, "Saul Bellow and Norman Mailer: The Secret Sharers"; Ben Siegel, "Saul Bellow and Mr. Sammler: The Absurd Seekers of High Qualities"; Victoria Sullivan, "The Battle of the Sexes in Three Bellow Novels"; Ruth Wisse, "The Schlemiel as Liberal Humanist."

43. *Saul Bellow: Herzog: Text and Criticism*, ed. Irving Howe. New York, 1976: John Aldridge, "The Complacency of Herzog"; Gordon L. Harper, "Saul Bellow: An Interview"; Irving Howe, "Down and Out in New York and Chicago"; Gabriel Josipovici, "Bellow and *Herzog*"; Alfred Kazin, "The Earthly City of the Jews"; Frank Kermode, "*Herzog*"; Forrest Read, "*Herzog*: A Review"; Earl Rovit, "Jewish Humor and American Life"; Robert Shulman, "The Style of Bellow's Comedy"; Theodore Solotaroff, "Napoleon Street"; Tony Tanner, "The Flight from Monologue."

Single Items

44. Galloway, David. *"Mr. Sammler's Planet*: Bellow's Failure of Nerve." *Modern Fiction Studies*, XIX (Spring 1973). 17-28.
45. Hassan, Ihab. *Radical Innocence: Studies in the Contemporary American Novel*. Princeton, 1961.
46. Klein, Marcus. *After Alienation: American Novels in Mid-Century*. Cleveland, 1964.
47. Ludwig, Jack. "The Wayward Reader." *Holiday*, XXXVII (Feb. 1965), 16-19.
48. Podhoretz, Norman. *Doings and Undoings*. New York, 1964.
49. Tanner, Tony. "Saul Bellow: The Flight from Monologue." *Encounter*, XXIV (Feb. 1965), 58-70.
50. Poirier, Richard. "Bellows to Herzog." *Partisan Review*, XXXII (Spring 1965), 264-71.
51. Shechner, Mark. "Down in the Mouth with Saul Bellow." *American Review*, XXIII (1975), 40-77.

INDEX